**The Impure
Imagination**

The Impure Imagination

Toward a Critical Hybridity in
Latin American Writing

Joshua Lund

University of Minnesota Press
Minneapolis
London

Parts of the introduction to Part I and chapter 1 were published as "Hybridity, Genre, Race," in *Coloniality at Large*, edited by Enrique Dussel, Mabel Moraña, and Carlos Jáuregui (Durham, NC: Duke University Press, 2007); reprinted with permission from Duke University Press. Part of chapter 5 was originally published as "Reyes, raza y nación," in *Alfonso Reyes y los estudios latinoamericanos*, edited by Adela Pineda Franco and Igancio M. Sánchez Prado (Pittsburgh: Instituto Internacional de Literatura Iberoamericana, 2004), 191–220; reprinted with permission from Instituto Internacional de Literatura Iberoamericana. An earlier version of chapter 6 originally appeared in *Journal of Latin American Cultural Studies* 12, no. 2 (2003): 171–89; reprinted with permission from the Taylor and Francis Group, http://www.tandf.co.uk.

Published by the University of Minnesota Press
111 Third Avenue South, Suite 290
Minneapolis, MN 55401-2520
http://www.upress.umn.edu

Library of Congress Cataloging-in-Publication Data

Lund, Joshua, 1969–
    The impure imagination : toward a critical hybridity in Latin American writing / Joshua Lund.
        p.   cm.
    Includes bibliographical references and index.
    ISBN-13: 978-0-8166-4785-9 (hc : alk. paper)
    ISBN-10: 0-8166-4785-2 (hc : alk. paper)
    ISBN-13: 978-0-8166-4786-6 (pb : alk. paper)
    ISBN-10: 0-8166-4786-0 (pb : alk. paper)
    1. Hybridity (Social sciences)—Latin America.   2. Miscegenation—Latin America.   3. Latin America—Civilization.   4. National characteristics, Latin American.   I. Title.
    GN254.L86 2006
    306.098—dc22
                                            2006006212

Printed in the United States of America on acid-free paper

The University of Minnesota is an equal-opportunity educator and employer.

12 11 10 09 08 07 06   10 9 8 7 6 5 4 3 2 1

Contents

Acknowledgments

In writing this book, I relied on the help and encouragement of many people. To begin, the project would have been impossible without the intellectual and emotional support of Sarah Elizabeth Hultgren Lund, Benjamin Weldon Lund, and Natalie Elizabeth Lund. I owe them infinite thanks.

This book emerged out of conversations with friends and colleagues. Far too many people showed up at one or another crucial moment for me to thank them all individually, but a few must be singled out. Peter Hallberg has been a great friend and inexhaustible voice of reason from the very beginning of this project, responding with consistent good humor to anxious requests for last-minute readings and reassurance. I owe a special debt of gratitude to Carlos Jáuregui, who talked me out of giving up on the project at least twice. While I benefited from the comments of a number of critics, two sets of readers were absolutely essential. First, at the outset of the project, the interventions of Helen Kinsella and Adam Sitze allowed me to formulate the questions that would become the very center of the book. Second, the project never would have come to completion without the help of María del Pilar Melgarejo and Ignacio Sánchez-Prado. Nacho's seemingly limitless bibliographic memory and intellectual camaraderie made him an interlocutor on whom I came to depend. And Pilar's talent for identifying an argument's edge (and demands for rigor and clarity in highlighting it), her commitment to critical work, and her generosity of insight have taught me a tremendous amount. A number of others offered valuable comments and critique on certain aspects of the book. Special thanks in this regard to René Jara, Fernando Arenas, John Mowitt, Joanna O'Connell, Juliet Lynd, Malcolm McNee, Joel Wainwright, Santiago Castro-Gómez, Caryn Connelly, Betsy Konefal, Julie Kroll, Ignacio López, Silvia López, Amy Robinson, Gabriela Valdivia, Lisa Disch, Amy Kaminsky, Patrick McNamara, Edson Nery da Fonseca, Nelson Pereira dos Santos, Nick Spadaccini, Hernán Vidal, Tony Zahareas, and all of the participants in my graduate seminars of 2002 and 2003. Thanks as well to Richard Morrison at the University of Minnesota Press for taking interest in this project, and to Laura Westlund and Salomé Aguilera Skvirsky for their help with the manuscript.

I benefited from two contexts of institutional support during the years that it took to write this book. The University of Minnesota was very generous, as parts of this book were facilitated by funding from a Thomas H. Shevlin Fellowship and a number of travel grants through the Department of Spanish and Portuguese. Special thanks are in order for the financial and intellectual support that I received as a Scholar in the MacArthur Program in interdisciplinary research at Minnesota. I have found myself in the midst of good fortune again since coming to the University of Pittsburgh, surrounded by a department of creative and energetic colleagues. The research leave granted by the university was well timed and allowed me to finish the manuscript. I also benefited from research funding from the Center for Latin American Studies and the University Center for International Studies. I am grateful for support from the Richard D. and Mary Jane Edwards Endowed Publication Fund.

Finally, I would like to thank all of the family and friends involved in my life as this project developed, and who didn't ever seem to mind that a book could take many years to write. Warm affection and gratitude to you all, and especially to Kristen and Kristofer Lund, Peter Lund, Karen Flannery, Seth "Hartsy" Hartung, Jamie Weid, August Hartung, Florence Lund and the late J. Benjamin Lund, Harold Acker and Natalie Acker, for inspiring me—indeed, telling me—to follow my passion.

Introduction
The Stakes of Hybridity

This book is about the concept "hybridity." It is a metacritical study, insofar as it takes as its object theories and narratives of hybridity, as opposed to empirical practices of hybridization (or mixing) that unfold at the level of cultural production and performance. My interest, then, is not concerned with collecting samples of hybridization, but rather with tracking the ways in which the idea of hybridity has been thought, specifically in Latin American writing. I will contest the common thesis that hybridity works toward (cultural, social, political) emancipation. My central argument is that Latin American theories and narratives of hybridity have been, and continue to be, structured by an insufficiently contemplated relation to what Aníbal Quijano has called the "coloniality of power."

Quijano's term adds needed life to the now somewhat sapped language of "colonial discourse." If colonial discourse theory helped point us toward the historical relations between writing and colonialism, the coloniality of power emphasizes the way in which colonially derived social relations underwrite our contemporary world.[1] The distinction is an important one for the purposes of this book, insofar as I focus on the ways in which norms, rhetorics, and assumptions of social exclusion inhabit and still animate the political—even biopolitical—commitments of hybridity theories.[2] Moreover, the source material that enables the book comes from a context that is no longer explicitly "colonial," at least not in the strict historical sense.

Hybridity means "genre mixing." Allowing this kind of broad definition to guide my thinking about the concept has the strategic advantage of framing hybridity as an aesthetic, philosophical, and critical tendency. Hybridity thus emerges as the name for a paradigm. Under this paradigmatic structure fall the various theories of Latin American cultural specificity that depend on the exaltation of what George Yúdice refers to as a generalized aesthetics of mixing (2001, xx). By expanding the word *hybridity* beyond its specifically critical function associated with 1990s-era debates in and around Latin Americanism and, more broadly, postcolonial theory and criticism, we can rearticulate that word and that moment to a much longer history. In short, rethinking the recent return to hybridity as paradigmatic brings to the fore its historical relation with a number of "older" key words, most prominently *mestizaje*.

The acknowledgment of this history was implicitly reiterated throughout the past decade. It could be heard every time the resurgence of hybridity in the human sciences—especially in its postcolonialist mode— was met with the incredulous response in Latin Americanist circles that can be summed up by the question "So what else is new?" Hybridity, suddenly everybody's favorite new toy, had always been the generic mark of Latin America's geocultural singularity. And yet this Latin Americanist recoil before hybridity's resurrection missed, or rejected a priori, a novel claim that almost always accompanied its reinvocation. The new hybridity, specifically in its Latin Americanist context, purported to delink itself from its own conditions of possibility: the interaction between discourses of race, gender, and social reproduction. It is thus that Néstor García Canclini could announce, in the opening pages of his influential *Culturas híbridas* (1989), that his turn to hybridity should not be confused with a return to mestizaje, especially and precisely given *mestizaje*'s explicit commitment to race (1989, 14–15). Jesús Martín-Barbero, in a book that would also be decisive for rethinking Latin American cultural production in the 1990s, chose to maintain the language of *mestizaje*, but was careful to note that his plural *mestizajes* should not be confused with the old, racialized version (1987, 2). And Serge Gruzinski, in *La pensée métisse* (1999), a momentous work that capped the decade, went so far as to call the historical relation between the aesthetics of mixing and the aesthetics of race "embarrassing" (2002,

19), best left behind, like Hegel's Old Europe, in the lumber room of exhausted ideas.

But one might be suspicious of this revalorization of hybridity theory that, perhaps too optimistically, pretends to abandon the material conditions of possibility that underwrite its critical force. As we know from more than two decades of particularly intense anti- and postcolonial historiography and criticism, the coloniality of power is tenacious, and sticks to cultural forms (which, of course, include critical discourse) in often discrete ways. The entanglement of hierarchical ideas of race and gender, as Quijano reminds us, is always at issue here. Paradoxically, it is at the gesture of abandoning, or even disavowing, the force of coloniality at play in these social relations that current theories of hybridity announce their commitments to those same earlier formulas (for example, "race") that they wish to transcend.

This book asks in what ways these structures of coloniality continue to operate on the site of hybridity. That the past persists in the present, and that old conventions always haunt critical innovations, is no secret. That they do so accompanied by all sorts of anxiety and disavowal may present obstacles for realizing the emancipatory potential (intellectual, cultural, social) of today's critical efforts.

A number of key terms enable this book. We could begin with the most basic of identity markers that will be in play throughout these pages, namely, race, gender, nation, culture, tradition, history. Rather than turn a brief introduction into a lengthy and tedious glossary, I will simply assure the reader that problems of meaning will be taken up as particular concepts intensify. *Hybridity*, as the key word around which all of the others circulate, will be exempted from this deferral. Let me pause, then, and briefly introduce what hybridity has come to signify in the human sciences today.

Although it first became an important scientific term during the nineteenth century, in the fields of botany, biology, and natural history, today hybridity has returned in the service of disciplines more explicitly engaged in the study of human cultural practices, notably in literary theory and criticism, cultural studies, communication studies (especially in Latin America), and anthropology. I noted at the outset that hybridity has to do with "mixing." As a way of talking about mixing, hybridity has three central implications—empirical, methodological, and critical—in contemporary academic work.

Empirically, descriptively or referentially, hybridity denotes a general condition of "mixedness" (the term is Stam's [2000, 85]) or a process of mixture. A study of actually existing hybridity would be interested in those objects whose generic parameters explicitly exhibit their dependence on appropriation and internalization. An obvious example of a hybrid object would be the novel as theorized by Mikhail Bakhtin, as that literary form which owes its existence to the appropriation and recombination of other forms. American jazz or the Cuban *son,* generally understood by musicologists and novices alike as felicitous mixtures of African and European musical traditions, could represent hybrid forms in another artistic medium. Andean, Brazilian, and Mexican baroque styles of architecture are often noted for their formal hybridity. It is easy to complicate and throw into doubt the utility of this referential aspect of hybridity that pits mixed things against things not mixed. This aspect of hybridity will be discussed in chapters 1 and 2. For now, let me simply acknowledge that although hybridity today still has an empirical value, it has also come to imply much more.

Methodologically, the invocation of hybridity, especially in Latin Americanist fields, signals studies that are attentive to the "in-between" spaces of cultural production and practice: studies that think about what happens as culture moves from the big house to the slave hut, *ciudad* to *campo,* center to periphery, and, of course, vice versa. These kinds of studies focus their methodological apparatus on the problematization of purist notions of popular, elite, and mass culture, assuming that, in real life, each contaminates the others. In this sense, hybridity does not name static ends but rather signals an emphasis on the mobility of processes and circuits, and often implies a sense of interdisciplinarity.

Critically, hybridity has evolved into a concept that is often invoked as a kind of deconstructive lever, as a way to reverse and displace authoritative rhetorics and discourses. Indeed, the kind of critical impurification suggested by hybridity theory is a basic operation at work in deconstruction from its earliest moments (Spivak 1976). More than the objective mixing of disparate elements, hybridity in this sense describes or effects a movement by which the cultural and social practices traditionally constructed as "low" within a particular context (e.g., a society or a literary community) come to infiltrate and impinge upon the "high." Hybridity thus acts as what Robert Stam has called a kind of "jujitsu," turning the cultural energy of colonialism (that is, theories and practices of forced acculturation) back against itself and thereby destabilizing the culture of the colonizer (what Fernando Ortiz [1940] discerns as the unexpected emergence of *transculturation*). It is at this level of critique that hybridity becomes most explicitly oppositional, and is even theorized as a kind of subversion, thereby tracing a remarkably resilient trajectory in Latin American writing. Thus, in 1933, Gilberto Freyre could still agitate sectors of the local elite by demonstrating the extent to which Brazilian culture rested not on a European tradition but on that tradition's scandalous hybridization with Africa. Decades later, Silviano Santiago would radicalize this notion, making a case for the critical power of Latin American literature by linking it to the "savage mind" that seditiously infiltrates both Bible and dictionary. These "older" invocations of hybridity's critical force share a common quality with many of today's rearticulations of the term in that they appropriate for hybridity a notion of opposition, or even transgression. They posit that the insistent mixture—cultural, generic, genetic—that defines hybridity leads to a total collapse of the purist categories on which authoritative power and signification arguably rest.

It is the efficacy and implications of this last aspect of hybridity—that is, hybridity as a critical tool in the service of emancipatory, cultural affirmation within the context of Latin American writing—that I take as my general object of critique. I organize that critique by first homing in on the basic idea that escorts hybridity from its origins in empiricist scientism to interpretivist culturalism: the category of race. Given what is known about the history of the concept "hybridity," this articulation of hybridity to race is not difficult to demonstrate (see chapter 1). However, I want to be clear that the motivation of my critique of hybridity in its relations to race is not to argue that hybridity, or the theories and practices of mixing in general, are somehow essentially racist. I will not be calling for an erasure of race. Nor will I propose the need for more race. Rather than discover or denounce race in hybridity, the central goal vis-à-vis race will be to examine the mechanisms through which it has been thought—or gone unthought—within theories and narratives of hybridity, and to ask after the cultural, social, and political implications of this thinking, or unthinking.

Permutations of the literal word *hybridity*—*la hibridación, lo híbrido*—as a means for speaking of intercultural mixture are not new to Latin American writing. As early as 1916, the Mexican anthropologist Manuel Gamio made a key distinction between *hybridization* (which he associated with the artificial, the foreign) and *mestizaje* (which he associated with the organic, the authentic, the national). In the early 1930s, the Brazilian writer Gilberto Freyre would refer—in a chapter title, no less—to Brazil as a "hybrid society." Although these invocations were exceptions to the rule of *mestizaje* and, later on, especially in anthropological circles, *sincretismo* and *transculturación*, it is today hybridity that holds the greater critical currency. It is adopted by the widely cited cultural theorists Néstor García Canclini and Homi Bhabha, whose work is the subject of chapters 2 and 3 and remains in play—sometimes implicitly, other times explicitly—throughout the book. And although there certainly are conceptual and historical differences between hybridity and, say, *mestizaje*, those differences are neither clear nor stable, and are ultimately unmanageable. Moreover, because I aim to confront those differences with the repetitions that recur within a generalized discourse, the fantasy of precise distinction or autonomous singularity is far less interesting to me than the conceptual articulations and fusions. Therefore, to invoke *hybridity* in the generic sense is simply another way of saying "the theory, practice, and representation of mixing" and includes the other terms within its paradigm.

Before moving on to a brief description of the chapters, let me quickly pause to address an important point. Stuart Hall has argued that the kind of critique that I propose here might be too narrowly philological, and may only demonstrate a failure to fully grasp the radical transformation of the word *hybridity* over time (1996b, 259).[3] In the following chapters I argue that, at least in Latin American writing, this semantic transformation is less drastic than Hall suggests, and that it has entailed a historical forgetfulness that has allowed the trivialization of real social exclusions to persist. Although demonstrating the workings and implications of this dynamic is the task of the book itself, I would like to quickly register here the value of rethinking hybridity today. I maintain that the interrogation of *hybridity* is precisely the kind of project that productively situates itself at, and attempts to go beyond, a crucial problem. Let us summarize this problem as the impasse between representation and action that has reemerged and proven to be a flash point for rancorous debates about the political effectivity of postcolonial and cultural studies over the past two decades, and about the nature of deconstruction for much longer. Hybridity, in many ways, has become a critical tool that marks this site of contention, and is today employed, in a postcolonial mode, as a way of debunking the purist claims of authorities and authoritarianism (as we will see in the work of

Homi Bhabha, chapter 3). And yet we also witness today another kind of postcolonial reappropriation of theories of hybridity, one that invokes it as a strategy bent on undercutting the case for slavery reparations in the United States, and thwarting the struggle for the land, civil, and national-political rights of marginalized subjects in Brazil, Colombia, Guatemala, Mexico, South Africa, and elsewhere.[4] As we will see, *hybridity*, with its contradictory stakes in an entire range of biopolitical projects—from subjective emancipation to ethnic cleansing, from eugenics to social transgression—finds itself explicitly positioned at this impasse: an articulation of identity (gender, race, nationality, culture) to economy (production, consumption, reproduction), discourse to structure, representation to power. Thus the concept "hybridity," including its long association with the (re)production of bodies, forces us to confront identity, discourse, and representation in the context of the tenacious naturalization of colonial structures of power and social (re)production.

The following pages are organized into three parts. The three chapters of Part I fall under the heading "Theorizing Hybridity Today." They are, in effect, a critical reflection on the 1990s, insofar as that decade represented the canonization of "hybridity" as a key word in contemporary Latin Americanist literary and cultural studies. Whereas the purview there is transnational and contemporary, chapters 4–10 deal with earlier historical moments and two particular national contexts famous for their long, intense, and multifarious projects of theorizing and narrating hybridity: Mexico and Brazil.

Part I is framed by an analysis of the contested relations between Latin Americanist and postcolonial criticism that flared up during the 1990s. The concept "hybridity" emerged as a leading protagonist within these debates. How can we account for the tense relationship between these competing hybridities? I argue that it has to do with hybridity's complex entanglement with a Eurocentrically determined logic of race. Chapter 1, "Genres Are Not to Be Mixed," represents the necessary groundwork for establishing the relations between hybridity and race. Hybridity's stake in race is explicit in classic hybridological writers such as José Vasconcelos or Fernando Ortiz. In an attempt to account for and trace the tenacious and sometimes surprising ways that a logic of racial marking underwrites major Latin American intellectual signposts that appear to have nothing to do with it, I look to texts that may be less obvious: a famous essay by Jorge Luis Borges and a less famous one by Antonio Candido. The implicit functioning of race within these texts requires me to unearth its operations obliquely. The mediating term that I appropriate for this endeavor is the concept of genre as set forth in Jacques Derrida's essay "The Law of Genre" (1980). Via this route, I show how Latin Americanist theories of hybridity are tightly bound up with a rhetoric that, while deriving its intelligibility from race, simultaneously obscures that relationship through strategies of exceptionalism and exemplarity. Ultimately, the same principle of racial marking that enables the naturalization of exclusionist social reproduction is that which administers both the cultural marking of genre and its ostensible transgression via hybridity.

This demonstration of the particular relations between hybridity, genre, and race in the context of Latin American writing is decisive for the chapters that round out Part I. Those chapters each turn on critical rereadings of leading theorists of hybridity whose work generated significant debate in Latin Americanist fields during the 1990s. Chapter 2, "Erasing Race and the Persistence of Teleology," takes up Néstor García Canclini's now famous *Culturas híbridas*, as well as a number of its opponents, by asking after the implications of actively forgetting race in theories of hybridity. In chapter 3, "The Ambivalence of Theorizing Hybridity: Coloniality and Anthropology," I refocus on the relations between Latin Americanist and postcolonial theories of hybridity through an analysis of key essays by Homi Bhabha and their relevance for Latin Americanist criticism.

After tracing the implications of the relations between hybridity and race at the level of transnational theory—in Borges, Candido, García Canclini, Bhabha, and others—I take the insights gained through that conversation and ask how (or if) those problems emerged in earlier historical moments where the concern was less about postnational fragmentation than about national consolidation. The first historical context through which I read earlier theories and narratives of hybridity is Mexico, specifically the Mexican intelligentsia that mediates the transition from a state-sponsored, hegemonic positivism to postrevolutionary idealism: roughly 1867 to 1925. One of the supposed innovations of the new hybridity as theorized by García Canclini and Bhabha is its rigorous attention to questions of time, that is, the ways that distinct modes of interaction with the temporal can coexist spatially (García Canclini calls this phenomenon "multitemporal heterogeneity"; Bhabha tends to refer to it as a "time lag"). It is thus somewhat surprising to discover the same preoccupation with the temporal among the positivist liberals of nineteenth-century Mexico, and their postrevolutionary opponents. As is well known, the dominant mode of theorizing hybridity during this period happened within the framework of *mestizaje*. If the old *mestizaje* and the new hybridity are separated by radically different preoccupations with *nation*—the former concerned with challenges to formation and consolidation, the latter with the emancipatory potential of dissolution and dissemination—they seem to return to the common ground on which race meets time. It is this relationship that I seek to account for in Part II, "Mexico."

The Mexican discourse of *mestizaje* assumes as its object the "mixing" of differentially constructed categories of people, often generalized as "Indian" and "European." Of these categories, it is the production of the figure called "the Indian," and that figure's problematic inscription into modern society, that has always been at play in the Mexican intelligentsia's long-standing preoccupation with *mestizaje*. As a way of framing the specifically Mexican problematic of hybridity, I begin in chapter 4, "New Cultural History and the Rise of Mediation," by examining the historical emergence of the indigenist–*mestizaje* couplet and its relevance today. I read the recent turn to new cultural history in Mexicanist historiography as a sublimation of the logic of *mestizaje*, and argue that its critical innovations share an unexpected resonance with a moment of theorizing hybridity that came one hundred years earlier. This was the hybridity, as theorized by the Mexican positivists, that dominated the Porfirio Díaz regime. Chapter 5, "Back toward a Positive *Mestizaje*," examines the spirit of synthesis with which the liberal positivists articulated time to race in their reformation of national identity. By turning to the problem of multiple temporalities as the symptom of national fragmentation, the positivists demonstrate the long-standing Mexican rhetoric that euphemizes racially marked difference as a question of heterogeneous time. The overcoming of this problem—that is, the articulation of race and time as the realization of national consolidation—would be thought in terms of *mestizaje*.

The *mestizaje* solution, with all of its biopolitical implications intact, achieved the kind of ideological strength such that even the opponents of the state were tied to its terms. It is within these terms that there emerges a devastating critique of the genocidal policies of Porfirian militarism, in the form of Heriberto Frías's novel *Tomochic* (1893). This novel, its conditions of production, and its reception today are the subject of chapter 6, "They Were Not a Barbarous Tribe." Framing the Porfirian crackdown against a rebel village as a kind of anti-*mestizaje* that belies the state's commitment to mediation, Frías's ambivalence around the questions of Indianness and the proper modes of national subject formation speak to the ideological effectivity of *mestizaje* in the Mexican scene, not only then but also now. Frías is also prescient, insofar as he expresses the melancholy of foundational failure that seems to only intensify in the wave of *mestizaje* aesthetics that would arise in the wake of the Mexican Revolution. José Vasconcelos and Mariano Azuela are two icons of postrevolutionary cultural production that return to the problems of race–time disarticulation as a national crisis, but now in a notably anxious tone. I read this particular dynamic of hybridity theory in their signature works—Vasconcelos's *La raza cósmica* (1925) and Mariano Azuela's *Los de abajo* (1915)—in chapter 7, "*Mestizaje* and Postrevolutionary Malaise: Vasconcelos and Azuela."

If race is at stake in hybridity, it is insofar as race acts as a name for the normalization of hierarchical social reproduction. While rules of social reproduction tend to enter discourse through rhetorics of normality, the relations between hybridity and race always also resonate literally insofar as they pertain to the reproduction of national populations: this is to say that race in hybridity—indeed, race in general—is unthinkable without gender. Although the gendered operations of hybridity theory will be implicit throughout the preceding chapters, Part III, "Brazil," brings the relations between hybridity, gender, and social reproduction to the fore. This critique of hybridity theory will revolve around Gilberto Freyre's monolithic cultural history of Brazil, *Casa-grande e senzala* (1933). It is not a narrow interpretation of the work, however, as I articulate *Casa-grande e senzala* to a broader trajectory of thinking hybridity in Brazil, reading it through and against an influential predecessor and an insightful successor.

Taking its title from a classic essay by Antonio Candido, chapter 8, "The Brazilian Family," offers an introduction to Freyre's role in the construction of what I call the "national family." Although the figure of the family has always been used in metaphorical invocations of national community, this is not the sense in which I use it here. Rather, I speak of the nation–family relation in the sense that Hannah Arendt uses the concept (1958, 28–37, 256–57), as a name for a normative discourse insofar as it does not simply "represent" the nation but rather *natural-*

izes a structure of power on which social relations and reproduction are carried out. A specific kind of *mestiçagem*—the language of race and culture mixing of Freyre's Brazil—mediates this naturalizing process. In chapter 9, "On the Myth of Racial Democracy," I consider the famous Freyrian formulation of race and social reproduction, canonized as "racial democracy." I argue that the Freyre of *Casa-grande e senzala* has been largely misread, and that to understand the full significance of his critique one must abandon the insistence on Freyre's unchecked "celebration" of Brazilian race relations by looking instead to its profound ambivalence. Finally, in chapter 10, "The Iracema Effect in *Casa-grande e senzala*," I consider Freyre's treatment of the "classic" hybridization between Indians and Europeans by reading his representation of a foundational *mestiçagem* against two famous texts that stand in dialogue with his: Silviano Santiago's "O Entre-lugar do Discurso Latino-americano" (1971) and José de Alencar's *Iracema* (1865). The task, still, is not to expose formative errors or reveal past advice as misguided. It is to ask after the ways in which those errors and that advice still guide our own thinking.

Hybridity's operations within a Latin American coloniality of power that naturalizes hierarchy and divides resources unequally are not unknown. At the same time, the persistence of these operations has not been systematically delineated, historicized, or analyzed. This study attempts to do so through a critique of hybridity in Latin American writing. By critique I do not simply mean that it is negative vis-à-vis hybridity, though, of course, a gesture of negativity—a response of "no"—brought to bear on the received affirmations of a certain concept, theory, or idea is an act of resistance crucially important to, and that even propels the politics within, critical thought. But the point here is not to deny or negate or stake a position *against* hybridity, a move that would be as impossible to execute effectively as opposing speech, or land, or love, or terror. We might quarrel over its essence, its knowability, its legitimacy, or its material effects, but once we commit ourselves to the study of culture, hybridity in the most literal sense—as the formation of cultural objects out of heterogeneous elements—describes almost all things and certainly all human beings. Obviously, the object of critique here is not hybridity the thing or the word, but rather the mechanisms and processes through which the concept "hybridity" enters into discourse.

A "critique," following Jacques Derrida, seeks to construct an "interpretative and meaningful evaluation" of its object without rejecting or exteriorizing its object (1990, 989). Critique is at once interested and vertiginous: in order to provide such an evaluation, a critique questions identitarian foundations and methodological assumptions while recognizing its own dependence on those foundations and assumptions. It puts its own conditions of possibility under erasure: in Spivak's formulation, "[s]ince the word [all received metaphysical categories] is inaccurate, it is crossed out. Since it is necessary, it remains legible" (1976, xiv). It is, in short, the ambivalent refusal of obviousness. It is thus that hybridity today lends itself to critique. Hybridity has become conventional in Latin American writing: its critical force is self-evident, and its undeniable productivity quickly becomes synonymous with affirmation and even emancipation. On what does the self-evidence of hybridity's critical force rest? What does its affirmative function negate or deny? What remains outside of its emancipatory effects? Why? These are the kinds of questions that a critique of hybridity asks. I formulate these questions as an *immanent critique*; that is, I am putting into question the innocence of the genealogy of the basic concepts of the institutional field in which I dwell and through which I articulate my own commitments and interests: U.S.-based Latin American literary and cultural studies. There is thus an affirmative aspect to my own critique, in that I sense that hybridity could and should be sharpened within Latin Americanism. But far more important, I maintain that the pressing objective is to rethink the function of academic work in its complicity with institutional and international hegemony, such as the "racial axis" that Quijano has identified as central to the continued unfolding of the coloniality of power. Moreover, this rethinking means thinking through how that hegemonic complicity might be dialectically rearticulated with what I would say *could* be the motivating force of Latin Americanism: the realization of a material and political alliance with the institution's others.

What is at stake, then, in hybridity? I argue that it is the necessary unlocking of the dialectical reversal of a concept historically dedicated to the formation of a hegemonic subject position. It is a concept that works—not unlike the global expansion of U.S.-driven, liberal (and now increasingly conservative) pluralism—through what writers such as Jesús Martín-Barbero and Giorgio Agamben have called, in different contexts, a logic of inclusive exclusion. This logic unfolds in a number of ways, many of which will be described and analyzed in the pages that follow. As a theory of aesthetic production, hybridity has been an effective—if ultimately unsustainable—strategy for affirming the cultural singularity of Latin America vis-à-vis the rest of the world, and its cultural solidarity as a region. As a theory of social (re)production and political policy, hybridity quickly reveals itself as useful to a kind of eugenic discourse: as the biopolitical means for engineering the desired ends of "good births." I posit that these two aspects of hybridity—cultural production and social reproduction—are not necessarily distinct, and indeed traditionally overlap. In Part I, I will argue that this overlapping, in often covert and surprising ways, is still very much in play. In Parts II and III, I will try to unravel some of the political implications of this historical alliance. I will be arguing, then, that the ambivalence of hybridity theory toward (trans)nationally marginalized subjects articulates it to a coloniality of power, and that this articulation suggests not a haphazard coincidence but a cultural logic whose operations can be described, analyzed, and potentially stopped. The relation between theories of hybridity and the coloniality of power speaks to—even in the production of newness—the process by which the multiplicity of "other" identities, epistemologies, and cultures that define and inhabit the nation-space are effaced, sometimes quite literally.

In turning to the study itself, let me finally claim that my critique does not imply an overwhelming gloom hanging on the horizon of the current phase of globalization and the future of hybridity. In a world that has been pompously reinscribed with a deceptive division between "us and the terrorists" and injected with a new paranoia over national purity—such as the international return to nativism in the global economic centers, exemplified in Samuel Huntington's concern over the prolific birth rates of brown immigrants to the United States (2004)—hybridity may find itself with a new critical life. Thus it would seem crucial to take seriously Arendt's premise and acknowledge that even while repetition grounds worldly life, so is there always the possibility of repeating with a difference. If hybridity has returned today as a watchword of our times, again pronouncing itself as the pure transcendence of old purisms, then the activity of rethinking hybridity by looking into its history is part of the process of questioning, fragmenting, and perhaps redirecting the teleology of its cultural, social, and political force.

Part I
Theorizing Hybridity Today

The peasant—remote, conservative, some-what archaic in his ways of dressing and speaking, fond of expressing himself in tradi-tional modes and formulas—has always held a certain fascination for the urban man. In every country he represents the most ancient and secret element of society. For everyone but himself he embodies the occult, the hid-den, that which surrenders itself only with great difficulty: a buried treasure, a seed that sprouts in the bowels of the earth, an ancient wisdom hiding among the folds of the land.

—*Octavio Paz,* The Labyrinth of Solitude, *1950*

Here I am a barbarian, for men understand me not.

—*Ovid*

For underneath that codification of relations between Europeans and non-Europeans, race is, without doubt, the basic category.

—*Aníbal Quijano, "Coloniality of Power, Eurocentrism and Latin America," 2000*

Theorizing Hybridity Today

A **discourse of race** underwrites theories of hybridity. There is nothing shocking or extravagant in linking hybridity to race, so let me emphasize that I am not simply noting a conceptual coincidence. Rather, I am beginning by asserting a general principle: *to theorize hybridity is to operate within a discourse of race*. I announce this rule immediately, and even somewhat polemically, for a reason: in spite (or because) of the obviousness of the relationship between hybridity and race, in Latin Americanist criticism that relationship has sunk to the level of the implicit, whereby its force has gone underestimated, and in some cases disavowed.[1] This structural condition has frustrated the emergence of an effectively critical theory of hybridity in Latin American writing, to the point that failed theories of hybridity are now constitutive of the basic concepts of Latin Americanist literary and cultural studies. In what sense do these theories "fail"? In the sense that, despite repeated claims to the contrary, they can never succeed in going beyond the discourse of race in which they dwell.

How can this be? The attraction of hybridity is precisely its utility as a discursive, rhetorical, and conceptual anchor in constructing a language *against* the exclusionary implications of race. Hybridity, understood in its most explicit sense, signals a process or condition of cultural mixture. We exemplify it by pointing to established cultural forms. For

3

example, the Cuban *son*, the Colombian *cumbia*, the Brazilian samba, or the Argentine tango, are variously understood as hybrids of African, European, and sometimes Amerindian musical traditions, as a negotiation and tense agreement between canonized and popular forms. Latin American literary trends, such as magical realism and the multiple *vanguardias*, tend to be explained in similarly hybrid terms. It is no exaggeration to say that for the past five hundred years, the geographical landmass that we today call "Latin America" has been theorized as a space that compels writers to produce "mixed" forms and genres.[2] Hybridity (and by extension, Latin America), then, should be precisely that which trumps the racialization of culture by transgressing and overcoming the purism of generic restrictions, static traditionalism, and strict formalism. Moreover, hybridity seems to indicate a decentering and even displacement of the purist standardization and canonization of culturally authentic artifacts established in the name of colonial or national authority. To be sure, some of the most innovative concepts that attempt to explain Latin American cultural singularity—on bases that can appear to have nothing to do with race—are frequently premised upon a mixing that effects a counterhegemonic transgression against cultural purity: *mestizaje, criollismo*, transculturation, Luso-tropicalism, racial democracy, heterogeneity, syncretism, *nuestra América*, the baroque, *antropofagia*, di- and heteroglossia, *lo real maravilloso, modernismo*, the postmodern, and *culturas híbridas*, to name only fifteen.

But hybridity, saturated in a racialized history, also points to the inseparability of race and culture. The genealogy of the term itself, imported to the study of culture from the biological sciences, is directly bound up with the elaboration of race science, especially in England, France, Germany, and the United States. It became a key concept in the nineteenth-century debate over human origins carried out between monogenists (who believed in a common, familial origin of all humans) and polygenists (who believed in multiple local creations of different kinds of humans). This debate was linked directly to justifications of slavery and largely turned on the question of the fertility of interracial offspring, or "hybrids." These old implications die hard: not long ago, Antonio Cornejo Polar noted that "[a]s for hybridity, the almost spontaneous association has to do with the sterility of hybrid products" (1998, 7).[3] In short, scientists, jurists, and essayists begin discussing cultural hybridity as they begin to cast a biopolitical gaze upon the reproductive intercourse between Africans, Amerindians, Asians, and Europeans, and to question whether or not this practice is a good idea.[4] This history, conscious or not, enables the current usage of the term (Young 1995; cf. Hall 1996b, 259).[5] It is worth noting that this biopolitical theorization of mixing has a much longer history in the Ibero-American world, especially within the language of *mestizaje*.[6] Nevertheless, even there, framing the question of "mixing" specifically in the terms of "hybrids" rises in concert, and in dialogue, with nineteenth-century Euro- and Anglocentric race theory: the naming of *mulatos* and *mestizos* as such is an enabling prelude to the history of *cultural* hybridity.[7]

While this history is known, it tends to be elided, or at best glossed, in current elaborations of the critical potential of hybridity. What typically goes unrecognized, then, is the uncomfortably close relationship between hybridity and segregation. If hybridity is rooted in a notion of blending, these same roots are nourished by a concept that always returns to segregation: the category of race (Balibar and Wallerstein 1988, 22–23, 103). An impasse arises: hybridity as the incessant process of mixing traces its condition of possibility to a discourse—race—that legitimates and institutionalizes separation.[8]

This impasse surprisingly reappeared at the level of academic argument during the 1990s. In contemporary humanistic criticism, *hybridity* usually indicates the dynamics and implications (political, aesthetic) of intercultural mixing *in general*. Yet in Latin Americanist fields, *hybridity*—as the name for a paradigm of culture mixing—stands as the sign of Latin American cultural production *in particular*. Thus, as hybridity became more and more entrenched as a "key concept" in the loosely related, Anglophone and Francophone reading strategies that, over the past two decades, have come to be known as "postcolonial theory" (Ashcroft, Griffiths, and Tiffin 1998, 118–21), interdisciplinary tension began to build. Within the many and widely cited debates that revolve around the contested relevance of postcolonial theory for the study of Latin America, only the category of the "subaltern" can rival hybridity as a flash point for controversy and polemics.[9] Out of these conversations has arisen the conventional notion that the postcolonial idea of hybridity is at best an imprecise fit for Latin American discourse and society, and at worst effaces a long tradition of specifically Latin American ideas about culture mixing articulated under thematic cognates such as *mestizaje, antropofagia, sincretismo, transculturación, lo real maravilloso, heterogeneidad*, and so on (e.g., Franco 1992, 76; Moraña 1998, 217; Stam 2000, 83, 91). It would seem that theories of hybridity—categorized under the sometimes competing banners of Latin Americanism and postcolonialism—have found it difficult to hybridize. Why has this encounter proven so problematic?

This is a question worth asking: at stake is nothing less than the production of a truly internationalist critique of the globalization of liberal multiculturalism in its imperial mode, one that can resist the centrifugal pull toward a divisive territorialism. In other words, at stake is the formation of an effectively critical project that refuses to take the bait of an old colonial lure that leads only to an insistent particularization of protest, revolt, or even just criticism. In response to that question are a number of possible lines of analysis, perhaps necessarily beginning with the historical fact that what is proposed in mid-1980s postcolonial theory as a vehicle for counter-Eurocentric subversion (e.g., Bhabha 1994) is *already* a generic mark of cultural production in Latin America (e.g., Reyes 1936, 232–33) that has also already been redeployed as a sign of cultural resistance (e.g., Santiago 1971). This fact has been widely noted. But the challenge of postcolonialism for Latin Americanist criticism is not (or should not be limited to) the naming of a difference, a historico-cultural incommensurability. The more urgent work for Latin Americanism might be to take the recoil provoked by postcolonial key words—in this case, *hybridity*—as a cue to revisit its own founding principles. This is the task of Part I, in which I take as the object of my critique the Latin Americanist commitment to the "production of theories of hybridity," what might be called *hybridology*. Against the current trend to think theories of hybridity "beyond ethnicity" (or, for that matter, to think Latin America "beyond hybridity"), this will entail placing hybridology back into dialogue with the condition of possibility that determines its modern intelligibility: a Eurocentrically articulated theory of race.

Let me be clear: I will not propose a rereading of hybridological texts in the name of "exposing racism." Nor will I denounce hybridology as "fundamentally racist," as something that needs to be exorcised from a conceptual field. Rather, I embark from the idea that, given that "hybridity" historically enters into cultural discourse as a contested term within the racialized and transnational debate over human origins, the necessary reframing of hybridity is not best accomplished by placing it under (or against) the terms of *the nation* (cf. Larsen 2001) or even the more broadly construed *popular subject position* (cf. Beverley 1999).[10] Rather, hybridity will be best (re)thought in its emergence through a field of *biopolitics*.[11] To rethink hybridity in terms of biopolitics is to bring back to the fore the social contracts that govern the naturalization of differential relations between subjects, bodies, and the state, and that articulate race to nation.[12] This has always been hybridity's domain and, I argue, it is this domain that still enables the conversion of hybridity into the generic mark of Latin American cultural production, whether the institutional host of this conversion coalesces at the level of the state, the academy, the mass media, or their complex and historically variable articulations.[13]

And yet it is the field of biopolitics that is effaced in the often insightful critique of the new hybridity that focuses exclusively on its alleged abandonment of the nation(-state) as a workable arena for the articulation of culture to politics. The reduction of hybridity to a confrontation with "nation" leaves the call to historicize materially in the paradoxical position of having forgotten the material history (that is, the historical conditions of production) of hybridity's function within Latin American discourse and society. These conditions are meaningless if extracted from their biopolitical history that runs directly through race and, by extension, through the idea of nation itself.

It is precisely the ill-advised, momentary suspension of this contradictory history—hybridity as both built upon and transcending race—that has left cultural theorists stalled in their attempts to move hybridity "beyond ethnicity." One could amass citations, but for now let me put forth one outstanding example. I think it is precisely through the evasion of the biopolitical commitments of hybridology that Serge Gruzinski, in an ambitious attempt to take hybridity beyond ethnicity, can begin his narrative by first unselfconsciously detailing as the original agents of hybridity the forced "deportation of populations," the emergence of "centers of [European] penetration," and arranged marriages between "Portuguese soldiers" and the "daughters of indigenous dignitaries" (1999, 13), and then in the next breath refer to hybridity's roots in racialized differentiation as "embarrassing" (19). This relation, he concludes, is something to be "avoided like the plague" (ibid.). But this might be just the problem: disavowing that which embarrasses may in fact lead the embarrassing object to reemerge at a later, unexpected, and perhaps inopportune moment. *Embarazoso*: hybridity, like race, ensures the "properly" gendered, socialized, and strategic modes of (re)production.

To emphasize: confronted with a postcolonial appropriation of hybridity, I am arguing for neither a change in Latin Americanist terminology

nor a recovery of Latin American intellectuals who theorized it better, first, or more accurately for particular national-historical contexts.
Rather, I am arguing for a sustained engagement with and critique of
hybridology in the persistence of its uninterrogated biopolitical mode.
One place to see this persistence in action is in writing. The kind of
critique that I have in mind would require Latin Americanism to take
seriously the unfinished work of Ángel Rama and Antonio Cornejo
Polar by heeding the call for historical specificity and hence rereading
America within its internationalist context, in other words, *in its dialectical relations with Eurocentrism*. Latin Americanism's most prominent
participants in the postcolonial conversation—Walter Mignolo (1995),
Santiago Castro-Gómez (1996), Fernando Coronil (1999)—do precisely
that. But although writing this history *as* a Latin Americanist critique of
Eurocentrism is key, this project will remain unrealized or, at best, weak
if not accompanied by a critique *of* its own self-evidence, that is, a critique
of Latin Americanism as a kind of Eurocentrism. And this shift changes
the terms of the Latin American dialogue with postcolonial theory. In
short, both Alfonso Reyes's old call to provincialize the metropole (1936)
(which is precisely the space of the reading strategies today called "postcolonial") and Aníbal Quijano's new one (2000, 544) must be effected
through a critique of the efficacy of foundational, or "local," alternatives. The modest contribution to that task put forth in Part I is a critical reconsideration of the ways that "hybridity" functions as the generic
mark of Latin American writing.

I maintain that a rigorous confrontation of hybridity with its history will ultimately open up avenues for (re)thinking the postcolonial
in Latin America, by which I mean to indicate the intersections of cultural inclusion and political exclusion not only on a north–south axis,
but also within and between Latin American societies, *in the context of an
ongoing colonialism*. This framework is what I understand Quijano to be
theorizing as "the coloniality of power," and which, following Stuart
Hall (1996b, 248, 250), is also precisely what postcolonial reading highlights. In the Latin American context, this project, now well under way,
will be long and collective, requiring not only a rethinking of García
Canclini through and against Vasconcelos, but also the rereading of the
nineteenth-century archive of Latin American identity construction at
the biopolitical articulation of race and state formation. My goal in Part I
will be to try to get at the inner logic of a problem: the alliance of "hybridity" and "Eurocentrism" at the core of Latin American intellectual

identity and thought (ontology and epistemology), countercolonial or otherwise. This will require a critique of hybridology's stake in race. Writers such as Quijano and Roberto Schwarz (1992) have drawn out the specifically American articulations of race to colonial–national modes of production in powerful, if still schematic, ways. The task now is to trace how that socially embedded naturalization of (hierarchical) difference installs itself not only within bodies, but also within the structures of ideas, at once enabling and frustrating the Latin Americanist critique of Eurocentrism. The claim, then, is not that "race relations" go ignored in Latin America(nism) (they do not). Rather, I would argue that an account of the discursive maintenance of race, as the production of naturalized cultural differences, has gone understated, and is still too easily subsumed within the racial exceptionalism of Latin American racial democracies.[14] In order to begin tracing race as it clings to the very writing of hybridity in Latin America, let us begin by moving to the most explicit and general site of hybridity's critical action today: genre.

1. Genres Are Not to Be Mixed

At least since **Mikhail Mikhailovitch Bakhtin's inquiry** into novel-istic structure (1935), artistic and literary genre has been one of the most common sites at which to propose the critical potential of what is today called "hybridity." It has also been one of the most difficult.

The nature of these difficulties can be readily demonstrated through Néstor García Canclini's ephemeral turn to "impure genres" (1989, 314–22). García Canclini identifies certain generic practices and forms (e.g., video [282–88], graffiti [314–16], and the comic strip [316–22]) as effecting a kind of cultural impurification in their modes of material production, critical strategy, and public reception. Productively, "they bring the artisanal to industrial production and mass circulation" (315). Strategically, a genre such as the comic strip exhibits its impurity in the way that it draws on multiple generic canons (316–17), only to impurify them with strategies such as parody (317), anachronism (ibid.), hyper-bole (e.g., unapologetic commercialism) (320), resignification (322), and social critique (317, 321, 322). Receptively, this impurity delinks culture from class (281–88, 314): the comic strip is literature for everyone, as it speaks to both popular and elite sectors of society (316–17); it decenters the location of culture, moving it from the library to the street cor-ner. For García Canclini, then, an impure genre is essentially a genre that mixes, or one that is mixed. He asserts this point by noting at the outset of his discussion that ostensibly impure genres such as graffiti or the comic strip are in fact "constitutionally hybrid genres" (314). Upon suggesting this synonymous link between impurity and hybridity, however, the concept of the "impure" immediately vanishes from his text. The "impure," in fact, only appears in the title of a subsection (ibid.), henceforth usurped by the presence of the "hybrid." If hybridity is, or can stand in for, impurity—as this shift in signifiers leads us to conclude—then the hybridization of genres must be a kind of impurification. Thus the *act* that propels this transitive *process*—to "hybridize *x*," to "impurify *y*"—must be carried out upon or against something that is not yet hybrid, not yet impure. The object of this transgression, it stands to reason, will be pure genre.

The problem within García Canclini's account of genre is signaled in this inability to delink his notion of the "impure" from the purist implications of "genre." The comic strip, as the impure genre that he addresses most explicitly, is, of course, a universally recognized genre in its own right (317), making the function of the tag "impure" somewhat dubious. Moreover, the specific example that he offers—Fontanarrosa's *Inodoro Pereyra*, a savvy and widely read Argentine comic strip, published serially beginning in 1972—is no less a canonical cultural artifact than the foundational text that it most insistently impurifies or hybridizes: José Hernández's *gauchesco* classic *Martín Fierro* (1872). Furthermore, the comic strip is no more hybrid than gaucho literature itself, which was never reducible to anything like a "pure genre," as Borges implied when, in "La poesía gauchesca" (1932), he called *Martín Fierro* a novel disguised in epic verse (1964, 32–33). In fact, as García Canclini admits at an earlier point in his narrative, transgressively hybrid forms reconvert into the same old class-based hierarchies of institutionally sanctioned genre relatively quickly, if not immediately (287–88). By bracketing and eventually discarding this moment of hesitation, however, his critique arrives at an impasse in which hybridity merely hybridizes that which was once hybrid, but to which we now ascribe the purity of genre. In short, the critical force of his "hybridization" proves brittle at precisely the point that one might hope to find its strongest edge.

Let me set aside until the following chapter a more thorough consideration of García Canclini's text, and say simply that his theory stalls in the one-way street that it maps for the operations of hybridity's transgressive function. Its critical force undercuts itself by producing a model that poses hybridity as a kind of automatic transgression against its other, coming after or in opposition to the implicit purity of genre or generic formalization, and by extension, against the purist segregationism of class stratification and hierarchy (258).[1] As I will demonstrate more fully in the following chapter, rather than a critical unveiling, García Canclini's configuration precisely obscures the kind of interdependency that governs the relations between "hybridity" and "purity." Let me also point out that his sublimation of mixing is a common one in Latin Americanist criticism, and constitutes, as writers with projects as diverse as Alfonso Reyes (1936), Silviano Santiago (1971), Ángel Rama (1982, esp. 173–93), Jesús Martín-Barbero (1987, 2–3), Nelly Richard (1993, 456–58), and René Jara (1996, 10) have all insisted, a founding principle of Latin American cultural identity: genre mixing becomes the generic mark of *all Latin American cultural production*.[2]

Drawn into this complex Latin Americanist staging of cultural identity by way of impurity, hybridity, transgression, and genre, a question posed by Jacques Derrida is especially provocative: "And suppose for a moment that it were impossible not to mix genres. What if there were, lodged within the heart of the law itself, a law of impurity or a principle of contamination?" (Derrida 1980, 204). Might that "counter-law, an axiom of impossibility" (ibid.), find its explicit reconversion into natural law within the Latin American intellectual tradition? The prominent roll call of modern Latin American participants in various "aesthetics of hybridity" (Yúdice 2001, xx)—which is essentially an aesthetics of mixing—has led generations of artists, essayists, and critics to suggest as much.

But before rushing into an essentialist, even exceptionalist, foundationalism, let us recall that Derrida first illuminates genre as a limit, in the sense that it can be formulated as a norm and carries with it the force of law (203). No sooner has he accounted for this disciplinary quality of genre, however, than he exerts against it the counterforce of its constitutive opposite. The limits established by genre only exist as such through the inherent possibility of transgression: any such transgressive admixture "should confirm, since, after all, we are speaking of 'mixing', the essential purity of [a particular genre's] identity" (204). But, in general, "[g]enres are not to be mixed" (202). Genre in the generic sense should then require a kind of discipline; or, more precisely, discipline—as a heterogeneous field that is at once regulatory and productive (Foucault 1971a, 1978; Mowitt 1992, 31–32)—becomes the necessary companion of genre. The anxious question that arises is whether the artistic mixing of genres (as hybridity), or its scholarly correlate found in the movement between and across disciplines (as interdisciplinarity), can have any legitimacy at all.

I do not exaggerate when I characterize this question as "anxious." There persistently emerges, throughout the recurrent theorization of hybridity in Latin America, an explicitly articulated anxiety. The reiteration of this anxiety is precisely that which most symptomatically speaks to, and also suggests the danger in sublating, the links between the will to mix of hybridity and the segregationist impulse of race: the act of theorizing hybridity participates in a racialized discourse. Prominent theorists of hybridity provide some illustrations. In the preface to an English translation of *Casa-grande e senzala*, Gilberto Freyre gives as the fundamental inspiration for his mammoth inquiry into the hybridization of Brazilian culture the following: "of all the problems confronting Brazil there was none that gave me so much anxiety as that of miscegenation" (1946, xxvi).[3] In a prologue to the 1948 edition of *La raza cósmica* (1925), José Vasconcelos similarly recalls "the question that the mestizo has frequently asked himself: 'Can my cultural contribution be compared with the work of the relatively pure races that have made history up until our day, the Greeks, the Romans, the Europeans?' And within each nation *[pueblo]*, how do the periods of *mestizaje* stack up against the periods of creative racial homogeneity?" (1925, 43–44). Octavio Paz seems to be working through similar questions in his momentous treatment of the "pachuco" and the "hijos de la Malinche" (1950). Writing in a different political context, Roberto Fernández Retamar, at the outset of his famously polemical *Calibán* (1971), would equate the question of whether there exists a singular "Latin American culture" as tantamount to questioning the very existence of Latin Americans as such (1971, 7). That he proceeds, echoing Martí and Bolívar, by delineating a cultural program based upon a specifically *mestiza* America (8) again betrays the anxious link between cultural and racial legitimacy. Lest all of this be written off as a transcended history, recall that the racialized hybridity deemed "embarrassing" by Gruzinski still implies, as the late Antonio Cornejo Polar once put it to García Canclini, the age-old question of the productivity of hybrids (1998, 7).

If Derrida's account of genre is useful in this Latin American scene, it is because it confronts us with the dialectical relation by which the rule (law, pure genre, pure race) depends on its exception (transgression, hybrid genre, *mestizaje*). *Mestizaje*, in this model, rather than being an alternative to racial purity, instead reinforces it. Cultural hybridity, in a similar way, and as we saw in García Canclini, mirrors the taxonomic gesture of the law of genre.[4] To argue for the hybridity of *mestizaje* as the legitimizing mark of a kind of exceptional status or identity becomes a tacit recognition and admission of the preeminence of race. In other words, *mestizaje* as the exception to racial purity ultimately makes possible, legitimates, and reconfirms that purity. Understood as such, it comes as little surprise that the early Spanish colonial taxonomies of racial mixture mingled with and appropriated the force of law through the normative "society" or "regimen" of *castas*.[5] With this cluster of juridical norms regulating many aspects of colonial life (handling of arms, access to wealth, commerce, and social ascension), its multifarious recodification—spanning dozens of racial categories—at once exposes the impossible fluidity of racial classification and reconfirms the social force of race.[6] Centuries later, in an attempt to forge the *patria* by redefining a nationalist cultural specificity, Manuel Gamio would refer back to that colonial mixing as the originary mark of Mexico's national protagonist, what he calls the "mestizo type," in its "pristine purity" (1916, 66). Whether the terms of production are racial or cultural, imperial or national, to argue for the hybridization of genres and practices as the Latin American exception speaks to a *genus universum* whose parameters are defined elsewhere: the metropole, the political and economic center (cf. Fernández Retamar 1971, 7).[7]

Positing hybridity as exemplary of an exceptional cultural singularity (exceptionalism) obscures the fact that that "elsewhere"—the site of genre—depends on that very exceptionalism to maintain its legitimacy. This is what the early work of Homi Bhabha theorizes by pursuing the ambivalent operations of colonial discourse.[8] The crux of the matter is as follows: The persistent rearticulation of hybridity as exceptionalism, even as a gesture of contestation, is a structural necessity of Eurocentrism. The ramifications of this structure are not all gloomy: much in the same terms as the critical advantage of marginality that Hegel found in the perspective of the "slave," or Bourdieu in "female intuition" (1998, 31), Borges will argue that the inner exteriority of Latin America lends its writers a certain edge. But the constant failure of attempting to overcome this marginal position through hybridity, which

Derrida's account of genre helps us see, suggests the need not so much for an interrogation of *hybridity* the social phenomenon as for a reconsideration of *hybridology* by thinking through the political-cultural legacies of its historical conditions of possibility. Asking after those legacies and conditions forces a confrontation with the racialized logic of exemplarity—and its attendant discourse of typification—on which the logic of hybridity is premised. Furthermore, it throws into question the very foundations of the "genre" of Latin American writing per se.

The question, then, is not (or no longer is), How can a Latin Americanist epistemology stand up to, or even overcome, a Eurocentric tradition that excludes it? Rather, it might be worth asking: How does that Eurocentric tradition depend on Latin America as its inner exterior that *will always fail* at "standing up to it" (whether, to paraphrase Santiago, as deficient economy or deficient intellectual production)?[9] Propelled by this question, let us turn to a pair of essays by Borges and Candido that engage the issue of genre and Latin American writing.[10] The objective of this reading is to help construct a frame for rethinking the legacy of earlier moments in theorizing hybridity with which modern Latin Americanist theories of hybridity always dialogue. At issue will not be an exposé of a "racism" that is always ultimately (and somewhat tediously) exploitable; rather, the issue is to rethink an assumed distance that separates the new hybridology from its precursors. For now, however, let's see how this chain of signifiers—genre, race, *mestizaje*, hybridity, example, exception—plays out in the very limited, but exemplary, set of essays by Borges and Candido put forth here.

The transgressive potential of the critical force unleashed by the mixing of genres is a recurrent theme in Latin Americanist literary and cultural theory. Whereas Borges harnesses this force and strives to explode a chauvinistic limit, Candido uses it to establish a basis for epistemological revalorization. Together, their distinct national perspectives conjoin in making an influential, exceptionalist case for Latin American singularity: Latin America constitutes a narratological terrain where theory and fiction hybridize, where boundaries blur, where genres mix. The kind of genre blurring that Borges and Candido posit, however, does not portray Latin America as one pole in a Manichaean dichotomy external to and premised against its European opposite. Rather, they represent Latin America as that discursive space, *within Europe* (cf. Dussel 1995, 134), where European discourse—tradition, universality—experiences its most radical exteriority. In other words, they suggest (and, in their own critical work, confirm) that Latin American writing is the practice wherein the tacit contracts of Eurocentrism are most strongly felt and explicitly thought. The most immanently critical practice of European writing, in this sense, is outside itself.

In his 1951 lecture "El escritor argentino y la tradición," Borges expresses this problematic through a consideration of the signs of purity known as tradition and genre. Against the apologists for a nationalist parochialism, he famously argues that anything resembling a regional literary "tradition" emerges only through inauthenticity (1964, 129–30). The gaucho literary mode, as the mark of generic *argentineidad*, is a bastard. Its canon resonates with the cultured spirit of Kipling as much as the earthy spirit of the pampa (133–34). In a move predictably similar to Derrida's critique of genre in general, Borges shows how the specificity of a *gauchesco* genre asserts itself through its own transgression (130–31).[11] For Borges, then, any authentic genre only comes into its own by recognizing its constitutive inauthenticity: it is precisely the foreignness of the *gauchesco* that makes it Argentinean. A pure Argentine genre, in effect, must be willing to disown its own claims to purity.

A year earlier, in "Literatura e cultura de 1900 a 1945" (1950), Antonio Candido had already proposed the obverse of Borges's thesis, here for the Brazilian intellectual scene. For Candido, something like a genre of Brazilian writing achieves its apotheosis through its persistent impurification and hybridization of received epistemological standards. Noting the strong literary (by which he means subjective or poetic) and weak scientific (by which he means objective or empirical) evolution of Brazilian intellectual production, Candido suggests that the implicit generic terms—"literature" and "science"—and the epistemological weight that they each carry have been misapplied. Without the necessary socioeconomic conditions to foment adequate institutions of scientific and philosophical advancement (1950, 154), Brazilians have always looked to a canon of fiction and rhetoric in order to know themselves and their world (155).[12] What goes by the name of Brazilian literature (e.g., Romantic *indigenismo*, Alencar, Machado) serves the empirical function of a sociological science (154). Brazilian science, in its turn, cannot resist "the powerful magnet of literature" (153). The most productive investigations into the Brazilian national psyche and social life—Candido mentions Cunha's *Os sertões* (1901) and Freyre's *Casa-grande e senzala* (1933)—are both: hybrids, occupying "that mixed genre of essay . . . which combines . . . imagination and observation, science and art" (ibid.).[13] His insight is perceptive and critical. He is perceptive in that he understands that the rules of positive scientificity—legislated and executed elsewhere—adjudicate what counts as scholarship. He is critical in that he interrogates the essentially rhetorical nature of all scientific endeavors. Candido here identifies in an entire national-cultural tradition the same kind of constitutive interdisciplinarity—and its critical force— that Michel de Certeau would later find in Freud's axiom "the novelist has always preceded the scientist" (de Certeau 1981, 19, 27).[14]

Borges and Candido are both participating in an old ontological problem produced through the tension between the particularity of Latin American knowledge and the universality of Eurocentric tradition, understood here as the universalization of local European norms of science, philosophy, historiography, and reason (Mignolo 2000a). Each attempts to solve this problem by diagnosing it as a kind of belonging without participation. In other words, they both assert Latin American cultural Westernness against what they perceive as a bad-faith, self-imposed stance of nonparticipation, or even exile, a stance that achieves "like existentialism," Borges concludes, only "the charm of the pathetic" (1964, 135); thus Borges's conclusion—readable as either a postcolonial reversal of, or a neocolonialist deferral to, Eurocentrism[15]—that Argentine "tradition is all of Western culture, and [that] we have a right to this tradition" (ibid.); thus Candido's assessment that the best Brazilian literary works are those prodigies that exhibit a new voice while not rejecting their European and "Portuguese fathers," that assent to participate in the "family dialogue" (1950, 129–31). Years later, he would define Latin American literary maturity as the achievement of a cultural "interdependency" with the metropole (1970, 133), echoing a long-standing promise by Reyes (1936, 235).

A deconstructive perspective, however, would reverse the reading of this problematic, reformulating it as one of "participation without belonging" (Derrida 1980, 206). This "taking part in without being part of, without having membership in a set," links up with the "principle of contamination" (ibid.) that both founds and confounds the integrity of genre, and hence, the intelligibility of the work that should be contained within this or that genre. That principle of contamination, which governs the discriminatory effects of *genre*, is the same inner principle that enables the formulation of *genus*, a genus that we might here call the "Western intellectual tradition." If we understand genus, in its classical Aristotelian sense, as the original container that holds all things of a common set or class (Agamben 1994, 80–81; Gruzinski 1999, 26), then we see that even this speciously self-evident concept is in fact, as Darwin understood, that which enables the metaphysical fiction known as "taxonomy." As a guiding principle, then, for taxonomic thinking, genus—the naming of categories—will produce not only generic commonality, but also effective differentiation. It can produce, for example, the difference between man and animal (a historically confusing and problematic endeavor, especially intense in the Judeo-Christian West, *Genesis* notwithstanding; see Agamben 2002; 1994, 80). Now, this same principle governs the intelligibility of *writing* insofar as generic categories determine the distinguishing marks of legitimate and illegitimate production of knowledge.

In more Foucauldian language, genus, like its derivative *genre*, will require a disciplinary (and ultimately imperial) production of plurality— and mixing—that it then surveys and regulates.[16] Within this logic of genus, all common things, including all mixed things, define themselves through, while participating in the constitution of, the genus (Agamben 1994, 83). Via this taxonomic framework, then, perhaps we can argue that *el pensamiento latinoamericano*, like any other postcolonial epistemology, has always participated in that genus called "Western tradition," but under the terms of a Eurocentric contract that presupposes its status as a constitutive peripherality (Dussel 1995, 134; Said 1989). Constitutive in this sense implies a productive agency that acts upon (participates by constituting) (see Agamben 1994, 83), but finds no home within (does not belong to), the genus. If, as Giorgio Agamben has argued, the construction of a Western philosophical tradition has consistently—from Aristotle to Marx—rested upon defining the genus "man" as that being whose generic mark is the constitution of its own genus through production, praxis, action, and will (1994, 68–93), then it is not surprising that the epistemological status of the marginal (here, Latin American) "work" would be revealed as a site of identitarian contest, and even as a source of anxiety.

Following the "logic of the example" (Derrida 1980, 206), this problematic status frames Latin American cultural production and intellectual practice as at once exemplary (of the "set") and exceptional (from the "set") vis-à-vis "the Western tradition." Agamben helps us put a finer point on this paradox of exemplarity when he demonstrates the inextricability of *the example* and *the exception* (or "the special case"). For

Agamben, although the example may participate in the exemplification of commonality, it is ultimately outside the bounds of the normal case. The example, "excluded from the normal case" insofar as it "exhibits its own belonging to it," becomes the exception. The example's *exemplarity* makes it precisely *exceptional*, that is, *unnatural*. The rhetorical mode of the example–exception relation, then, is one of *denaturalization*.[17] All of this is very abstract, but Agamben's referent is not: the Jews in Nazi Germany, in the most literal sense, were *denaturalized* insofar as they were, as a prelude to their literal extermination, *denationalized*, stripped of their status as "German nationals" and hence rendered exceptional, that is, expendable, or, in Agamben's terms, killable. We will return shortly to the figure of the Jew, but for now let us stick to the context of Latin American writing. For the "Latin American writer" (here understood on Borges's and Candido's terms), then, to participate without belonging is to occupy a subject position whose exemplary participation is also the sign of its awkwardness, its unnaturalness, its exceptionality, that which throws its status of belonging into doubt.

I think this is the impasse before which Borges and Candido find themselves stalled. They attempt to overcome a tradition of Latin American exceptionalism, in other words, the thesis that poses Latin America as an epistemological and geographical site where universal theories both fail and fail to be produced (see Schwarz 1992, 23). In failing, however, these attempts posit the exemplary limit without which the universalism of Eurocentric discourse could not define itself: exceptionalism becomes the constitutive limit case of the universal rule.[18] Latin American exceptionalism stems, paradoxically, not from an active exclusion, but rather from a constitutive exemplarity.

What constitutes Latin America's exemplary status, or, what does Latin America exemplify? Savagery.[19] Within this historically sedimented identification, the Latin American agent of knowledge production—the intellectual—is caught in a double bind. On the one hand, the nobility of the savage springs from an ignorance of the universal (as culture, civilization, and politics), and a wholeness that is particular (the bodily experience of nature): "The 'simple' man . . . admits the particularity of his place and his experience; by virtue of this, he is already something of a savage" (de Certeau 1986, 72).[20] De Certeau's savage is one that exemplifies an anthropological notion of culture (through a lack or an idealization) but is banned from culture's realm—the city, the metropole—for precisely that exemplarity (Agamben 1995, 8). If discourse limited to the particular, experiential, corporal, domestic, and "simple" is the mark of pure savagery, then to exit from the idiocy of savagery is, as Avital Ronell shows (1996, 3), to join the polis, the politics of the cosmopolitan dialogue (Arendt 1958, 38). To do so as equals might require asserting either universal rights (Borges, Candido) or something like the oxymoronic legitimacy of a "barbarian theorizing" (Mignolo 1998a). Whatever the case, this exit will thus also be an entrance, a route maintained today, as we will see in the following chapter, in the undeconstructed binary of tradition-and-modernity that underwrites García Canclini's account of hybrid cultures (e.g., 1989, 221–23).

Hence, while on the one hand exemplifying savagery, on the other hand Latin America will also transcend the limits of the savagery that it exemplifies. This transcendence has been most explicitly theorized as the struggle against (e.g., Sarmiento) or incorporation of (e.g., Martí) *la barbarie*. But now, vis-à-vis the geopolitical center, this disavowal or resemantization of barbarism yields nothing like the kind of "interdependency" that Candido will later have in mind. Rather, the residue of a savagery corrupted (i.e., "interdependent"), or only partially abolished, reconverts into a new exemplarity.

What now does Latin America exemplify? Hybrid monstrosity.[21] Borges's vision of the caudillo, the Latin American strongman operating as both national essence and margin, is archetypical here: "Azevedo Bandeira gives, even though well built, the unjustifiable impression of being mismade *[contrahecho]*; in his face, always a little too close, one sees the Jew, the Negro, and the Indian; in his gait, the monkey and the tiger; the scar that crosses his face is just one more adornment, as is his thick, black mustache" (1949b, 30). As hybrid monster, Latin America becomes a negation, the taint of a prior essence, neither one nor the other, in between this and that, at once exemplary and exceptional; in other words, a hybrid that participates precisely by exemplifying what pure genus *is not*. Just as Latin American intellectual production participates in the constitution of the genus "Western tradition" but finds no home there, so is the topos "Latin America" constructed as a kind of savagery, but one damned to immediately evacuate that space of infantile, illiterate, idiotic wholeness.

Latin America's hybridity soils the Eurocentric rule of genre, reveals its degeneracy, but also ensures its integrity against accidents. In that sense, the two are complementary and interdependent. Genre domesticates the wild energy of hybridity by making an example of it; conversely, hybridity's very existence as an anomalous exemplarity, like Azevedo Bandeira, lends credibility to the law of generic purity (i.e., the interests of the authorities). Each participates in the definition of the other, yet through an unequal relation of power. There is no genre "hybridity," just as there can be no real hybridity within "genre." Hybridity, like the social heterogeneity it negotiates (Bakhtin 1935, 360–61), can never stand alone as its own genre: the point at which a hybrid form becomes generic is precisely the moment that it overcomes its hybrid status (Beaujour 1980, 16). The transgressive, generic hybridization that once made the *Quixote* a heresy, we now call "novel." But what of the relations between hybridity, genre, and race? In what ways are all three concepts conditioned by discourses of typification and exemplification?

Borges is on to something when he asserts that literary genre is an "artifice" (1964, 130). "Genre" is as arbitrary and imagined as "nation" or, more precisely, "national unity" (de Certeau 1981, 25), and attains coherence only through the totalitarian, organizing mark imposed by "fakes," "tourists," and "nationalists" (Borges 1964, 132–33). His next move is to discard the problem as irrelevant and exhort us to "abandon ourselves to that voluntary dream called artistic creation" (137); in other words, just write. There is something of the sleight of hand, however, in this writing away of the "pseudo-problem" (128) of nation, national identification, and, by extension, the taxonomania of genre.[22] Simply because we can unmask genre and expose it as a fiction (a made object) does not mean that we disable its authoritative effects; one does not so easily disarm the force of law. It is in this way that the impossibility of "genre," whose conditions are arbitrary (Borges) and depend on their own instability (Derrida), operates along the same lines as the impossibility of race. Both are metaphysical conventions, always open to deconstruction (Hall 1996a). Nonetheless, both gain their social force through the taxonomic logic of (post-)Aristotelian, Western discourse that monitors what counts and what doesn't, which artifact or which body fits in where, who participates, and who belongs. Vigilance over both genre and race will guard against, as Derrida puts it, the "risk [of] impurity, anomaly, or monstrosity" (1980, 204).

Derrida sheds light on this necessary link between genre and race: "[I]n nature and art, genre [is] a concept that is essentially classificatory and genealogico-taxonomic"; hence, we are not surprised to find genre, through *genos*, linked to the "generous force of engenderment

or generation—*physis* [nature], in fact—as with race, familial membership, classificatory genealogy or class, age class (generation), or social
class" (208), and, of course, gender (221). He then speaks of a *mark* of
genre as "the identifiable recurrence of a common trait by which one
recognizes, *or should recognize*, a membership in a class" (210–11; my
emphasis). Derrida's brief hesitation ("should recognize") calls our attention. The remarkable trait that determines "whether this or that,
such a thing or such an event belongs to this set or that class" is also the
quality that cannot, in and of itself, be classified (211). Thus the mark of
exemplarity is also the condition of exemption, the trait that exemplifies
membership in a set, but that enigmatically does not belong there itself,
that participates without belonging (212). It is the foundational gesture
of deconstruction: the same kind of trait that generates identification
degenerates into differentiation (221). This trait or mark is managed,
even if unmanageable (or, not containable), by (or within) an authority
whose force resides in coloniality: it is that on which (neo)colonial authority *depends* and must insist. As Bhabha has argued, the power-laden
construction of difference does not stem from empirical "cultural differences" that are "simply *there* to be seen or appropriated," but rather is
structured by the ambivalent operation that enables "the production of
cultural *differentiation* as signs of authority" (1994, 114). Among these
signs we find the categorical matrices of genre, race, and the movements
between and within genres and races.

Let us return to Borges and Candido. Derrida seems to be saying
that the "mark" (that which we *should* recognize) of identification or
commonality is ultimately uncontainable; and that any such identifiable trait will only succeed in producing or demarcating a difference.
Candido also speaks of a mark that confirms a genre that we might call
"Brazilian writing." It is, unsurprisingly, a mark of distinction through
which he attempts to overcome the unequal order that regulates the dialogue between a marginalized Brazilian epistemology and its objectify-
ing, Eurocentric Other. He argues that the interdisciplinarity of the essay
produced in the confluence of "purely [segregated] scientific research
and literary creation" that gives, through "its syncretic [hybrid] character, a certain unity to the panorama of our culture" is what "constitutes
the most characteristic and original mark [*traço*; mark, characteristic,
line, or trace] of our [Brazilian] thought" (1950, 153). Borges (following
Thorstein Veblen) famously suggests something similar when he states
that Argentine writers take as their example the Jews—the "first" marked,

constitutive others of modernity—who are "outstanding in Western culture, because they act within that culture and at the same time do not feel tied to it by any special devotion" (1964, 136). His conclusion that, like the Jews (he also mentions the Irish), "we [South Americans] can handle all European themes, handle them without superstition, with an irreverence that can have, and already has, fortunate consequences" (ibid.), defines a stance that resonates throughout the modern trajectory of Latin American hybridology. The Latin American innovation (Borges) effected through an insistent interdisciplinarity (Candido) that *should* mark out something like a genre of Latin American writing instead displays a difference, a state of exception. As with the Jew ("outstanding in Western culture"), the exemplary participant of the set doesn't belong there ("do[es] not feel tied to it by any special devotion").[23]

There is perhaps an even "more exemplary" subject in this regard (curiously replaced by Borges with Jewish and Irish cultural producers), one that implicitly hovers in and around the discourse of Borges, Candido, and all Latin Americanist theorists of hybridity. That figure is the mestizo or *mulato*, specifically as embodied in this caricature offered by Sigmund Freud in 1915: "individuals of mixed race who taken all around resemble white men but who betray their coloured descent by some striking feature or other and on that account are excluded from society and enjoy none of the privileges" (cited in Bhabha 1994, 89).[24] Borges's and Candido's Latin American writer, while not "excluded from society" like Freud's "individuals of mixed race," nonetheless finds himself participating in a genre (the genus "Western tradition," wherein he "resembles" the standard "white men") to which he does not belong (enjoys "none of the privileges"). The genre mixing that stands as the striking feature of Latin American production (cultural, discursive, epistemological, generic, genetic) begets a distinguishing mark that makes it both exemplary and exceptional within the genus that we understand here as "the" Western intellectual tradition, as the arbiter of Culture and Civilization.

The hybrid as "distinguishing mark" claimed by the transnational intelligentsia of Latin America for most of the twentieth century reappears today, where it holds fast not only at the aesthetic level, but also (re)sublimated (as it was, e.g., in Porfirian Mexico) as the basic, epistemological key to interpreting Latin American sociocultural life.[25] That Freud's anachronistic configuring of the "mestizo" is still with us—its biologism repressed yet not absent, now masquerading as a new culturalism—can be verified in almost any of the generic images trotted out as "evidence" of today's hybrid cultures. In the Latin American scene, these invariably lead to some variation of "Mexico City's mélange of Indian women strolling among Reforma's high-rise buildings," which Gruzinski goes on to classify as an example of the "surprising and sometimes awkward juxtapositions and presences" that "shatter" what he calls "standard frames of reference" (1999, 20). But his frame of reference seems to be misplaced, and his standard extremely contingent. Given that the neoexotic "hybridity" put forth here does little more than describe a pedestrian scene in many major Latin American cities at any time during the past hundred or so years, the value of calling it "hybrid" as opposed to simply "everyday contemporary urban life" seems questionable. Perhaps the more interesting, and socially pressing, question provoked by this scene is not how it allegedly shatters Western frames of reference (which it does not), but rather how it came to be representable as exceptional, or "awkward," *at all.* To pursue this question is to pursue the history of the out-of-place-ness of this scene: if various ideologies grounded upon various hybridities ("mestizo Mexico," "Brazilian racial democracy") mark Latin America's modernity whereby, as García Canclini shows, the Latin American modern is unthinkable without the hybridization of cultures, races, and spaces, then from whence does the remarkableness of the "mélange of Indian women" walking around in a modern city spring? In other words, how is it that these women are marked as "other," and thus cast into the "awkward," almost the same but not quite, space of the old mestizo monster? How is it that their presence "shatters" the modern, as opposed to precisely confirming the condition of possibility of *all modernity*? How is it that their mark of exception becomes a mark of exclusion? At issue in answering, I think, will be the norms of cultural representation and material access that play out in a biopolitical field that regulates who participates, who belongs, and the naturalization of this inclusive exclusion. The cultural history of race is in play here: whether sublimated to the level of the exemplary mixing of epistemological genres or debased to the terms of a sociocultural and, moreover, political "exception."

The relationship between cultural mixing and racial marking is intimate, indeed inextricable. Given this relationship, what are the risks in theorizing *cultural* hybridity while resisting an interrogation of the *racialized* conditions of possibility that enable theories of hybridity in the first place? Provisionally, I will answer that the racialized structures that undergird hybridity will reemerge, intact, and in undesirable ways: theories of hybridity will find it impossible to erase race without leaving a trace. This impossibility creates unwanted problems for García Canclini's theorization of hybridity, and is the joint point around which my critique of his *Hybrid Cultures* will turn.

2. Erasing Race and the Persistence of Teleology

Néstor García Canclini's *Culturas híbridas: Estrategias para entrar y salir de la modernidad* (1989) was a well-timed arrival on the academic scene. Its circulation, which really took off after its English translation in 1995 (as *Hybrid Cultures*), precisely emerges from the rubble of the Berlin Wall and the fragmentation of a world once clearly divided in two. Its dissemination thus accompanies the crisis of the international, political left—hegemonic in Latin Americanist literary and cultural studies—as it struggled to define new strategies in the context of the Clinton-era political landscape. The international turn to a Third Way politics—whose rhetorical emphasis on mediation, "the market," and the fusion of public service with private gain, seemed to undermine, and even blatantly contradict, socialist solutions to social problems—resonated well with García Canclini's book. Indeed, as demonstrated by Alan O'Connor's review (2003), García Canclini's own professional trajectory is reducible to a certain "type" of Latin American leftist intellectual whose critical focus began to shed its commitments to Marxian-inflected analysis with the consolidation of neoliberal globalization (Cardoso, Castañeda, and Vargas Llosa are some of the exemplary names often invoked here). The cultural-political project of *Hybrid Cultures* apparently rejected hard "binary struggle" in favor of the fluidity of a hybridity strongly articulated around the nexes of cultural consumption and social class. Although reviled in some circles, it was widely and quickly acknowledged (even by its opponents) as a kind of watershed in the study of Latin American cultural politics. The prominent Latin American Studies Association awarded the book its Premio Iberoamericano for 1990–92.

It is perhaps unsurprising that although *Hybrid Cultures* and García Canclini's subsequent work has been roundly criticized and corrected for the way that it treats the articulation of economic agency and political power (e.g., Yúdice 1993; Larsen 1995; Jameson 1998; Beverley 1999; López 2000; Kokotovic 2000; Kraniauskus 2000; O'Connor 2003), a similar critique has not coalesced around its treatment (even elision) of race.[1] Indeed, one could argue, at first glance, that to indulge in such a critique would be precisely to commit the faux pas of engaging a text on terms that are not its own. At the same time, this critical vacuum could also be understood as emerging from the very logic of the text itself: in order to explain what García Canclini means by hybridity, we need to speak in categorical terms other than those of race. Yet if this is indeed the case, we must also insist on the fact that García Canclini himself insists on the abilitity of hybridity to both include and surpass its own stake in the theorization of race. This is an important move for García Canclini, and although lodged in a footnote, the note itself (the first of the book) is now commonly cited as an example of how hybridity allegedly extricates itself from its own genealogy. Here is the note in full: "I will make occasional mention of *sincretismo, mestizaje,* and other terms employed to designate processes of *hybridization.* I prefer this last term because it encompasses diverse intercultural mixtures—not only the racial mixing to which '*mestizaje*' is usually limited—and because it permits the inclusion of modern forms of hybridization better than '*sincretismo*,' a formula that almost always refers to fusions of religion or within traditional symbolic movements" (1989, 14–15).[2]

This note explicitly announces García Canclini's desire to depart from the "older" and more widely invoked Latin Americanist theories of *mestizaje* and *syncretism* on the grounds of race (i.e., in order to exempt it from the discussion) and temporality (reduced here to the binary modern versus traditional).[3] As Christopher Chiappari points out, one advantage of this move is that it emphasizes "the conscious or intentional aspect of cultural fusions" (2000, 227). *Mestizaje* and syncretism, in this view, both tend to infer an organic or unconscious (respectively) notion of cultural mixture and transformation (ibid.). Hence, they can gloss important questions such as political and cultural violence, collaboration and historical contingency. At the same time, of course, García Canclini's terminological disclosure reveals by association the theoretical turf that hybridity shares with *mestizaje* and syncretism: all, in fact, can "designate the processes of *hybridization*." Ten years after his book was published, García Canclini seems to have given up on the distinction altogether: "In today's condition of globalization, I find . . . [good] reasons to employ concepts of *mestizaje* and hybridization" (García Canclini 1999, 56).[4]

In the 1989 *Hybrid Cultures*, however, García Canclini found it necessary to distinguish his thinking on cultural mixture from thinking about racial mixture as such (what he understands as *mestizaje*). To what specific phenomena, then, does his theory of hybridity point?

The question of culture mixing is so deeply embedded, so persistent, and so dominant in Latin American cultural theory that I find it a reasonable decision on García Canclini's part to resist anything like a totalizing, definitional statement of what, specifically, hybridity *is*.[5] He has gracefully conceded this point to his critics, acknowledging that he should have gone further on the epistemological question, and has since offered a more explicit, albeit vast, definition of what he means by *hibridación* (2001b, iii). But even in the first edition of *Culturas híbridas* it is already clear that hybridity, for García Canclini, represents a flexible concept that helps him rethink the organization and practice of culture in contemporary Latin American society. It becomes a strategic site for pursuing two of the principal objectives in his study of Latin American cultures. The first objective, as the subtitle of his book suggests ("strategies for entering and leaving modernity"), is the interrogation and reconceptualization of the dominant notions of Latin American modernity. Second, he wants to formulate a more productive and theoretically sophisticated method for accessing, in the age of the North American Free Trade Agreement (NAFTA), the cultural practices and artifacts typically categorized under the rubric of "the popular." Toward these ends, he both calls for and deploys an interdisciplinary perspective that will focus on disassembling the ideological structures that police and segregate the defining terms of two entrenched binaries: on the one hand, *traditional and modern*; on the other hand, *popular and elite*. Hybridity is the concept that facilitates this project. Hybridity is at once referee and blacksmith, in that it not only mediates, but also pries apart and recasts, those binaries.

How does it work? At an elemental level, hybridity operates referentially. It describes what is often perceived as a basic contradiction
of modern Latin American societies: "Contemporary Latin American
countries are the result of the sedimentation, juxtaposition, and intersection of indigenous traditions (especially in the Mesoamerican and
Andean regions), of colonial, Catholic Hispanism, and modern political, educational, and communicational movements" (1989, 71). This
identification of the mixing of traditions—"indigenous traditions,"
"Catholic Hispanism"—itself walks on the hallowed ground of tradition, placing García Canclini in a literally centuries-old trajectory of
thinking about Latin American cultural identity.[6] Moreover, by coupling the indigenous to the traditional, and then posing it as against or
mixed through the countervailing Hispanic and Catholic, he suggests
that racial difference (inflected through ethnicity, geography, religion,
language, culture, in short, the basic elements of "tradition"), far from
left behind to the theorists of *mestizaje*, will be a central, if implicit,
aspect of his thinking about hybridity.

The next passage, however, reveals the more immediate concern, and
begins to yield the critical aspect of hybridity: "Despite the attempts to
give elite culture a modern profile, relegating the indigenous and the
colonial to the popular sectors, an inter-class *mestizaje* has generated
hybrid formations at all social levels" (ibid.). Whereas the first citation
indicates García Canclini's concern with the tension between cultural
tradition and cultural modernity, here a clearly articulated discourse of
social class is submitted to the mixing actions of hybridity (and, indeed,
mestizaje). Hybridity, then, is not *merely* a description of the obvious:
that Latin American racial, ethnic, and cultural heterogeneity exist,
and that Latin American aesthetics—from high art to everyday life—
is implicated in this heterogeneity. Rather, hybridity names a strategy for García Canclini to approach and rethink the extent to which,
despite this constitutive heterogeneity, the dominant conceptualizations
of Latin American cultural production and forms persistently slide into
what Pierre Bourdieu calls a class-based "ethnocentrism" (1968, 217):
the naturalization of the authority and value of *aesthetic* distinctions in
convenient correspondence with *social* class stratification and hierarchy.
García Canclini's *hibridación* looks after the ways in which hybridity
erodes these hierarchies.

The important, even if conventional, move here, evidenced in the
above citations, is the temporal pivot around which hybridity's critical

action turns. The problem is not simply the empirical existence of old traditions within the newness of modern life: a peasant, in traditional dress, hauling industrially produced handicrafts to market, in a horse-drawn cart, on a highway. Neither is it the appropriation of "popular" cultural forms by the "elite" sectors of society, or vice versa: a popular *milonga* performed in a concert hall; bootlegged copies of García Márquez novels sold at a popular newsstand. Rather, the problem is how to analytically approach and draw social meaning from these cultural juxtapositions. In other words, as he states in a chapter subtitle, "How to Interpret a Hybrid History" (69), or more precisely, how to reinterpret *"the intersection of different historical temporalities"* (71). Hybridity, in this sense, becomes a critique of teleology: "traditions" and the "colonial" are juxtaposed with the "modern," not in a dialectical contradiction to be resolved in synthesis, but palimpsestically, layered and linked in a schema that signals the contemporary as the constant reconfiguration of old and new.[7]

The hybridity of temporality thus intervenes in the historicist teleology that equates the movement from the traditional to the modern with the distinction between popular and elite culture, between folkloric craft and vanguard art, between rural and urban social life. Each end of these binaries exists within the other. Hybridity becomes the third term that both mediates and challenges those binaries. It reveals the interdependence of their component parts and the ways in which their tenacity conceals a more realistic model of "multitemporal heterogeneity" that emerges out of "a history in which modernization rarely operated through the substitution of the traditional and the old" (72). Hybridity, as multitemporal heterogeneity, denotes the coexistence, within the same *national-cultural* worlds, of differently modernized *social* sectors of societies. It fractures Latin American constructions of cultural unicity, homogeneity, and segregation both nationally and regionally (15–16).

If "older" theories of hybridity (like *mestizaje* or syncretism) asked "How do cultures mix?" or "What is the effect of cultural mixture?" García Canclini's work seems to supplement those questions with a demand for attention to how we conceive of the condition of cultural mixture *at all*. If the modern already contains the traditional, and vice versa, what use is served by models of teleological development, such as modernization, historicism, enlightenment, or acculturation? By tapping into this shift in perspective, García Canclini contributes to an invigoratingly decultured paradigm for the study of cultural production and practice. This hybridity-driven paradigm, although not doing away with categorization (see the discussion of "impure genres" that opens chapter 1 of this book), favors questions of negotiation and mediation (over domination) for reconceptualizing the ways that popular classes participate in modernity.[8] In this sense, hybridity is unapologetically "postmodern" in that it "refutes the originary status of traditions and the originality of innovations. At the same time, it offers the opportunity to rethink the modern as a relative, doubtable project, one that is neither antagonistic to traditions nor destined to overcome them by some unverifiable evolutionary law" (190). This critique of historicism—often missed by his critics—is García Canclini's strongest move, and leads to much insight. It is also the point where his theory of hybridity exhibits its most debilitating blindness. At the root of this problem is the practically total elision—even disavowal—of race from his hybrid equation: race understood not as self-evident "cultural difference," but as the dominant mode of producing and naturalizing cultural difference historically. This is a *constitutive* omission given the choice of "hybridity" as his preferred mode of engaging cultural mixture.[9] Indeed, it is precisely at this gesture of attempting to wipe away the teleology of modernity that the uninterrogated persistence of race reasserts its own teleological governance over the logic of hybridity. Race, in short, becomes the organizing mark whose reappearance will signal the tenacity of historicist teleology within García Canclini's own system.

The dichotomous components embedded within García Canclini's theory of hybridity highlight this problem. A hybrid, at the most basic definitional level, implies a structural whole (usually organic, but not necessarily) resulting from the combination of two generically distinct parts (in the classical sense, the offspring from a wild boar and a tame sow). Since he does not pursue these philological details, let's assume that this dominant, conventional notion of the hybrid pertains here. Hybridity, in this reading, could be interpreted as a kind of marital, or accidental, bliss.[10] This implication raises all kinds of red flags for those interested in history. It has contributed to frequent criticism of the alleged "celebratory tone" (Cornejo Polar 1998, 8) of *Hybrid Cultures*.[11] Perhaps it is this failure to explicitly disclose and problematize the enabling dyad within hybridity that has led to the widespread suggestions or assumptions that García Canclini is inattentive to unequal relations of power and the ensuing exploitation that the convivial implications of hybridity would seem to hide.[12] Although this generalized critique is important and not inaccurate, I think it could be at once sharpened—by reading García Canclini not so much for "tone," but instead reading him to the letter—and expanded to rethink the logic of hybridity in general.

In order to explain what I mean, let me briefly draw upon the critique of García Canclini posed by John Beverley in *Subalternity and Representation* (1999, 115–32), a work that went a long way toward clearing the ground for a new phase in an entire range of debates within Latin Americanist criticism. Against García Canclini, Beverley concludes that civil society and social struggle (the latter of which, we should add, is not exactly a key term for García Canclini) are "*binary* rather than (or as well as) *hybrid*" (129). At least within the context of *Hybrid Cultures*, this assertion presents us with a false choice.[13] Despite García Canclini's sometimes scornful stance toward anything redolent of essentialism, hybridity, in *Hybrid Cultures*, is not automatically a way of negating or totally defusing binarism and the us-versus-them political efficacy that wars of maneuver can sometimes yield, as Beverley's (and O'Connor's [2003]) critique seems to presume.[14] The role of hybridity in García Canclini's paradigm of cultural analysis is not diametrically opposed to binarism, forcing us to decide between *either* hybrid *or* binary. Rather, hybridity is essentially a way of *interrogating binarism*, as a cultural model, from within its own terms. Specifically, García Canclini invokes hybridity in the interest of problematizing the many instances in which binarism fails as an approach to the study of culture, as a reflection of Latin American socioeconomic, lived reality, or as a political strategy. Hybridity, as I maintained in chapter 1, arises alongside *and* within genre, not only (or not so much) in belligerent contradistinction to it, but also as its constitutive opposite. Hence, the binaristic choice between hybrid (mixed) or binary (pure/impure) presents itself as if it were, in fact, a real choice. In so doing, it conceals the fact that hybridity and binarism are functions of each other. The critical action of hybridity explodes binarism *from the inside* by destabilizing the categorical foundations of binary couplets: the ways in which those categories are constructed and segregated, where they intermingle or conflate, how they are consistently disfigured and reconfigured. Beverley's hesitation—"rather than (or as well as)"—is symptomatic of the impossibility of his position. To accuse García Canclini of privileging the hybridity of an object that is binary *rather than* hybrid is a charge whose reversal is easily accomplished, and the beginning of an argument that he will always win, and relatively quickly at that. To argue that his object of analysis is binary *as well as* hybrid lends strength to his appropriation of hybridity as a way of complicating deeply entrenched binaries.

An effective terrain of critical dialogue with García Canclini, then, is not established by noting his dependence on, or attempted rejection of, binaristic antagonism as such.[15] Rather, I argue for advancing a critique toward the categorical poles that constitute the binaries that attract his attention. The most notable of these materialize in his hybridization of *time* through the notion of *multitemporal heterogeneity*. And here we find an easily identifiable set of binaries against which García Canclini takes aim: old and new, traditional and modern, and eventually, rural and urban. All of these terms, as any serious reading of the trajectory of Latin American cultural history will show, are enabled by a racially marked subtext.

García Canclini problematizes these temporal categories primarily by exposing the folklorist fallacy that imposes a simplistic teleology on the relationship between peasant-indigenous cultures and the processes of modernization. Far from being necessarily crushed and extinguished by modernization, indigenous and peasant—what García Canclini will eventually summarize as "traditional"—artisans participate in the process by continually reinventing their cultural practices and products:[16] "traditional" (folkloric) arts contain, dialogue with, and participate in modernity, just as "modern" institutions express traditional relations of power.[17] As we can see, embedded within García Canclini's hybrid model there are "old" (traditional, rural) and "new" (modern, urban) times. Now, he is clearly arguing that the modernizing tradition depends on the confluence of both (multitemporal heterogeneity, what the concept of the "postmodern" brings to light), and arguing *against* the evolutionist-Enlightenment notion of one, synchronic "time" progressing to, accumulating upon, and being replaced by the "next" (the denial of coevalness).[18] However, his recourse to a temporal configuration fails to resolve the problem: the binarism whose limits García Canclini attempts to contort springs back into place, reasserting its tenacity. In fact, as John Kraniauskus has pointed out (2000, 130), he merely ends up reproducing, in another form, the dialectical kind of teleology that he wants to vaporize: social reality and cultural practice are hybrid constructions that ultimately consist of *different* temporalities, some "older" and some "newer," all always becoming mixed, the one sublated into the other (cf. Williams 1977, 122). But, as Silvia López indicates, these "different temporalities that coexist in Latin American culture are not a state of simple difference but reflect [and produce; or better, name] the state of social inequality that formal cultural politics cannot resolve" (2000, 258).

Race reemerges here. Within the operable poles of García Canclini's undeconstructed (and unequally valued) temporal binary—old and new, traditional and modern—it is the indigenous and peasant cultures and cultural producers that seem to always fall to the left: "tradition" is the time from whence they emerge, "modernity" is something toward which they progress, or at least, as the title of the book suggests, *entrar*. Whereas Borges's confrontation with "tradition" can be understood as a cultured attempt to escape the tyranny of purity (see chapter 1), García Canclini's decultured invocation of tradition unexpectedly reasserts it: "traditional cultures" for García Canclini—who is here following standard social anthropological practice (Quigley 1993, 41)—is simply another way of saying "indigenous culture" (see esp. 221). It is in this way that hybridity's unstated conceptual stake in racial and ethnological discourse structures the pluralization of time and the hybridization of high and low aesthetics that enable García Canclini's multitemporal heterogeneity.

Indigenous-peasant communities, over and over again, are proposed as "entering modernity"[19] when they *(a)* move to the city, or *(b)* "reconvert" their modes of handicraft production for the tourist market.[20] Before they become a constitutive element of the "hybridity" that undergirds Latin American modernity, or before they themselves experience hybridization, they exist somewhere else, a place—a *pure* place—that we might call, with García Canclini, "the traditional."[21] And this place is directly associated with an aesthetics of oldness, belatedness, and arrested development: "[The] difficulties of the ethnicities *[etnias]* in *relocating* themselves within modernity keeps them in chronic poverty" (221; my emphasis). Numerous examples of this move punctuate the text. In one short section he notes, on the one hand, that it is not "the fatal destiny of traditional groups to remain outside of modernity" (ibid.). But, on the other hand, even though these "traditional groups" sometimes "skillfully insert themselves within modern commercial rules" (222) and "integrate themselves into modernity" (223), relatively few "artisans or ethnic groups have achieved a decent standard of living with their traditions or incorporated themselves into modern development" (221).

García Canclini seems simultaneously dubious of, yet trapped within, the developmentalist model of tradition-to-modernity. He goes so far as to reject and embrace the teleology in a single gesture: "The problem is not reducible, then, to conserving and rescuing *supposedly unaltered traditions.* It becomes a question of asking ourselves how *they* [i.e., those previously "unaltered traditions"] *are being transformed*, and how *they* interact with the forces of modernity" (203; my emphasis).[22]

This configuration of the relationship between modernity and the once "supposedly unchanged," but now clearly changing (that is, modernizing), "traditions" (indigenous, peasant) is enabled by the discourse of race located at the heart of modernity. The failure to interrogate that discourse as hybridity's condition of possibility conceals an important aspect of those sociocultural processes whose confluence we name "modernity." "Traditional groups," "ethnic groups," "artisans," in short, marginalized sectors of society such as the Nahua protagonists of García Canclini's fifth chapter, do not *only* hybridize, integrating into modernity even as they preserve what they remember and appropriate as their "traditional" cultural identity. They also resist the dominant structures of modernity, and refuse hegemony through a variety of strategies and tactics, from cultural activism to productive inefficiency, from rowdy uprisings to purposeful nonparticipation. What García Canclini's model obscures is the long-standing fact, unveiled through four decades of Latin Americanist and postcolonial criticism, that *both* the "traditional" otherness of marginalized actors *and* their hybridization vis-à-vis their social Other are constitutive and complementary processes of modernity. This constitutive process is indivisible from the modern racial contract itself, brokered at the dawn of modernity with the institutionalization of the enslavement and degradation of African and indigenous American people, and sealed in the colonial projects of primitive accumulation beginning in the sixteenth century. In short, Latin American social life and cultural production are not containable within the trajectory that García Canclini at once wishes away and reasserts, the movement *from* tradition *to* modernity. Rather, they exist in a matrix that would look more like a field of competing modernities, unequal, and always in various phases of dialogue, repetition, and differentiation.[23] To paraphrase Roberto Schwarz (1992, 47), the crucial point is not the hybridizing effects of modernity, but rather the segregationist marginalization of differentially constructed subjects that persists within that hybridization.

García Canclini's theory of hybridity represents an important intervention against purist culturalism and orthodox Marxism for understanding the ways in which Latin American popular cultures participate in modernity. But its critical force is limited to precisely *that* intervention. It might upset the aesthetic sensibilities of some anachronistic sectors of an elitist-culturalist academy—by rethinking the relationship between modernity, art, and artisinal production, or showing the sophistication and cultural, even literary, relevance of "impure genres." It might also deflate the revolutionary dreams of academics who would find in the oppressed an automatic site of cultural resistance and pretheoretical, militant raw material (though this critique of the left, is, in itself, beginning to wear thin). If, as George Yúdice claims, García Canclini's hybridity is ultimately the "undoing" and subsequent reconstruction of representation (2001, xvi), and hence, I would argue, simply names the modern tendency to undermine stable categories, then this destabilization is only really felt at the epicenters of enemy camps that subscribe to a war that fewer and fewer are interested in fighting anymore (and yet that, with the rise of neoconservativism in the United States, suddenly *everybody* seems interested in fighting again). In the end, then, García Canclini's is a very easy, and very traditional, move. Asserting and even demonstrating how some supposedly marginalized cultural actors participate in modernity only contradicts the absolutist thesis that *all* "traditional" cultures *must be* crushed by modernity. At the same time, however, it still fails to heed García Canclini's own proscription of "unverifiable evolutionary law[s]" (1989, 190). The hybrid alternative that García Canclini proposes does little to get beyond the assertion that popular, peasant, or indigenous cultures get into modernity: in that sense it reiterates a theme of developmentalism that makes it unfortunately reducible to a theory of evolutionist integration—in a word, a teleology, with all the tired inevitability of progress that the term implies.

Although his arguments are more than a decade old, later work by García Canclini does little to revise their basic structure. Indeed, I would argue that the implications set forth in *Hybrid Cultures* have been exacerbated by the persistence of another teleology that arises in García Canclini's writings: that of high cultural theory itself. Throughout *Hybrid Cultures*, the strong constructivism to which García Canclini subscribes is represented as a kind of theoretical end (or beginning) that leaves behind the naive essentialisms of nationalist "fundamentalists"

(1989, 149–58). Increasingly, however, he adopts a similar attitude toward more broadly framed "sociopolitical movements" that convene around a perceived common identity, reducing their discursive and material claims to "fundamentalist doctrines" (1995b, 9–10; 1995a, 91–92). Although he has refrained from explicitly indicating the authors of this sociopolitical and activist fundamentalism, he does mention Peru, inferring the confluence of radical social demands and sometimes apparently indiscriminate violence that came to define the Sendero Luminoso movement during the 1980s and 1990s (1989, 167; 1995b, 10). Now, nobody, save the converted or the radically unfashionable, endorses the methods of the Sendero Luminoso. Even its goals of social transformation through armed revolutionary action have been eclipsed by the rise of the so-called New Left in Latin America and its commitment (e.g., in neighboring Bolivia) to fomenting change through social pressure and electoral politics. Nevertheless, this should not dissuade us from critical analysis of the social and cultural processes that led the Sendero Luminoso's grievances to find a receptive and once relatively widespread national base.[24] On the contrary, in other words, what should be vociferously rejected is the totalitarian reduction of social movements to "fundamentalism"—today growing in frequency and volume—that is essentially a call to forget history.

All of this aside, it must be added that the Sendero Luminoso, for many students of Latin American culture, is not the first "sociopolitical movement" that comes to mind on the contemporary scene. García Canclini has remained notably silent on multiform movements such as the pan-Mayanists in Guatemala, the Movimento Sem Terra (Landless Movement) in Brazil, and the new Zapatistas in Mexico.[25] All of these social movements subscribe to doctrines that draw upon a politics of identity and posit various essentialisms to ground their political positionality.[26] One wonders if these new social movements are also to be written off as fundamentalist. The chain of signifiers that closes García Canclini's preface to the translation of his *Consumidores y ciudadanos* (1995) (*Consumers and Citizens*, 2001) suggests that they are. On the one hand, he notes the "analogies between . . . the separatist emphasis that takes self-esteem as a key factor in the rights claims of women and minorities of the United States, and . . . some Latin American indigenous and nationalist movements that interpret history in a Manichaean manner, reserving all virtues for themselves and blaming others for the problems of development" (2001a, 11). This canned reduction of U.S.

feminism and multiculturalism and Latin American rights-oriented socio-political movements to questions of blame is an empty (if often effective) rhetorical move. It would find its equivalent in proposing that García Canclini's hybridity, or Vasconcelos's *mestizaje*, is simply a strategy to assuage an inferiority complex that afflicts "Third World intellectuals," a mere excuse to lend relevance to the periphery. Obviously, this line of critique is less than convincing.[27]

If it is indeed a fair charge to argue that one of the functions of García Canclini's hybridity is to reduce identity-based resistance to fundamentalism, then he effectively negates the legitimacy of an agency that would move in any direction other than what he perceives as "forward." Hence any critical propulsion of this move forward—that is, toward the totalization of the norms and aesthetics of modernity as global capitalism—stalls in the one-way street that García Canclini's theory of hybridity maps.[28] Like the disconcerting inability or refusal to distinguish resistance from barbarism on the part of many on the academic right and left today, equally disconcerting is García Canclini's lack of differentiation between fundamentalism, on the one hand, and organized, collective action, on the other. Although this is to be expected from, say, the Bush administration, it is a disappointment, to the say the least, when it comes from the pen of one of Latin America's leading cultural theorists.[29]

Although García Canclini's theory of hybridity offers insight on many levels, it is also limited by its own conceit that, despite what appear to be the best of intentions, aligns progress with successful integration into the global capitalist market economy. Of course, such integration does represent a kind of "progress" for those who succeed in reaping its economic benefits. Yet there are many ways of imagining such integration and of mitigating its harshest effects: this is what indigenous social movements have been arguing for decades.[30] Indigenous social actors do enter into García Canclini's discussion, but only as an underdeveloped outside, or, conversely, when they participate in the commodifying impulse of modernity by selling their stuff. In what way, then, does García Canclini's hybridity participate in a specifically Latin American discourse of race? It is not a move away from the abstract inclusion with concrete exclusion that governed the political project of Enlightenment (Martín-Barbero 1987, 7) and defined national consolidation in nineteenth-century Latin America. Rather, hybridity is the postnational correlate of that project. The specter of race returns when we ask the question of agency and insist on knowing who is hybridizing whom. When we do ask this question, we find that there is very little new in the world: as they always have, "traditional communities"—indigenous, African, peasant, and generally marginalized sectors of society—are interpellated by and participate in global modernity, some of them very efficiently and to profitable ends. This participation, however, can not be equated with an unequivocal welcome that would lead to a feeling of belonging.

It is thus that García Canclini's *Hybrid Cultures* effectively "makes race" even in attempting to transcend it (by abandoning a vocabulary of *mestizaje*). Recall that we are being guided by a *constructivist* notion of race here (see the introduction to Part I), wherein race names not objective difference but rather the practice of producing categorical human difference *as race*. The point, then, is not to criticize García Canclini's constructivism for destabilizing the idea of "pure" race; the point is that he is *not constructivist enough*; that is, he forgets the subject's (in this case, his) role in *making race*. This historically sedimented consolidation of the idea of race relies on uncritical reiteration and repetition. *Hybrid Cultures* participates in this process, not, of course, as "racism," but as producer of cultural difference. The point is not that García Canclini could have elected *not* to produce cultural difference; the point is that he seems to mistake the contingencies of a historical racialization of culture for social-historical fact. When García Canclini produces the particular place of the "indigenous peasant" in his hybridist framework, it is not enough to simply say that "not all peasants are Indians" or "many Indians are *mestizados*." Objective "impurity" does not erase the social contracts and exclusions that govern race. Rather, the opportunities for critical reflection arise when we ask after the conceptual conditions of possibility that allow us to think the indigenous peasant in the first place. Displacing this actor away from the modern and into the pure place of tradition (even, or especially, as a place that the Indian will abandon)—that is, the past—is one of the generic operations of producing the Indian in Western discourse. That García Canclini does not use his considerable insight to fully displace this displacement diminishes the critical force of his work.

In an influential and timely attempt to rethink the specificity of Latin American modernity, García Canclini's recourse to hybridity repeats the now familiar failures of *mestizaje*, transculturation, *antropofagia*, and all the rest. The otherness of Latin America is premised on a hybridization of Latin America's others. Like the relationship between Latin

America and Western tradition that Borges and Candido confront, the traditional, racialized others of Latin America participate in the globalization of culture as the embodiment of precisely that limit without which we can neither exit nor enter modernity.

If it is undeniable that all people feel the force of globalized modernity, to what extent does globalized modernity feel the force of all people? More specifically to the project at hand, how do cultural theorists get a handle on these forces? García Canclini's hybridity, while not openly negating, and in fact even acknowledging this force that often folds into resistance, tells us very little about it, or about the possibility of a contestatory mode of subjectivity. To pursue this question, we need to expand his framework by looking elsewhere. In the age of late-modern globalization, can a theory of hybridity generate a theory of resistance? At what point does hybridity become heresy?

3. The Ambivalence of Theorizing Hybridity
Coloniality and Anthropology

When can hybridity be thought in terms of resistance? The short answer, from Homi Bhabha, is when it writes back: "Hybridity is heresy" (1994, 225) when a subject (doubly inscribed as sovereign and subjugated) relocates the symbols of authority, reappropriates them dialogically, and redeploys them in a mixed-up discourse that displaces orthodoxy and deconstructs the rules of identity formation. Hybridity, in Bhabha's complex and multilayered schema, confronts the official discourses that constitute the coloniality of power with themselves: that is, with their own essentially ambivalent nature. In sites of territorial aggression, hybridity thus becomes at once the source of authorization and of authoritarianism's unraveling. While both link hybridity to power, García Canclini's sociological and empirical perspective is rooted more firmly in symbolic production, communication, and reception, and speaks thus of how the people *participate* in modernity. Bhabha's approach, stemming from the nexus of psychoanalysis and literary criticism, changes the terms to performativity and, most succinctly, representation (as both portrait and proxy), emphasizing the *circumvention* of modernizing authority.[1] Here is a long quote, extracted from the relatively early "Signs Taken as Wonders" (originally published in 1985), which I think still stands as Bhabha's most rigorous and useful—if exceedingly difficult—formulation of the operations and stakes of the hybridity of colonial discourse:[2]

[Hybridity] is a problematic of colonial representation and individuation that reverses the effects of the colonialist disavowal, so that other "denied" knowledges enter upon the dominant discourse and estrange the basis of its authority—its rules of recognition . . . [It] is not simply the *content* of disavowed knowledges . . . that return to be acknowledged as counter-authorities . . . [Rather, w]hat is irremediably estranging in the presence of the hybrid—in the revaluation of the symbol of national authority as the sign of colonial difference—is that the difference of cultures can no longer be identified or evaluated as objects of epistemological or moral contemplation: cultural differences are not simply *there* to be seen or appropriated . . . To see the cultural not as the *source* of conflict—*different* cultures—but as the *effect* of discriminatory practices—the production of cultural *differentiation* as signs of authority—changes its value and its rules of recognition. Hybridity intervenes in the exercise of authority not merely to indicate the impossibility of its identity but to represent the unpredictability of its presence. (1994, 114)

The appearance of two kinds of hybridity floating around this passage, at once contradictory and complementary, may be less problematic than it first seems. As Bakhtin illustrated in his essay on "Discourse in the Novel," hybridity, as a representational quality that is always both aesthetic and social, can be understood as a process that simultaneously seeks out and resists mixture (1935, 304, 360). Bakhtin's hybridization is the construction of a "double-languaged" discursive space where "two socio-linguistic consciousnesses . . . come together and consciously fight it out on the territory of the utterance" (360). Thus the oft-cited oppositionality of Bakhtinian hybridity depends on an equivalent gesture of constructing a common ground—the utterance—where contesting languages or consciousnesses will "come together" *before* they (or in order to) "fight it out."[3] Hybridity—or, more specifically, what Bakhtin calls *intentional hybridization*—is thus not simply resistance, but rather develops as a theory of simultaneous cultural integration and opposition, of conviviality and contest.[4]

Bakhtin's seminal articulation of cultural, literary, and linguistic hybridity is suggestive for reading Bhabha. What it suggests is that the emergence of two kinds of hybridity visible in Bhabha's work may have less to do with the undecidability of a psychoanalytic critical apparatus that is attentive to deconstruction, and more to do with a kind of ambivalence, or at least doubleness, that undergirds hybridity itself. Not coincidentally, it is this structural ambivalence that lends Bhabha's hybridity its critical thrust. Before moving in that direction, however, a quick explication of his double use of hybridity is in order.

First, for Bhabha, hybridity (as we just saw) is a question of discourse or, as he puts it, a "problem of colonial representation" (1994, 114). It describes the way in which the voice of authority splits—or hybridizes, in Bakhtin's diffusive sense—at its locus of enunciation, and thereby undermines its own position. Attempting to construct a univocal site of legitimacy, the subject of authoritarianism (the colonial functionary, for Bhabha) relies on a "doublespeak" in which "[t]he 'part' (which must be the colonialist foreign body) must be representative of the 'whole' (conquered country), but the right of representation is based on its radical difference" (111). With this representational disconnect colonial authority attempts to construct referential "transparency" (reason, right, objectivity) through a "discursive closure—intention, image, author," which for Bhabha amounts to the exercise of power itself.[5] This move, however, founders as it simultaneously "discloses" the rules of a rigged game, or of "recognition—those social texts of epistemic, ethnocentric, nationalist intelligibility . . . the voice of modernity" (110). In other words, authoritative discourse *discloses itself,* revealing the fact that what it calls universal right or law or ethic depends on the recourse to violence and subjugation: the hybridity of colonial address yields a kind of hypocrisy. This colonialist hypocrisy is, of course, well known.[6] What Bhabha brings is a greater insistence upon, and demonstration of, the hybridity of colonialism's very enunciatory moment.[7]

Second, hybridity is explicitly material. This material aspect is exhibited as the authoritative effects that govern the "production of cultural differentiation": "the colonial hybrid is the articulation of the ambivalent space where the rite of power is enacted on the site of desire, making its objects at once disciplinary [pedagogical] and disseminatory [performative]" (112). In other words, the movement of containment within colonial discourse *disrupts itself* through "the articulation of the ambivalent space" of power: authority can never be total, complete, whole. Equally, however, colonial discourse *is disrupted* by an other, the living matter of the embodied object produced at the confluence of its discipline and desire: "faced with the *hybridity of its objects,* the *presence* of power is revealed as something other than what its rules of recognition assert" (ibid.; my emphasis). Suddenly, Bhabha's critique becomes far less abstract, and far more immediate; for the living embodiment of this "hybrid object," in Bhabha's system, is nothing less than the colonial subject: that which he will characterize in a later essay as "almost the same, but not quite . . . almost the same but not white" (86, 89).[8]

As a literary critic, Bhabha derives the empirical evidence for these psychical transits through the contrapuntal appropriation and redeployment of the colonial archive and contemporary cultural theory and philosophy. He draws upon moments of colonialist anxiety.[9] He homes in on what Jean Franco calls "those moments when dissident subjects appear in the social text and when the struggle for interpretive power erupts" (1989, xii). Exemplary in this regard is Bhabha's famous group of "partially" Christianized Indians under the tree in nineteenth-century Delhi who subtly yet aggressively renegotiate the hegemonic pact sealed in the English book: noting the blasphemous dietary habits of the English, they circumvent colonial authority and establish a direct relationship with a higher power; they assert their conversion, but "politely refuse" the offer of baptism; "maybe next year," they say, and so on (1994, 102–4, 116–21).

While hybridity is thus identifiable on several levels (hybrid enunciation; hybrid objects), its complexity endows the postcolonialist with a kind of heroism, as the critic who takes on the task of unearthing and revealing its critical operations. Hybridity comes between ("intervenes") colonial discourse and its desired object (the colonial subject, colonized space) by destabilizing the unicity of both. Harnessing hybridity, then, yields results similar to the deconstructivist critic's strategies of reversal and displacement which can unmask the positionality and split nature of subjectivity, and hence, the instability of not only authority, but also of identity in general. In this sense, as John Beverley correctly observes, hybridity stands in for the deconstructive act itself (1999, 102). However, it should be pointed out that Beverley only reads the 1994 version of "DissemiNation" in his critique of Bhabha, and thus provides us with only half of hybridity's double-edged critical force when he states that "the collapse of the pretension to signify . . . is for all intents and purposes what Bhabha understands by hybridity" (ibid.). As we have seen, however, for the postcolonial Bhabha hybridity is also precisely the opposite: the emergence of the *pretension to signify*, a problem of colonial representation.

Against Beverley (among others), I would argue that this unhidden genealogical relationship to deconstruction does nothing to reduce the critical—even political—potential of Bhabha's model for reading authoritative discourses. Beverley, drawing on the work of Ernesto Laclau and Chantal Mouffe, asserts that a politicized cultural studies must convert its critical energies into the construction of a popular subject position

(Beverley 1999, 93–94, 106). Bhabha's project, from this perspective, does not escape the culturalist elitism that always dogs avant-garde critical movements. Hence Bhabha effectively enacts "a kind of recontainment or reterritorialization of the subaltern within, so to speak, the MLA [Modern Language Association]" (100). The two, then, are divided over how to pursue what Beverley calls the need to "adequately [represent] the dynamics of 'the people'" (113).[10] As we see here in Beverley's own comments, however, constructing a critical politics *is* a question of representation. The fundamental problem, then, is not a lack of an actually existing political potential in Bhabha's discourse. Rather, the problem emerges through Bhabha's complication of any desire to totalize his discourse by locating it within the boundaries of an explicitly defined camp.

Hybridity and hegemony, for Bhabha, are not questions of pure domination. Neither do they imply a pure resistance: "The place of difference and otherness, or the space of the adversarial, within such a system . . . is never entirely on the outside or implacably oppositional. It is a pressure, and a presence, that acts constantly [as hybridity], if unevenly [here complicit, there rebellious], along the entire boundary of authorization" (1994, 109). Bhabha's politics, then, do not operate through diametrical opposition and direct contestation (157). His is a revolution based not on negation, but on problematization and, ultimately, dialogue. Therein, the critic can play a crucial role (12, 121). What Bhabha's writings will *not* afford the critic is a user-friendly handbook of revolutionary action. Indeed, his writing itself exemplifies the fact that effective critique, like revolution or even just modest social change, will only be wrought with great difficulty and through much effort.

Within the vast Latin Americanist bibliography of critical colonial-discourse studies, one can find many potential allies for Bhabha's persistent complication of the relations between subjectivity and social struggle. Signature works such as Silviano Santiago's critique of lazy reading (1971) or Antonio Cornejo Polar's theory of nondialectical heterogeneity as a migrant subject position (1998) are two examples that immediately spring to mind. Nevertheless, Bhabha has not exactly received the warmest of receptions in Latin Americanist criticism.[11] Although I will not dwell on empirical examples, Robert Stam summarizes the situation nicely when he notes that "[f]or those of us working in the area of Latin American culture, where 'hybridity' and 'mestizaje' have been critical commonplaces for decades, it is always surprising to learn that Homi Bhabha, through no fault of his own, has been repeatedly 'credited' with the concept of 'hybridity'" (2000, 91). As Stam exemplifies (83, 91), and as I have mentioned, this criticism revolves around a demand for historical specificity and a perceived postcolonial hijacking of hybridity. It is hard to tell if this position wants to frame Latin American and postcolonial theories of hybridity as fundamentally the same or fundamentally different.[12] One assertion that has been repeatedly made clear within these debates, however, is the idea that Latin Americans were theorizing hybridity first. Even though this is a difficult point to sustain empirically, there may be little harm in accepting it at face value.[13] What seems unacceptable, however, is to use this assertion as an excuse to wall off Latin American hybridity from geoepistemologically disparate theories that go by the same name and that can perhaps be appropriated for the productive analysis of aspects of Latin American cultural, social, and artistic phenomena. This, after all, is the internationalist message of many of Latin America's finest hybridist movements, whether articulated along the lines of nationalism (e.g., the Brazilian anthropophagists) or cosmopolitanism (e.g., Borges and Candido). If hybridity is critical at all, its critique stems from its incessant disruption of authoritative legitimacy (e.g., pure race, pure genre, pure canon, pure reason). This disruption is effected by a repetitive aesthetic invocation and practice of what Stam calls "mixedness" (85). As such, if Latin American hybridity is a theory that only works in Latin America, and if Latin America is a geoepistemological space that will only accept a hybridity as theorized within Latin Americanist fields, then what Latin Americanism calls hybridity is not really hybridity at all, but rather a new purity.

I hope that it is clear that the idea here is not to embrace Bhabha, or postcolonial criticism in general, as some kind of improvement upon and potential replacement of Latin Americanist strategies of cultural analysis. Nor am I interested in sketching a Latin Americanist family tree into which we could appropriate Bhabha's critical hybridity as a kind of forgotten cousin. I am simply interested in asking how Bhabha's insightful and suggestive work with "hybridity" can contribute to reading Latin American writing and culture, if in fact it can at all. How, specifically, does Bhabha help us read the archive of Latin American theories of hybridity? I will argue that the most important contribution is the self-critical move implied by his postcolonial engagement with the psychoanalytic account of ambivalence.

Classical psychoanalytic ambivalence, most explicitly developed through Sigmund Freud's elaboration of Bleuler's term in *Totem and Taboo* (1913), typically refers to an unconscious conflict between an abomination and a wish.[14] Many of us are familiar with this phenomenon via the modern Judeo-Christian restrictions against onanism: "[In the neurotic,] [t]he opposition between these two streams [desire to touch, abomination of touching] cannot be easily adjusted because . . . they are so localized in the psychic life that they can not meet. The prohibition becomes fully conscious, while the surviving pleasure of touching remains unconscious" (Freud 1913, 830). Contemporary thinkers would rework this psychic basis of taboo as the subjective simultaneity of repulsion and attraction. Well-known examples would include Stallybrass and White's notion of the debased *low* that always retains the "imprint of desire" (1986, 191), or Kristeva's *abject* that confronts our attempt to look away with the compulsion to look back (1982). Postcolonial ambivalence maintains that structure by showing how the debasement of the slave obscures the desire of the master, especially clear in the general feminization and homoeroticization (combined, as we will see in Part III, with a specifically gendered desexualization) of colonized cultures within the patriarchalism of colonial discourse.[15]

Bhabha, however, also works ambivalence in the other direction. Freud's clinical research led him to conclude that ambivalence can also express itself as an act of tenderness that provides a thin armature against feelings of hostility (1913, 853–54). Although there is no need to pause and amass examples, one remembers the myriad representations of the kind slave owner or the conflicted position of the ethnographer vis-à-vis the object of study:[16] that which is loved, even revindicated, but simultaneously feared, degraded, or ultimately contained.[17] In Bhabha's colonial scene, the motivation to *include*, to produce sameness and promote moral progress through missionary enlightenment and bureaucratic employment, is always tempered by the drive to *exclude*, sparked by the paranoia-inducing disintegration of difference.[18] Thus the colonialist-nationalist gesture of inclusion is exposed as a power move that fails— that *must* fail—or that at least can never succeed totally: as mimicry becomes mockery, and as hybrid objects proliferate wildly, the moral force of colonial discourse erodes along with its inability to maintain its difference. Ambivalence reigns.

What Bhabha does, in effect, is turn Freud's most anthropological theory on its head, reversing its direction and displacing its critical force. Almost without exception, Freud finds the raw material for his theory of ambivalence in the others of masculinist-colonialist and scientific discourse: in the "pathological expression of mourning" that he identifies in women (1913, 854) and in the centrality of taboo in primitive societies, both of which he persistently links to sickness (neurosis), immaturity, and infancy. What Bhabha helps us see more clearly is the ambivalence expressed by a figure such as Freud himself; in other words, the ambivalence that governs the relations between the subject of authority and its object of investigation.

Now, in this respect, the impossibility of disentangling Bhabha's notions of ambivalence and hybridity becomes quite suggestive. The taboo object, for Freud, is both the object and source of ambivalence (ibid., 832, 859). Likewise, for Bhabha, the hybridity of colonial discourse seems to be something that acts as both effect and cause of ambivalence. Or conversely, the ambivalence of colonial discourse serves as both cause and effect of hybridity. It is hard to tell which direction has priority. This exceedingly nebulous division between hybridity and ambivalence is worth a brief pause. Whereas "hybridity represents [portrays and/or stands in for] that ambivalent turn," Bhabha also speaks of "the ambivalence of hybridity" (1994, 113). Bhabha's standard gesture of radical metonymy is obviously in full effect here, and teasing out its distinct strands is a difficult and probably not very interesting task. What *is* interesting, for my purposes, is that this relationship suggests that *theorizing hybridity itself* is, like deploying the rhetoric enabled by colonial discourse, a profoundly ambivalent practice.

After a long detour, we now need to remember hybridity's articulation to race, and recognize that cultural theories of hybridity are always, even if obscurely, bound up with discourses on the racialized other. Moreover, despite vertiginous levels of abstraction, these discourses always express a desire to access the referential, indicative, reified *thing* behind hybridity: the radical heterogeneity of colonial, national, or civil society shot through with sociocultural intercourse (sexual, communicative, narratological, economic) between differentially constructed social actors. As we have seen, even Bhabha, who has been called a "master of political mystification and theoretical obfuscation" (Dirlik 1994, 333), is quite explicit in making this etymology of objective mixture a foundational element in his critical scheme: as in Santiago's model of the "entre-lugar" (1971) (to which we return in chapter 10), Bhabha says that "the knowledges of cultural authority may be articulated [as in mixed, connected] with forms of 'native' knowledges or faced with those discriminated subjects that they must rule but can no longer represent . . . The *display* of hybridity . . . terrorizes authority with the *ruse* of recognition" (1994, 115; my emphasis). Thus, while hybridity signals both a referent that is uncontainable ("the display of hybridity") and a point of enunciation whose splitting produces its own resistance (the hybridity of colonial authority), the critic's *desire for hybridity* cannot be assumed to eclipse the ambivalence of other desiring machines that propel their force, such as colonial discourse as such. In this sense, theories of hybridity speak to the theorist's desire to access and appropriate the heterogeneous, subalternized, multitudinous other of official speech and knowledge. Various expressions of this desire include obliging the subject of that otherness to listen, allowing it to speak, or insisting upon its fundamental irrepresentability.

Configuring hybridity as not only resistant to colonial discourse, but also ambivalent like colonial discourse, helps remind us of its excluded others left underdeveloped as a requisite nod to conflict, or simply left unstated. In other words, it may remind us that hybridity's commitment to production and reproduction historically emerges through theories and practices of genocide and rape. As many have demonstrated (e.g., Stepan 1991; Franco 1992, 67–68; Klor de Alva 1995; Gould 1998, 260; Canessa 2000), the *mestizaje* with which hybridity overlaps has historically tended to euphemize a process of whitening, Europeanization, and primitive accumulation (e.g., Sarmiento 1845; Vasconcelos 1926), and today is sometimes redeployed in a sophisticated discourse of ethnopolitical delegitimation.[19] Thus it is not particularly surprising when we find especially politicized theorists who couch their discourse entirely or partially in collective identitarian claims—pan-Mayanists in Guatemala, Zapatistas in Mexico, *o movimento negro* in Brazil—to be less excited about the emancipatory potential of hybridity than some academic postmodernists, even as their various social movements participate in a patent "hybridization" along discursive, political, aesthetic, ideological, and ethnic lines.[20] And vis-à-vis these same postcolonial actors whose discourse is analyzed and explained, hybridist frameworks may find themselves challenged and mistrusted on grounds of history (e.g., Sáenz 1936; Hewitt de Alcántara 1984; Gould 1998), political strategy (e.g., Oliveira e Oliveira 1974), or both (e.g., Cojtí Cuxil 1996; Henríquez and Rojas 1996).[21]

What does all of this imply for rereading theories of hybridity? It suggests a need to take seriously the self-critical challenge announced by Ángel Rama (1984), Gayatri Spivak (1988), and Edward Said (1978). In other words, it suggests that we not lose sight of the critic's relationship to what Bhabha calls the "on-going colonial project" (1994, 128), what Santiago calls "neocolonialism" (1971), what Marx theorized as "primitive accumulation" (1867), and what in Latin Americanism we might still call (were it not for the embarrassment of anachronism) a kind of internal colonialism. The importance of whether or not we name this scholarly position taking "postcolonialism" is open to debate. After Klor de Alva's problematization (1995), it may be more efficacious in Latin America to speak in terms of a postnationalism,[22] or to think about what Roberto Fernández Retamar (1976), Fernando Coronil (1999), and Walter Mignolo (1998) have intelligently formulated as the epistemological need to construct a "postoccidentalism." Whatever the name, and despite divergences, these projects require at least two gestures: the continued and rigorous exposure and displacement of the foundational complicity of academy and (neo)colonial authority; and an uncompromising democratization—in the literal sense—of knowledge. Hybridity, whether from the perspective of García Canclini or Bhabha, attempts both moves at once. At the same time, as a kind of theorizing that strives to map the radical heterogeneity of social life, the ultimate and ultimately unattainable object of hybridity theory is the holy grail represented in Paz's peasant or Menchú's secrets. In Latin America, we could consider it a name for the perennial attempt, in the words of Mário de Andrade, at "getting control of a language that reconciles a nation horizontally across geography and vertically across classes" (cited in Martín-Barbero 1987, 171). The desire expressed in Mário's demand plays out ambivalently. On the one hand, to theorize hybridity is to enter into dialogue with the radical heterogeneity—and radical inequality—of the social and thereby take seriously the relationship of that heterogeneity to legacies of (an on-going) colonialism, that is, to confront and attempt to reshape the coloniality of power. On the other hand, to theorize hybridity is to participate in complicity with those same legacies: it becomes a question, as Mário puts it, of "getting control," of realizing the nationalist reconfiguration of colonialism's politico-economic consolidation. I do not think that getting beyond this impasse will entail erasing hybridity. Rather, we might begin by putting hybridity under erasure and analyzing its conditions of possibility. That is what the remainder of this book attempts to do, by reading the theories and narratives of hybridity as they emerged in an earlier historical moment.

Were an unproblematic Manichaeanism applicable here, one might make from the subject position of the Latin American intellectual—like Hegel's slave, Montaigne's cannibals, or a postcolonial Caliban—an epistemological advantage, in which only the oppressed other or outsider can really see through and unmask the reality effects of the oppressor or insider. As such, the Latin American writer would gain a kind of legitimacy vis-à-vis a "more Western" interlocutor, and seize a moral authority that would foment a "speaking back" to the exploits of Eurocentrism. Regardless of the geoepistemologial space from which they enunciate, however, the writers that I have focused on throughout these opening chapters, and those that produce the source material of the subsequent chapters, are unsustainably framed as such. Although they may or may not hail from nation-states that bear the brunt of the neocolonial, global economy, only the most extravagant theoretical leaps could read them as occupying the position of "slave." The implicit recognition of this problem by Santiago in his articulation of the "space-in-between" *(o entre-lugar)* (1971) is one aspect that lends his influential argument its deservedly widespread approbation. For Santiago, the discursive space occupied by the Latin American writer emerges in between the code and its transgression (28): "in between," that is, not always already a pure transgression. If the Latin American writer can be thought of as "subaltern," then, it is only within the most literal reading of Ranajit Guha's famously vast definition of that social category (1982). If, as Santiago argues, to speak is "to speak against" (1971, 19), we should also remember his insistence that this speaking against requires as its companion the action of constructing a politicized criticism. In other words, the task is not merely to assert the critical advantage of marginality, but to think through (in both senses) the politics of acting upon that advantage. Ultimately, this project would seem to require an alignment of the practice of critique with the nonexclusive inclusion of the discursively and materially dispossessed. To what extent, then, does theorizing hybridity act out this alliance?

In the subsequent chapters, I will attempt to put a finer point on Santiago's critique. Although avant-garde writers such as Borges and Cortázar helped Santiago find a critical space-in-between in which to situate Latin American writing, an equally strong current in Latin American letters suggests a different relationship with, for lack of a better term, the metropole (Europe and North America as world-historical, -political, -economic, and -cultural center). The discursive and institutional positionality vis-à-vis the metropole that I have in mind is not so much "in between" the code and its transgression, but rather *split between* a local centralization of cultural authority (Rama's *ciudad letrada* and its historical transformations) and the global bid for cultural hegemony embodied in a Eurocentric modernity located elsewhere. As I showed earlier, Latin American writing becomes a kind of inner exterior of Eurocentrism, the exception to the rule that yet defines the rule, becoming the rule's most extreme expression and necessary counterpart. The ambivalence that this positionality generates is important in that it suggests a subjectivity that is not necessarily oppressed. Rather, it is a subject position that looks simultaneously toward a Eurocentric modernity that eludes it (or that it willfully eludes) and toward the constitutive countermodernity that surrounds and undergirds it (orality, backwardness, poverty).[23] These partially integrated social realities are what García Canclini calls mixed times, or "multitemporal heterogeneity." The Latin American theories and narratives of hybridity that I engage throughout this book are more explicitly informed by the voice of modernity than by the voices of modernity's others. But it is from within this unequal multitemporal heterogeneity that their discourses are forged, as they emerge as an attempt to participate in the former without altogether effacing the latter.[24] The ambivalent negotiation (between indictment and endorsement) of this discourse of effacement—the genocide and primitive accumulation that marks both colonial conquest and national consolidation—will draw most of my attention in the remaining chapters of this book.

What foments the constant retheorization of hybridity? Or, what does "thinking hybridity" *do* for the Latin Americanist intellectual? I am highly skeptical of the kind of psychologizing that attempts to reduce it to a question of overcoming sensed inferiorities and social illnesses, extending the diagnoses of Samuel Ramos's *pelado* (1938) or Paz's "hijos de la Malinche" (1950) to far-flung and diverse intellectual movements. Although Latin Americanist hybridity has historically exhibited a consistent exceptionalism, the motivations behind its (re)theorization are not reducible to a version of Freud's "exceptional" patients from which he drew a tentative "analogy between deformities of character resulting from protracted sickliness in childhood and the behavior of whole nations whose past history has been full of suffering" (1916, 592).[25] Likewise, it is not only, or at least not so much, like the hybridity of Santiago's or Bhabha's colonized subjects, a convenient vehicle for undermining, destabilizing, and eventually overcoming the authoritative status of Eurocentric discourse. This is not to say that Latin Americanist theories of hybridity offer no challenge to that discourse. On the contrary: they represent early, agile, and doggedly sustained critiques of Eurocentrism, white supremacy, and cultural imperialism. This critical consciousness, however, does not ward off a profound complicity: in short, Latin American theories and narratives of hybridity almost always end up reproducing some form of the discourses that they are articulated against. In other words, they fail to entirely reflect back upon their own similarly articulated, institutionalized discourses of power. Rather than some kind of discourse of pure resistance, or defiant transgression, I would argue that a more suggestive and realistic reading would place the Latin American project of theorizing hybridity in the terms of renegotiating a hegemonic pact, heretofore sealed in the nexus of a knowledge that is Eurocentrism and a place that is the metropole. They are precisely attempts to elucidate a mark of difference that participates constructively, without necessarily belonging to a coloniality of power that persistently reduces the intellectual production of the periphery to a second-order copy.[26] This entails, both literally and metaphorically, a resemantization of Freud's "mixed race" represented in the gesture of transforming it from "excluded" into something dynamic, what Vasconcelos calls "cosmic," what Freyre calls "meta-racial." Those efforts are something like the construction and legitimization of *another* social and epistemological genre—emerging from a universal genus—that can get control of the materiality of a radical social hetero*gen*eity.

The structural difficulty before which we find the possibility of a critical hybridity now stalled is the coloniality of power and the common ground that its logic shares with the logic of exemplarity (see chapter 1). The hybridity that Latin American hybridologists have tended to theorize is an argument for the active participation in, *and* critique of, the ostensibly universal flow of Eurocentric history. But what if, as I have suggested, the inclusive aspect of structural Eurocentrism allows for, even presupposes, such participation? How do these thinkers address the question of (non)belonging to this *genus universum*, and yet strive to guarantee the vitality and agency of the truly excluded, the abject otherness of *pueblos enfermos*, that they perceive as forming the social base

of their societies? It is here, at the point of confrontation with real social difference—at the articulation of race, class, gender, and nation that
constitutes that differentiation—that the critical propulsion of hybridity
begins to sputter. What the critic seeks through hybridity, in essence,
is a unifying theory that emerges in relation to an "impossibly" heterogeneous social condition: impossible not through transparent "difference," but impossible in its differently experienced social inequality.

One way that Latin American writers have pursued this problematic is by appropriating the scientific authority that had consolidated
around anthropology, "the science of man," by the early twentieth century.[27] Anthropological discourse, however, like the colonial discourse
in which it participates, is similarly founded on the constitutive ambivalence that Bhabha theorizes.[28] This complicity with colonialism is, of
course, long known in the discipline of anthropology itself, where the
relationship between studier and studied, between "modern" and "primitive," has been widely problematized and thoroughly deconstructed. As
Claude Lévi-Strauss makes clear at the opening of his *Tristes Tropiques*
(1955): "The fact is that these primitive peoples . . . [that yield] noble
and profitable revelations . . . are all, in their different ways, enemies of
our society, which pretends to itself that it is investing them with nobility at the very time when it is completing their destruction, whereas it
viewed them with terror and disgust when they were genuine adversar-
ies" (1955, 33). Now, recall that I positioned the Latin American theorist
of hybridity as simultaneously in dialogue with the modernity of the
metropole and "dealing with" the contrapuntal alternative modernities
(which is not to say "nonmodernity") of local popular and peasant social
sectors. If acceptable, this configuration makes the ambivalent action of
an anthropologically oriented discourse particularly useful.[29]

On the one hand, the Latin American production of anthropological
discourse is capable of articulating a difference from, thereby grounding a critique of, North American and European hegemony: this is how
our heterogeneity becomes a productive hybridity, our cosmic race, our
racial democracy, "nuestra América mestiza." One of the ways that anthropological discourse does so is by signaling the cultural productivity and value of constitutive, nationally internal others. On the other
hand, however, the same discourse that rhetorically expands cultural
participation by articulating a national hybridization also enacts an ar-
chivalization and hence domestication of the threat of a politically charged
heterogeneity. The most extreme expression of this "other side" of valo-

rization is the resemantization of literal, physical *erasure* from the national scene. It is the discursive workings of this expression, and its founding ambivalence, that most interest me in the pages that follow. I argue that the rhetorical revindication of internal others is a rescue tinged by fear. Who is being variously rescued, hybridized, modernized, and (re)incorporated into national participation? Precisely the "new" social actors embodied in the materially abandoned (and emboldened by that same abandonment) as they begin to articulate forceful claims on the state.[30] Where do we find this theorizing most explicitly practiced? Although the ambivalence of theorizing hybridity appears in different forms at various points in Latin America's history, a moment of particular intensity is that which accompanies the foundational renegotiations of modern Latin American national consciousness of the late nineteenth and early twentieth centuries. Thus, for my purposes, the correlate of Bhabha's "ambivalence of colonial discourse" is not necessarily the theories of empire invoked by imperial Spain, but rather the theories of nation articulated by literate, bourgeois, modernizing Latin America. The historical articulation of these two modes of domination is summed up in Quijano's idea of "the coloniality of power."

The anthropological discourse through which Latin American theories of hybridity were (and usually still are) constructed rests on its own formal hybridization. Candido is one link in a long chain of Latin Americanist intellectuals who have sounded a certain skepticism toward the efficacy of the wholesale importation of Western philosophy and positive science for the study of Latin America. He is also one of many who signal "stories"—in his case, as told through literary narrative fiction—as perhaps the best, even only, means for thinking about and representing Latin American heterogeneity. Borges concurs, in his frequent reference to the theoretic power of "fictions" (*ficciones*). Martín-Barbero has argued that "only in literature does *mestizaje* [in the broad sense, as hybridity] cease to be an abstract theme and become a living actor who speaks with a distinctive way of perceiving, narrating, and being aware of the world" (1987, 188). Rama (1982) suggests something similar in his famous studies of Arguedas. In short, many have looked to the literary as the primary arena in which to effectively grapple with the problem of a specific Latin American identity and difference.

Anthropological description, in its turn, as a method that openly embraces narrative, throws into question the purist and fictive objectivity of scientism (de Certeau 1981, 17–34). Anthropological discourse, then, as Candido suggests in his reading of "Brazilian social science," must be science *and something else*. That something else goes by the name of literature. Although literature, as de Certeau has argued via Freud, "always precedes science" in understanding our social and psychical condition, the "science" that has most ardently challenged (and confirmed) the unicity and centrality of Eurocentric reason is that famous companion of the colonizer: ethnology, today generalized under the disciplinary field "anthropology." What Candido senses, and what the Latin American trajectory of theorizing and narrating hybridity has put into practice, is an insistent interdisciplinarity that has *always* blurred the distinction between those two modes of discourse, literature and anthropology, the humanities and the social sciences, the aesthetic arts and the exact sciences.[31] Whether masquerading as "literature" or "anthropology," anthropological discourse is a primary mode through which Latin American theorists and narrators of hybridity have engaged in rethinking a worn-out exceptionalism by constructing new versions of exemplarity. The results have been mixed.

Part II
Mexico

QUE NUESTRA MAYOR ESPERANZA DE SALVACION SE
ENCUENTRA EN EL HECHO DE QUE NO SOMOS UNA RAZA
PURA, SINO UN MESTIZAJE, UN PUENTE DE RAZAS FUTURAS,
UN AGREGADO DE RAZAS EN FORMACION: AGREGADO QUE
PUEDE CREAR UNA ESTIRPE MAS PODEROSA QUE LAS QUE
PROCEDEN DE UN SOLO TRONCO.

—*José Vasconcelos,* Indología, *1926*

They will Mexicanize this country!

—*Louis Agassiz, in despair upon being
informed of the outbreak of the American
Civil War*

America is therefore the land of the future,
where, in the ages that lie before us, the
burden of the World's History shall reveal
itself—perhaps in a contest between North
and South America.

—*G. W. F. Hegel,* The Philosophy of
History, *1837*

Mexico

Three themes dominated Part I. First, I argued that theories of hybridity, regardless of their stated objects of analysis (biological reproduction, generic forms, cultural processes, intellectual work, etc.), are underwritten by a discourse of race. Second, taking Néstor García Canclini's *Culturas híbridas* as an example, I analyzed the way in which this racialized discourse can nevertheless operate within theories of hybridity that explicitly reject their stake in race. Finally, I made a case for thinking about how the two fields of critique generalized under the names "postcolonialism" and "Latin Americanism" can inform and enrich each other. This led me to propose that paying special attention to how the symptomatic "ambivalence of colonial discourse"—understood as the unconscious conflict of love and fear that structures representations of colonized others—could be a productive strategy for rereading Latin American theories and narratives of hybridity. My critical apparatus, then, emphasizes the logic of cultural power that conjoins the practice of theorizing hybridity to discourses (literary, anthropological, or both) that I generalize as "colonial" in their general characteristics, including their material effects and political implications, even where their scene of writing is more precisely classified as "national." In this sense, theories and narratives of hybridity attract my interest insofar as they operate within the parameters of persistent colonialist structures that Quijano calls the "coloniality of power."

Over the following four chapters I will extend this line of analysis. While maintaining my focus on *race* as a necessary discursive thread that holds hybridity together, I will analyze the ways in which that thread is at once entangled with and conditioned by discourses of *time* and *nation*. Moreover, I will attempt to step out of (without altogether abandoning) the realm of Latin Americanist metacriticism that marked the first three chapters, and move to an analysis whose historical contextualization is more explicit. This will entail centering my consideration of hybridity theory on a particular mode, a specific place, and an exemplary case. The mode of theorizing hybridity at issue here will be *mestizaje*, translatable as "miscegenation," but typically carrying a Latin American positivity and general flexibility that the English term often lacks.[1] The context with which my remarks dialogue will be the place—and historical moment—that made *mestizaje* famous: Mexico during the late-nineteenth and early-twentieth centuries. Finally, the case study that will enable my analysis will be a formally heterogeneous set of texts (literary, anthropological, historiographical, political, in general "mixed") that precede, foreshadow, and attempt to sort out the Mexican Revolution. The trajectory of this analysis will run from a review of the function of *mestizaje* in Mexico's ninetheenth-century doctrine of positivism, to a reading of key "revolutionary" narratives of *mestizaje* by Heriberto Frías, José Vasconcelos, and Mariano Azuela. My concern is not the emancipatory potential of hybridity as a marker of the cultural specificity, or even oppositionality, of Latin American discourses and societies. Rather, I am interested in the ways in which the laws of hybridity operate as a discursive formation that can consolidate at the level of statist ideological function.[2] The Mexican discourse of *mestizaje* is a well-known example of this consolidation.

Central to my critique will be the fact that *mestizaje* in modern (post-independence) Mexico is not theorized solely, or even mainly, as a means to regulate, in a prohibitionary sense, the proliferation (actual or potential) of interracial and/or intercultural mixing. Although rooted in a concept of the biopolitics of interracial mixing, the discursive objectives of *mestizaje* tend to be displaced. My contention is that *mestizaje* is a metadiscourse that can enable the ideological articulation of a conceptual series crucial to the consolidation of the Mexican state: race, (historical) time, and nation. Although much criticism has been devoted to the discursive function of *mestizaje* in Mexico, the role of metaphors of time—and their articulation to race and nation—within this discourse has not been considered. As I will show, throughout the history of modern Mexico several generations of intellectuals have dwelled on the disarticulate status of race, time, and nation. It is this disarticulation that many have theorized as a hindrance to the formation of a durable state; a state that can make convincing claims upon both hegemony and sovereignty; a state, in short, that can interpellate its subjects into an integral body politic, and enforce its legitimacy as universal.

These problems of nation-state consolidation were widely theorized among the nineteenth-century positivists. How they harnessed *mestizaje* to these problems is the theme of chapter 5. That chapter will be dedicated to showing how the nineteenth-century positivists invoked the discourse of *mestizaje* as a means for articulating—that is, for putting back together—the perceived fragmentation of race, time, and nation. I take as my evidence a set of key positivist texts from various historical moments, but with particular emphasis on Gabino Barreda's groundbreaking discourse *Oración Cívica* (1867).

In chapter 6 I will show the ideological effectivity of this articulation on the part of the positivists. I do so through a reading of Heriberto Frías's largely forgotten, anti-Porfirian novel, *Tomochic* (1893, final revision in 1906). Frías's novel represents what I call a narrative of *foundational disarticulation*. Often associated with naturalism, the generic mark of the foundational disarticulation is an emphasis on the horrors, crimes, and violence of state expansion and consolidation, as opposed to national reconciliation. In other words, rather than strive for a tone of patriotic duty, or demonization of an antagonistic other, the contradictions of state expansion and consolidation themselves become the object of literary reflection. Frías's novel, which is presented as a critique of the positivist-oriented Porfirian state, nevertheless speaks to the effectivity of the ideological limits established by the positivists' construction of *mestizaje*, especially in the articulation of race and nation.

The full significance of the centrality of time within discourses of *mestizaje* becomes clear in chapter 7, and governs my comparative reading of some of José Vasconcelos's major works on *mestizaje*, and Mariano Azuela's classic "novela de la Revolución," the celebrated *Los de abajo* (1915). In reading them comparatively, I ask how they alternatively produce discourses of race, time, and nation in the context of postrevolutionary Mexican nation-state consolidation. Rather than read Vasconcelos *against* the positivists, which is standard critical and historiographical practice (cf. Hale 1989, 258–59; Zea 1943), I read him as a continuation of a key positivist intellectual project that distinctly marks positivism's intersection between philosophy and social politics: the attempt to reconcile the disarticulation of race, time, and nation through *mestizaje*. This reconciliation, I argue, is precisely what Vasconcelos strives for—and fails to realize—as I will show through a reading of his theory of *mestizaje*, most famously expressed in his treatise *La raza cósmica* (1925), but more elaborately theorized in lesser-known works such as *Indología* (1926). At the same time, Vasconcelos's failure, along with the critical force of Frías and the pessimism of Azuela, is indicative of a larger success that at first glance might seem like a paradox: the transcendental realization of *mestizaje* as an effective discourse of nation-state consolidation. I will attempt to explain how and why.

4. New Cultural History and the Rise of Mediation

Before introducing more fully the problematic entanglement of race, time, and nation that will govern my analysis, I would like to dedicate this chapter to addressing the basic question of why revisiting *mestizaje* and, moreover, some of its foundational narrations, might be a worthwhile project today. Two historiographical strains are most urgently at stake, and will stand as implicit objects of critique throughout Part II. The first has to do with the Eurocentric trajectory through which "the Indian" has been thought in modern Mexico, and that is very much in play in the increasingly volatile, yet often cautiously hopeful, politics that has engulfed Mexico's indigenous communities since 1992. The second has to do with the sublimation of what we might call something like "mediating subjects" as an increasingly privileged object of historical analysis in history writing both from and about Mexico.

If we read Latin Americanist theories of hybridity, among them *mestizaje*, as entangled in the coloniality of power, then the ethnocultural subject that has consistently (even if not exclusively) found itself colonized within this discourse in Mexico is traditionally known as "the Indian" *(el indio)*. Let us recall that the coloniality of power, the bare fact of the existence of an ongoing colonialism, signifies a generalized political project marked by an expansion of state sovereignty, accompanied by the institutionalization of an often privatized primitive accumulation that expropriates wealth on behalf of a politico-economic center. If these terms are acceptable, then I think it is reasonable to claim that many indigenous people in Mexico live in a situation of ongoing colonialism.[1] This was certainly the case at the dawn of the Mexican Revolution (Knight 1990, 79). And although the postrevolutionary state to some extent reformed both attitudes and policies toward indigenous communities, the statist discourse on the Indian continued to be regulated by a marked ambivalence (ibid., 98–102).

The Mexicanist discourse of *mestizaje* has a stake in constructing the figure of the Indian as an ambivalent object of desire.[2] *Mestizaje*, as a concept, develops around, through, and against indigenous communities. These real and imagined, compact and diffuse communities—here embattled, there flourishing—are the material substrate that always exceeds the discursive construction of "the Indian." This subjectivity called the Indian is the product of a representational violence that homogenizes and reifies a dynamic multiplicity of ethnocultural communities. Indeed, as Guillermo Bonfil Batalla has pointed out, the Indian did not exist before Europeans invaded the New World (1981, 19). And, as Judith Friedlander has shown (1975), the denomination "Indian" *(indio)* is extremely shifty, and runs up against all sorts of economic and political appropriations and disassociations. Hence, just as this book rests on a constructivist view that understands "race" as a historically dynamic social relation (as opposed to a historically transcendent fact· of biology, geography, climate, culture, language, psychology, or Spirit) whose analysis is best carried out on the plane of discourse, so do I invoke "the Indian" here as a discursive formation that serves an array of ideological purposes. In other words, I am interested in thinking about the social construction and rhetorical deployment of the Indian as an essential component in a system of representation.

That system is *mestizaje*. And if *mestizaje* is underwritten by a discourse of race, the racialized figure with which it has been most obsessively preoccupied in the Mexicanist scene is the Indian. Almost all of the most vigorous contemporary arguments over *mestizaje* hinge on questions of *mestizaje*'s implications for living indigenous communal or individual actors. So, whereas Néstor García Canclini's account of hybridity (1989) opens toward a notion of cultural *mestizaje* as a framework for intercultural democratization and greater social fluidity, George Yúdice points out the "*mestizo* normativity" that complicates the access to social benefits for individuals identified as *too Indian* (2001, xxxviii).

And whereas Enrique Krauze argues that the successful negotiation of cultural *mestizaje* is the positive mark of Mexican national identity (1997, xiv), for Bonfil Batalla *mestizaje* also euphemizes "de-Indianization" *(la desindianización)* and, by extension, ethnocide (1987, 17). Within and alongside these debates, much attention has been given to the difficult task of positively formulating a clear definition of "the Indian," or some kind of standard that would indicate when a person can in fact be deemed "indigenous." Although this question often has urgent political and economic consequences, I want to emphasize that it is not a question that these chapters will address in any systematic sense.[3] Not only are the empirics required by these questions outside of my field of critique, but Alan Knight has discussed and summarized their major points of contention in a far more thorough fashion than I will here, in a widely read essay titled "Racism, Revolution and *Indigenismo*: Mexico, 1910–1940" (1990, 72–78).[4]

In that very same discussion, however, Knight also suggests something that I do want to pursue in these chapters, and, moreover, to write against. In the essay, Knight convincingly identifies the ways in which theories of *mestizaje* and *indigenismo* formed a powerful discursive couplet in the service of postrevolutionary nation building (86).[5] If the cult of *mestizaje* enabled the construction of a national identity marked by mixing, then *indigenismo* provided the framework for pulling the internal exteriority of the Indian into the national mix. The former exalted a national trait; the latter interpellated a heretofore alienated national subject. Together, they worked in the service of hegemony: the forging of an integral body politic. As Luis Villoro long ago pointed out, the Indian would serve as a resource for a hegemonic identity construction, "charged with reminding us [*recordarnos*: by "nos" he means mestizo Mexico] of our specificity vis-à-vis the foreign" (1950, 190). And yet, alongside this abstract sacralization of the Indian, a concrete denigration of indigenous cultures, communities, and individuals would persist. This situation produced a gap, Knight writes, whereby "official ideology," which "may . . . have softened . . . some of the earlier excesses of full-fledged biological racism," would find itself "at odds with social reality" and an "intractably racist society" (1990, 100, 101). Moreover, this official articulation of *mestizaje* and *indigenismo* would exhibit "its own contradictions . . . [and] devise racist formulae of its own" (101).

My objective will not be to identify this contradiction in literary texts, or to confirm new subtleties of its various instantiations. The contradiction has, in fact, been identified to the verge of becoming a disciplinary convention. It is generally noted in the many critiques of integrationist or corporatist *indigenismo*. Villoro offers a classic, though uncritical, formulation of what he calls the *indigenista* "paradox" at the heart of *mestizaje*: "now the Indian is no longer only alterity; we see him at a distance, but at the same time, he forms part of our spirit" (1950, 192).[6] My task will be to show how this contradiction is in no way contradictory, if by that we mean a conceptual phenomenon dependent on an irreconcilable set of statements and enunciations. Rather, what appears as a frustrating contradiction is in fact a productive irresolution, the very link between *mestizaje* and *indigenismo*, whose apparent paradoxes are in fact symptoms of the ambivalence that governs all colonial discourse. Far from contradictory, the simultaneous exaltation and denigration of the Indian is the postrevolutionary recodification of what Martín-Barbero calls the intersection of "abstract inclusion and concrete exclusion" that served as the Enlightenment's "legitimization of social differences" (1987, 7).[7] There is nothing illogical or contradictory about the Indian's symbolic function here: it is the object of ambivalence that makes *mestizaje* work, allowing it to articulate race, time, and nation in a particularly effective way.

At the risk of belaboring the point, I want to make clear that all of this talk about representation makes it easy to lose sight of the more urgent political relevance of invoking the Indian today. Although indigenous communities of the Americas have always been active participants in the defense of their own social and communal integrity, over the past couple of decades they have been mobilizing in innovative and very visible ways. Obvious examples would include the momentum that ushered forth from the congresses and demonstrations around the Quincentennial; land- and resource-rights activism (and even some legal victories) in Bolivia, Canada, Ecuador, Guatemala, and the United States; the indigenous-dominated alliance associated with the Zapatista uprising in Mexico; and the 2005 election victory of Evo Morales in Bolivia. Nonindigenous social movements and intellectuals have allied themselves with these struggles on various levels.[8] I want to emphasize, however, that although my critique may have something like a historical affinity to these struggles, it is not *about* them. There is nothing, at least at the analytical level, about real indigenous cultural practices, or resistance, in the following pages. My object of study is not indigenous peoples. My object is the symbolic economy of *mestizaje*, an economy in which trafficking in "the Indian" has historically yielded significant discursive dividends. If what follows can be linked to the contemporary political relevance of indigenous struggles, it will be at the level of shedding light on the history of a representation, albeit one whose effects play out in the physical and political world.

A second point of contemporary relevance for these chapters is what I might call, if not an argument, then a certain tension that I sense between my critique of *mestizaje* and the emphasis on *mediation* within the increasingly prominent historiographical orientation that is sometimes generalized as "the new cultural history." A thorough review of this historiographical genre would take me too far afield here. Indeed, it would be easy to stumble at the first hurdle, as some have gone as far as to question its very existence. However, for something whose existence is questionable, the new cultural history has kicked up an impressive amount of dust, especially in recent Mexicanist historiography.[9] Let us admit, from the beginning, then, that the new cultural history is neither stable nor homogeneous, yet at the same time has practitioners who do not hesitate to classify their work as "new cultural history." For now, all I want to do is to acknowledge a kind of anachronism, vis-à-vis the new cultural history, in the "top-down" approach to reading *mestizaje* that I engage in here, and to explain how and why I think it can be a productive anachronism.

The new cultural history draws heavily on poststructuralist, postcolonialist, feminist, and neo-Gramscian innovations in the transnational fields of literary criticism and anthropology, and is strongly informed by the culturalist turn in British Marxist cultural studies (e.g., Thompson, Williams, Hall, Anderson) and French cultural history (e.g., Chartier, Veyne, Darnton).[10] As such, a central feature of the new cultural history is a vigorous drive to rethink the workings and locations of culture, power, and social struggle. A study in the new cultural history would seek to complicate, or even reject, models that posit struggles for social hegemony as strict binaristic affairs, contests of total domination and total resistance. Rather than emphasize (at least exclusively) the emanation of laws, campaigns, or culture from a centralized seat of power (the *ciudad letrada*, in Ángel Rama's famous model), the new cultural historian would be more (or at least equally) interested in how those effects are received, reinterpreted, reappropriated, and even transformed in the periphery (Vaughn 1999, 274; Knight 2002, 141–42).

Rather than focus on the ultimate national consolidation imposed by a state sovereign, the new cultural history shifts the attention toward, in the hybridized phrase of Joseph and Nugent, processes of "everyday forms of state formation" (1994, 4). It is a profoundly *antiteleological* historiography, premised explicitly against "grand narratives" (Knight 2002, 153), giving far less value to the narration of epic struggles between domination and resistance, and placing a high premium on marginal perspectives, middlemen (and, very prominently, middlewomen), and communicational circuits. Terms such as "process," "relation," "negotiation," "dynamics," and "exchange" proliferate. Mexico, with its long history of national disarticulation—regional disputes, peasant uprisings, incomplete hegemony, and contested sovereignty—has been a productive object of study for the new cultural history; indeed, it has been the field where its most notable enthusiasm and debates have played out.

Subsumed within this historiography is an unselfconscious, or at least uninterrogated, commitment to "mediation." I would go as far as to call "mediation" the unthought of the new cultural history, as it shows up missing in even the most thorough delineations of the genre (e.g., Vaughn, Knight). The new cultural historian reworks often reified or fixed terms such as "state," "peasant," "popular," "mass culture," or "the people," at once putting them in motion and setting them in relation. In other words, the interdependent formations—the mediations—through which emerge elite and subaltern actors are historicized, their alleged atomization problematized. This is the implication of Joseph and Nugent's essay that introduces *Everyday Forms of State Formation* (1994). Here they clearly embrace Philip Corrigan's reminder (which they reproduce in the volume) that "the natural, neutral, universal—that is 'The Obvious'—becomes problematic and questionable" (1990, xviii). Mediation itself is the new cultural history's condition of possibility exempted from this exhortation to problematize and historicize. Not only does it stand, untethered, as "The Obvious," but it denotes the teleology of the antiteleologism of the new cultural history. Mediation, in short, becomes the orthodoxy of the new cultural history.

A symptomatic example of what I mean appears in a review essay of an issue of the *Latin American Research Review*. In the essay, Terry Rugeley (2002) comments on the transformed representation of "peasants" in Leticia Reina's work. Whereas in her early book *Las rebeliones campesinas* (1980) they "too often seemed angry reactionaries interested in little more than the restoration of communal lands," in a current study the focus is on peasants that "not merely survived but flourished during the years of [nineteenth-century] Mexican Liberalism" (Rugeley 2002, 247). Rugeley concludes that "[t]he distance between these two volumes underscores how much historians' perspectives have evolved over the last sixteen years" (ibid.). It is not clarified, however, why a shift in emphasis from struggles for communal lands to questions of cultural survival and tenacity should be considered an evolution (which implies an advance or improvement) or even a separate issue.

The same tone of continuous advancement runs through the Joseph and Nugent essay, wherein the new culturalist approach "goes beyond" (1994, 12), and its studies "go beyond" (ibid.), the revisionist and neo-populist approaches that preceded them, which in turn "represent significant advances over the earlier [pro-revolutionary] orthodoxy" (6) of the Mexicanist postrevolutionary historiography that preceded *them*.[11] Joseph and Nugent, however, are more explicit than Rugeley about the active agent of this transcendence. It is the methodological move from stasis to motion (16) that emerges out of the mediation between old methods: a new "analytical framework for simultaneously integrating views of the Mexican revolution 'from below' with a more compelling and nuanced 'view from above'" (12). The latter view they will take from what they call "revisionism," the former from what they call "neo-populism"; the mediation and merging of these perspectives begets what some have since gone on to call the new cultural history. Integration, a methodological *mestizaje*, begets improvement, an evolutionary step forward, and, in the end, a stronger analytical framework. I do not casually invoke *mestizaje* here; for Joseph and Nugent precisely recite the logic of Mexican *mestizaje*, complete with its evolutionary implications (which I will discuss extensively), as a method for writing the history of Mexico. Indeed, in the more broadly framed Latin Americanist approaches to the study of popular cultures that have emerged in the last two decades, mediation *(las mediaciones)* stands in analogous, if not synonymous, relation to *mestizaje*. This is why, at the opening of his influential *De los medios a las mediaciones* (1987), Jesús Martín-Barbero stresses the need to look at "the popular" not as an atomized unit, but as "the thick layers of *mestizajes* or mixtures" that mark the mediation between sender and receiver, between blacks, Indians, and whites, between modern and traditional, between popular, elite, and mass (1987, 2).[12]

As this citation of Martín-Barbero—who, it will be noted, has vastly informed my thinking on Latin American literatures and cultures—suggests, this book has its own obligations and commitments to the new cultural history. If this particular project in literary and cultural studies participates in that genre, however, it will not be by furthering the understanding of how popular (nonelite) actors negotiate *mestizaje*. Rather, its role will be that of critical interlocutor. The critical edge, of course, will not consist of invoking something like a "one-drop rule" or "guilt by association." The idea is not to "expose" the new cultural history's discursive stake in, or genealogy that leads to, a logic of *mestizaje*, and thus suggest that it must inherit all of *mestizaje*'s unwanted baggage, throwing the legitimacy of the entire project into doubt. My aim is not to indulge in a reactionary polemic "against mixing," methodological or otherwise. Instead, if there is relevance for the new cultural history here, it will emerge through an interrogation of the workings of *mestizaje* that may raise self-reflexive questions about the academic's ability to escape genealogies of repression. As will become clear in the following chapters, the cultural mixing mediated by the discourse of *mestizaje* in Mexico has traditionally served a repressive function, and participates in the coloniality of power that governs the relations between the state and nationally internal indigenous communities. It is this function that serves as the object of these chapters. The fact that the mediations of the new cultural history repeat its basic formula, especially in reference to Mexico, speaks to the ideological effectivity of *mestizaje*. In other words, while writing against the mythic centralization of power (the state, official history, etc.) in compelling ways, I maintain that the partisans of the Mexicanist new cultural history have reinvoked the basic structure of one of the most effective discursive modes of othering that undergirds that same centralization.[13]

I have noted several lines of dialogue in which these chapters on Mexico engage. At the same time, it is important to be clear that while it participates in, and draws from, all of them, its generic parameters are bound by none. Thus, what I offer from here forward is a critique neither of *indigenismo* nor of the new cultural history. Nor do I frame the following as a comprehensive or sustained study of Mexican nationalism, nation-state formation, racism, or the "novela de la Revolución." Rather, the generic space that these chapters inhabit is that of the larger project, a critique of hybridity. In these chapters, that critique will focus on a set of literary texts that emerge within the national context of revolutionary Mexico.

However, I want to stress that the questions that will govern the following pages will not revolve around striving for a positive definition or seamless mapping of hybridity by way of *mestizaje*. In the words of Partha Chatterjee, the object is not to "produce a new 'theory'" that could explain hybridity "by reducing it to something else" (1986, 42). Rather, I will ask how the mode of hybridity called *mestizaje* consolidates as a discursive formation that depends on its relation to a series of discourses (race, time, and nation). How does *mestizaje* mediate, and even articulate, discourses of race, time, and nation? How is that mediation represented and reproduced in literary texts? If *mestizaje* operates as part of a nationalist rhetoric in the service of the state, in what ways does it represent its national others? How does it contain and rearticulate that same otherness? How does it represent the nation as such? What kinds of power dynamics does it produce within that nation-space? In what ways does it depend on and reproduce the coloniality of power? How, ultimately, does *mestizaje* exemplify the transformation of the fact of hybridity into something like *hybridology*?

These are the kinds of questions that govern my analysis of *mestizaje* in Mexico. The first step, then, will be to defend the idea that the Mexican discourses of race, time, and nation have, in fact, been theorized as a problem. In order to read *mestizaje* as a system of representation that helps alleviate ideological dissonance around race, time, and nation, it is necessary to first show that there *is* dissonance. Thus, rather than simply assert, it seems wise to demonstrate that the articulation of race, time, and nation is in fact a problematic task, and that this task is something that state-sponsored intellectuals (and their critics) have long paid attention to. This will help reinforce my claim as to the importance of the dialogue between, on the one hand, race, time, and nation, and, on the other hand, *mestizaje*, in the work of Frías, Vasconcelos, and Azuela. I will also need to show how and why these discourses tend to emerge in concert. To begin, let us consider the problem as it applies to the positivist discourse on *mestizaje* in nineteenth-century Mexico.

5. Back toward a
Positive *Mestizaje*

It is well known that the modern history of Mexico—from the first significant mobilizations for independence (1810) through the last phases of the revolution (1940)—has been marked by a series of crises of national hegemony and state sovereignty. It is also well known that the intelligentsia has consistently thought about the Mexican "race problem" in terms of an "Indian problem." At the same time, it should be emphasized that accompanying this meditation "on the Indian" within the context of national crisis, there has existed a certain anxiety over the very possibility of constructing a coherent *Mexican* national identity. Why should these issues be formulated as a problem of race, time, and nation? And what do they have to do with hybridity?

The relations between race and nation present themselves as constantly transforming and always open questions. These difficulties are surely linked to the quagmire of territory, birth, citizenship, and sovereignty that complicates the modern nation form in its relation to national subjects (see Agamben 1995, 126–35). For the purposes of what follows, I will be operating from the basic theses that race and nation are interdependent, and that their articulation is thought in terms of their relations to a common historical time. There is a lot of current (and, indeed, not so current) theory that could be cited to support these claims.[1] But we can also stick to the context at issue here, and extract our evidence from the Mexican texts that were most explicitly engaged in this historical labor.

During the long and contested period of Mexico's nationalization (roughly, 1810–1940), intellectuals are keenly aware of these problems of race and nation. I will set forth many examples, but to begin it is worth pointing out Manuel Gamio's 1916 *indigenista* treatise, which is not for nothing called *Forjando patria: Pro-nacionalismo.* In the opening pages of that work, Gamio diagnoses as the greatest challenge to Mexican, postrevolutionary nation building its patent lack of racial and linguistic unity, and cites the well-forged nationalisms of Germany, France, and Japan as countervailing examples (1916, 7–9).[2] This challenge, he explains, is embodied in the living indigenous communities whose very existence presents an unwanted reminder of the ongoing colonial conditions of the modern Mexican state (9–10). Reifying or stabilizing the nation form, then, is the continuation of a colonial project. Interpellating the Indian as a national subject becomes synonymous with "pacifying" indigenous resistance.[3] Indigenous communities, as a political force, historically problematize—at least from the perspective of the political elite—the Mexican project of hegemony, by denying the horizontal unity of nationness. And they repetitively frustrate the realization of Mexican sovereignty by rejecting—through counterclaims, wars, uprisings, nonparticipation, and so on—the vertical authority of the state.[4] The revolution, in which many peasant and indigenous communities participated, on all sides, reasserted these realities in an urgent way for the postrevolutionary nation-building intelligentsia.

It is precisely here, at the impasse between alternative modernities (say, Gamio versus Zapata), that Étienne Balibar's following conclusion is relevant: "as social formations [economies, families, tribes, villages, trading networks, etc.] are nationalized, the populations included within them, divided up among them or dominated by them are ethnicized— that is, represented *in the past or in the future as if* they formed a natural community, possessing of itself an identity of origins, culture and interests which transcends individuals and social conditions" (Balibar and Wallerstein 1988, 96; my emphasis). Although Balibar's explicit concern is the discursive naturalization or erasure of social-class inequality that accompanies nation-state formation, the comment resonates with Mexican national consolidation on another level. In the Mexican case, I would change his diagnosis of the national will to ethnicize to read "represented in the past *and* in the future." If the very emergence of the national body politic produces a set of radical, racialized differences, then those differences are naturalized through their ascription to particular historical temporalities. Closing and transcending this temporal gap is the burden of nationalization. The work of this construction—the production of what Balibar calls a "fictive ethnicity" that can ground a *national* identity—in literate and semiliterate societies, as many have shown, often falls to writers: novelists, essayists, scholars, journalists, speechwriters, bureaucrats.[5]

Gamio is again illustrative here. In the rather hyperbolic introduction to his *Forjando patria*, he stages this discursive intersection of race, nation, and time: "In the great forge of America, on the gigantic anvil of the Andes, centuries and centuries have wrought the bronze and iron of virile races . . . They were miniature *patrias*: Aztec, Maya-Kiché, Inca . . . that perhaps later would have combined and fused until they embodied great indigenous *patrias* . . . It was not to be. Upon the arrival of Columbus with other men, other blood, other ideas, the crucible that unified the race was tragically overturned and the mold, where Nationality was forming and *Patria* was crystallizing, was shattered . . . Today it is the revolutionaries of Mexico who must grasp the mallet . . . of the ironsmith so that from the miraculous anvil will surge the new *patria*, fused of iron and bronze. There is the iron . . . There's the bronze . . . Stir forth, brothers!" (1916, 5–6).

At least three temporal vectors symptomatically conflate at this scene of nation formation sketched by Gamio, student of Franz Boas and Mexico's "first" modern anthropologist: the time of *history*, which narrates a series of moments (pre-Columbian, conquest, revolution)—at once destiny ("it was not to be"), contingency ("perhaps later would have combined"), and agency ("today it is the revolutionaries of Mexico who must")—that amount to the material conditions of possibility in which the nation resides; the time of *anthropology*, which constructs a scene of distinct national elements, heterogeneous in their cultures and "levels" (bronze, iron) of civilizational development; and the time of *national ideal*, which points the way to a future, articulate, and whole *patria*. America, realized in Gamio's Mexico, is a project, at once immanent and transcendent, whose participants emerge from a primordial past and an urgent present to propel the nation—Mexico—into the future: as Alfonso Reyes put it at about the same time, national participants that would "engender a common soul" (1915, 16). The old indigenous nations—flattened, "a race"—even in their false start must be made to participate in the shaping of the new, national race. And here we find the problem at the heart of the discursive intersection of race, nation, and time that the Mexican discourse of *mestizaje* strives to articulate. The Indian has historically named the problem—racially other, stuck in time, a national stigma—and *mestizaje* its solution, the motor that propels national consolidation, social evolution, and, in theory, political inclusion.[6]

When theories of hybridity say "mixed times" they also say "mixed races." We saw this dynamic at work in chapter 2's analysis of García Canclini's theory of *culturas híbridas*. But it is worth a quick rehearsal here, for it fits surprisingly well within larger historical trajectories of *mestizaje* and *indigenismo*. In chapter 2, I emphasized García Canclini's banishment of race from his hybridological framework. This expulsion could be said to operate along the lines of what Freud called a "disavowal." By this I mean that, although briefly recognized, the denial of race is then summarily, yet incompletely, "forgotten," with the object of that denial (race) later returning in the form of a substitute, or what Freud calls a "fetish" (1927, 152–53). Here that substitute is time. If, in García Canclini's hybridity, race is banished, and then that banishment forgotten, its trace is remembered as the temporality of "multitemporal heterogeneity." We saw, however, that as García Canclini's argument unfolds, the "multi" of temporality consistently slides into the "bi" of the old problematic couplet "tradition and modernity." And, as this binary reasserts itself, race returns by way of the now-temporalized notion of what García Canclini calls "indigenous and peasant cultures." These "cultures" find themselves reinscribed within a pure place called "tradition": indeed, as we saw, "indigenous and peasant cultures" eventually become for García Canclini indistinguishable from "traditional cultures." They leave this pure place, the realm of tradition, and enter modernity, as they impurify, or *hybridize*. Hybridization, in spite of García Canclini's repeated dismissal of teleologies, becomes something like the evolutionary law of modernization. It is important, and worth a pause, to note that this unwanted teleology becomes clearer and clearer as García Canclini's text becomes more and more ethnological; for it is precisely the resignification of savagery from an other in space (the savage "over there"), to savagery as an other in time (the savage "stuck in time"), that both marks the transformation of comparative ethnology into the modern discipline of anthropology and reveals anthropology's stake in the confluence of race science and various models of positive transformism (Spencerian evolutionism, progressivist historicism, developmentalism, etc.).

The point here is simply to underscore the tenacity of the race–time articulation that clearly emerges even in an analysis that precisely *attacks* the tradition of constructing the popular as tradition (García Canclini 1989, 178). Many productive subtleties emerge from García Canclini's emphasis on the participation of indigenous artists in modern circuits of communication and exchange. Nevertheless, he consistently defers to a metaphorics of temporality in which the naturalized space of indigenous (and peasant) cultures implies a kind of antiquity that stands not so much within as in relation to modernity. He is quite clear on this point when he claims as the condition of Latin American hybridity a set of multiple temporalities, whose elements include, on the one hand, "indigenous traditions," and, on the other hand, "modern . . . communicational actions" (71). Although "tradition" and "modernity" are difficult (even impossibly huge) terms that capture a range of meanings, García Canclini specifically links them to a question of the old versus the new, and then again to correspondingly racialized social actors. The question of time mixing is explicitly one of racial and cultural heterogeneity.

This conflation of multicultural and multitemporal heterogeneity exhibits a notable durability in Mexicanist discourse. For example, the positivists who dominated the Mexican intellectual scene in the latter third of the nineteenth century framed the problem in similar terms, even if with distinct motivations and solutions. In an 1898 speech honoring the late Comtian positivist Gabino Barreda, Ezequiel Chávez, a leading *Científico*, credited the venerable educator with insightfully diagnosing the symptoms of the "terrible scream of anarchy" that had plagued Mexico for much of the war-torn nineteenth century.[7] The "contradictory ideas" (e.g., Jacobin liberalism and monarchist conservativism) that drove national brothers to kill each other during the Wars of Reform and Restoration were merely symptomatic of a deeper impasse: "Mexicans . . . found themselves in diverse stages of progress, each one harboring a different conception of the world." For many of the Mexican positivists—whose materialist progressivism was always tempered by a deeper commitment to old metaphysical formulas—this crisis of "progress" had less to do with anything like the uneven distribution of material resources than with spirit or soul. More precisely, it had to do with that spirit's location in historical time. Chávez reports that the Mexican nation, as Barreda saw it, suffered from a "more deeply rooted insanity" that stemmed from its disarticulate condition of multitemporal heterogeneity, an "anarchy of thought" rooted in an anarchy of time. Chávez: "[Barreda] saw that the sickness was in the Mexicans' souls, which were distant from each other, belonging to different centuries; he perceived with certainty that in Mexico existed, side by side, prehistoric souls of the Stone Age . . . souls of sixteenth-century conquistadors . . . and the chosen sons of the nineteenth century [the Comtian positivists]" (citations from Zea [1943, 187–89]). Any contemporary reader would have immediately "recognized" the Indian in the "prehistoric souls of the Stone Age." Multitemporal heterogeneity is a long-standing strategy for thinking about the racialized social incommensurability that disarticulates the nation.

The race–time (dis)articulation is expressed as a historiographical problem. This expression is at the root of a striking discontinuity in the nineteenth-century Mexican discourse on the Indian. That discontinuous move is the thorough transformation of the young Indian of the New World that appears throughout colonial writing (children of God, innocent victims of Satan, etc.) and becomes a sign of the inclusive redemption of humanity (e.g., Las Casas, Vitoria, Montaigne) into an old, decrepit Indian that must give way to a vigorous, new social and cultural vanguard. I doubt that a pivot point signaling this shift could be identified with any precision (I have not been able to locate one), as its apparent discontinuity is the cumulative result of many sociohistorical forces and intellectual trends. However, Gabino Barreda, in his momentous *Oración Cívica* (1867), recites the shift succinctly, foreseeing the vogue in Spencerian evolutionism in spite of his own philosophical predispositions.[8] The speech is of great historic importance because it served as a de facto announcement of the liberal state's later appropriation of the positivist doctrine, converting it from an elitist and slightly esoteric philosophy of Masons to the social and political theory that would come to officially guide state policy over the following four decades, and, at least according to Charles Hale, unofficially guide it through the twentieth century (1989, 8, 12–13). President Benito Juárez was in attendance, and, after hearing the address, so the story goes, he promptly promoted Barreda to the commission charged with authoring the state's plan of education.[9] The speech gives no explicit attention to the Indian as an actual or potential actor on the contemporary scene, a practice of invisibilization that would persist, with a few notable exceptions, until the eruption of *indigenista* interest that would follow the revolution. As we saw with Chávez, the positivists theoretically understood the Indian problem as a problem of spirit and consciousness, and imagined that Mexico under the principles of liberal positivism was a world where no social barriers would hinder Indians who could accomplish the requisite spiritual evolution of leaving behind their "superstitions" (i.e., capitulating to the forces of acculturation). The republic's president and beacon of liberalism, was, after all, an Indian. Herbert Spencer's increasingly accepted naturalization of social "evolution" would take care of those who did not follow the upwardly mobile example of Juárez.

Barreda's one brief allusion to the Indian, then, especially couched as it is in the context of both race *(raza)* and time, is something to be considered.

The address is a liberal-positivist tour de force, in which Barreda hits most of the key notes: fervent anticlericalism; limited popular sovereignty and equal rights over monarchy and militarism; the rights of capital and private property; and, most important, history as a struggle between worldviews in which the progressive forces will always eventually triumph in the natural evolution (or transformation) toward eternal liberty, order, and progress. The end result of this emancipation will be the end of politics itself, with the emergence of an ideal civil society where ideas are exchanged, but never imposed, and where altruism reigns over egoism. The name of the ultimate expression of the progressive forces within this struggle is "science," and those most committed to its hegemony are the new liberals who call themselves "positivists."[10] Science, with its reliance on demonstration instead of revelation, submits to its laws the inferior sciences (1867, 76) of religion, morals, and politics (79–80). But positive science exhibits a mystical capacity of its own: the capacity—indeed, the responsibility—to organize a national history.

Barreda's bête noire, true to his Comtian doctrine, is "anarchy." His historiographical thesis is that anarchy of thought produces a falsely anarchic narrative of history, which in turn exacerbates the lack of order and liberty in Mexican society. Citing Comte, he asserts the need to triumph over the "painful collisions of anarchy that today reigns in both spirit and ideas" through a "truly universal doctrine [that] reunites all understanding *[inteligencias]* in a common synthesis" (1867, 73). History must be usurped from the novelists (75), and resituated in its proper domain of science: "subject, like all sciences, to the laws that govern it and that make possible the prediction *[previsión]* of events to come, as well as the explanation of those gone by" (72). A nationalist message frames this account of the visionary powers of science. Understood as a system, with a logic and purpose, as opposed to a "series of strange and exceptional facts" (ibid.), Mexico can take back its history, "terrible but fertile," from the "bad-faith politicians" who would represent the Mexican spirit as "a sad exception in the progressive evolution of mankind" (73). Reading national (pre)history as a formula, Barreda sees only one logical conclusion on Mexico's horizon: "mental emancipation" (75–76), an emancipation "characterized by the gradual decay of old doctrines and their progressive substitution by modern ones" (76).

Here we have a guiding dichotomy of old and new, within which the Indian will be ascribed a specific place. Barreda explains the condition of this "progressive substitution" by resorting to the standard dialectical notion of the *germ*, the seed of self-destruction already lodged in the heart of a project of domination. The agent of its transmission is a metaphor of "inoculation," whereby the contagious few transmit to the traditionalist multitude the germ of the modern, which, if properly nurtured, will overwhelm the decadent effects of "old doctrines." It was precisely this kind of mental and spiritual infection that caught hold of Father Hidalgo, inspiring a priest to spark the flames of independence that, according to Barreda's interpretation, would soon be turned against clerical privilege (71–77). Although Catholic clericalism and Hispanist conservatism are Barreda's explicit targets here, his metaphor of the germ is especially effective in resolving a deeper paradox of Mexican nationness. If the Mexican nation is to represent the ultimate expression of modern man, doing away with its traditions of clericalism and Hispanism, on what necessarily transcendent narrative can that nation's legitimacy possibly rest? Barreda's solution: even if its germination is new, in that it is only now being fully nourished by the rise of positivism, the germ itself is present at the very origins of the nation. It is, in fact, the timeless element of the Mexican race itself: "In that epoque [Renaissance Europe], the principal germs *[gérmenes]* of modern renewal were in full effervescence in the Old World, and it is clear that the conquistadors, already impregnated with them, inoculated them into the new population that would result from the mixture of both races" (78).

Three important things happen at this tropic invocation of the "germ." First, science, a "weak child" (79), is shown to have a gesta-tion period concomitant with that of the nation itself. Its youth echoes Mexico's claims to a progressive future, but also stretches back, time-lessly, to an Old World that predates the historical arrival of "Mexico." Second, Mexico's claim to racial singularity, *mestizaje*, is appropriated as the vehicle or medium for this development. The mestizo becomes the dynamic element in society, an extremely important quality for the posi-tivists, who framed their struggle with the church as a question of dy-namism (begetting progression) versus stasis (begetting retrogression). This mestizo dynamism would be echoed by Mexico's finest positivist thinkers, in the work of Vicente Riva Palacio, Justo Sierra, and Andrés Molina Enríquez.[11] Third, the indigenous inhabitant of the New World, the Indian, is suddenly no longer new, but old, placed alongside retro-grade forces such as the church and the landowning aristocracy (see Hale 1989, 4). This is the ambivalent condition of the Indian as con-structed in nineteenth-century Mexican discourse: the Indian as neces-sary participant in and erasure from the national project; an included exclusion that forms the very logic of *mestizaje*. The Indian participates in the building of a new race and a new spirit, yet is excluded from the modern on account of cultural antiquity: stuck, in the various positivist models, alternatively in a "theological," "mystical," or "animistic" stage of development. This foundational erasure is exemplified in Barreda's address, which nowhere mentions actual Indians at all, much less as part of the national project. Their participation is an allusion, a reference, a receptacle, the sublated element of that primordial dialectic, the synthe-sis produced through the "mixture of both races."

This theory of the Indian's oldness will prove tenacious, and is still in full force at the outset of postrevolutionary *indigenismo*. Gamio's early studies on the indigenous communities of the Valley of Teotihuacán, for example, issue a dire report on not simply the material poverty, but the general *decadence* of the Indian.[12] And reciting the oldness or an-tiquity of the Indian is still a powerful trope, showing up in the contem-porary and transnational Mexicanist canon in the work of writers from Paz to Anzaldúa.[13] But the figure of the decadent, or backward, Indian also responds to an influential current in greater Western philosophy: the general schematization of cultural difference that fixes the "races" at particular coordinates of geographical location and unilinear history. Versions of the teleological historicism that would emerge from this schema were strong in divergent thinkers such as Comte, Spencer, and Savigny who had a profound influence on Mexican positivism. But it is a logic of progressive transformism that first hits its stride during the

Enlightenment, a philosophical moment underwritten by more than two centuries of colonial expansion. If Kant worked to reify a European binary that distinguished, within Europe, the "modern" North from the "traditional" South (Mignolo 2000b, 732), as well as an Occident versus an Orient, then it is Hegel that would give this geotemporalized racism its most elaborate form on a global scale.

In both his *Philosophy of Mind* (1830) and his *Philosophy of History* (1837 [first posthumous edition]), Hegel clearly articulates the New World tension between decadence and vigor that the project of Mexican nationness will strive to resolve. Although he occasionally characterizes the Indians as "just like small children" (1837, 45), the far greater emphasis is on decadence and inviability: "with regard to the original inhabitants of America, we have to remark that they are a vanishing feeble race . . . When brought into contact with brandy and guns, these savages become extinct" (ibid.). Note the naturalization of the colonial project: not "are extinguished," but "become extinct." Yet this extinction is also a rebirth: "The indigenous races of this continent are dying out; the Old World is refashioning itself in the New" (41). America, in fact, is pure *future*, holding no interest whatsoever for a philosophy of History: "What *has* taken place in the New World up to the present time is only an echo of the Old World—the expression of a foreign Life; and as a Land of the Future, it has no interest for us here, for, as regards *History*, our concern must be with that which has been and that which is" (1837, 87). America, for Hegel, *had not yet been*.[14] The colonialist logic of modernity is clear: America, marching forward, does so at the expense of the airy, ahistorical (or prehistorical), native Americans. Although for Hegel the Indian is outside of History altogether, his nod to an *American* future—indeed, America as the place where "the burden of the World's History shall reveal itself" (ibid., 86)—simultaneously, and, I think, unintentionally, reinscribes the Indian as modernity's very condition of possibility; for it is the accumulation of indigenous land and blood that propels the Old World into *its* future. America moves forward in time, making History, at once leaning upon and effacing the Indian.

The problem with this model for the nineteenth-century Mexican intelligentsia—a problem that also displays the fantastic nature of colonial history that was accessible to Hegel[15]—was that the Indian had not met the philosopher's diagnosis of extinction, or even weakness. Although the various genocides carried out against indigenous peoples at several points in the history of the Americas had left their population greatly reduced, indigenous communities, especially in Mesoamerica, still composed a substantial part of the population, including a majority in several regions. Not only were their numbers vast, but their threat to the integrity of the Mexican state was very real. This threat was exercised with some frequency during the nineteenth century: in *guerras de castas*, implacable pockets of autonomy (in Oaxaca, Yucatán, and Sonora), and even in the 1810 outbreak of the War of Independence itself, whose main protagonist was not the emergent bourgeoisie—mostly cowering behind locked doors—but rather the largely Indian, peasant masses.[16]

The ascendant liberals, and later the positivists, attempted to meet this challenge to both national hegemony (horizontal identification) and state sovereignty (vertical authority). Their diagnostic efforts consistently reduced it to a problem of time, that is, multiple historicities or multitemporal heterogeneity. Thus José María Luis Mora, the most important theorist of early Mexican liberalism and a contemporary of Hegel, argued against the "revolution of men," which only brought about reaction and misery, and in favor of what he called a "revolution of time" (Mora 1830, 344–48). This revolution was a function of the state: "The ability of those that guide the State consists principally in knowing the necessities born of the degree of civilization to which men have arrived" (347). If the anthropological mandate on history is to understand the past as a foreign country, then for the Mexican urban intelligentsia, the past was the immediate countryside. The necessary task that Mora perceived was to get everybody on the same page, to the same "degree of civilization," the same moment in universal history. Again, in the work of Mora, as in the work of Barreda, the Indian is notable as an absence: Mora is specifically writing against clerics, conservatives, and caudillos, all of whom he understands as obstacles to progress. And yet it is the Indian that presents the greatest challenge to this revolution of time, as Mora suggests years later on a diplomatic mission to London, where he wrote of "the need not only to bring the Indian uprisings [*las sublevaciones de castas*] to a halt, but to make them impossible in the future" (1849, 277).

Just as their diagnosis of the problem of national hegemony was to some extent informed by their participation in the Eurocentric, world-philosophical subculture, so would the Mexican intelligentsia also find a solution there. That solution, as we saw with Barreda, was premised on the mixing of the races, or *mestizaje*. Its formulation, however, was not a mere repetition of European models. It was a repetition with a difference. Mexican *mestizaje*, when theorized as a potential route to national consolidation and as a positive mark of national identity, was typically opposed to the highly influential notion of a degenerate hybridity as theorized by famous proponents of racial inequality such as Gobineau, Le Bon, Spencer, Agassiz, and Gumplowicz. But rather than draw on those largely discredited voices, a more provocative argument would be to propose that the enthusiasm for race mixing corrected a racialized foundation of the Enlightenment itself. It did so by taking it at its word.

In his *Anthropology from a Pragmatic Point of View* (1797), Immanuel Kant briefly addresses the question of "the character of the races." The ensuing discussion, however, is limited to what Kant identifies as a contradictory law of nature that governs racial reproduction. He argues that "In fusing different races, nature aims at *assimilation*" (1797, 182). Because such mixture "gradually extinguishes [the races'] characters," it "is not beneficial to the human race" (ibid.). At the same time, however, "proximity of kinship, as is well known, results in infertility" (ibid.). How to escape this impasse and avoid both the assimilative dangers of hybridity and the sterilizing dangers of inbreeding?[17] Intraracially, Kant proposes, nature effects a miraculous reversal, and makes "the exact opposite [of assimilation] its law: that is, nature's law regarding a people of the same race (for example, the white race) is not to let their characters constantly and progressively approach one another in likeness . . . but instead to diversify to infinity the members of the same stock and even of the same clan" (ibid.).

The Mexican intelligentsia would finish the dialectic.[18] It was a strategic move, because assimilation was precisely what they sought. Given the alleged backwardness (yet self-evident tenacity) of the Indian, exogamic assimilation into Europe, via *mestizaje*, could be a route to historical, and hence, national—and, for the Comtian positivists, mental, political, and spiritual—emancipation. It was not an antiracist gesture. Rather, it was a correction of Eurocentric racism as read from within a specific set of historical conditions, that is, from *within* a legacy of colonialism and peripherality. Key theorists of nineteenth-century European race science—Gobineau, Gumplowicz—would reproduce a version of Kant's paradox, proposing that even the most homogeneous national races are in reality hybridized heterogeneities: for them, the gravest danger to national integrity—race mixing—was also its condition of possibility (Young 1995).[19] Mexican *mestizaje*, then, could be understood as a *neces-*

sary fusion whose assimilating effects held the key to producing a new race, that is, as with the goals of both Barreda and Gamio, a new *national* race. Once forged, Kant's law of intraracial differentiation could be invoked. By seizing the dialectical conflation of opposites in the racist contradiction, where hybridity is both condition and limit, they radicalize it. This was precisely the Mexican liberal-positivist reframing of the mestizo: the dynamic element of society, representing a radical move forward in a brand-new world.

The thinker who would bring this logic to its fullest and most systematic expression was the late positivist and *Científico* Andrés Molina Enríquez. Molina Enríquez, a perceptive and even visionary agronomist, sociologist, and political analyst, wrote creatively and methodically on a host of issues, from land redistribution to water rights. He consistently analyzed these themes through the lens of race, or, more precisely, "racial struggle."[20] He understood as the greatest challenge to Mexican national consolidation its lack of racial homogeneity. At this point in the discussion, it is unsurprising to find that he allegorizes racial heterogeneity as a problem of mixed times. Nor is it surprising that he proposes a kind of hybridity, *mestizaje*, as the solution to that problem. But going beyond the metaphorical, Molina Enríquez harnesses the logic of *colonización*—or state-guided *mestizaje* (see chapter 6 in this volume)—and makes a rigorous case for a forced *mestizaje*, proposing, in explicit terms, that intercultural and interracial mixing become a eugenic project of state.[21] A systematically encouraged *mestizaje*, he proposes, is the best way to effectively mediate between the vastly different interests and inequalities that emerge from Mexico's ethnocultural diversity. The result would be to reshape a fractured Mexico into the form of an "ethnographic nationality." A slightly misleading term, especially post-Boas, "ethnographic nationality" does not infer a plurality of ethnicities or nationalities that simply need to be cataloged, or ethnologized, under the rubric of a single state. Rather, it denotes a necessary formal homology between nation and race: the creation of a fictive ethnicity. Basave Benítez explains that, for Molina Enríquez, "ethnographic nationality" signals the "impossibility of a multiracial nation . . . [and] is the prelude to his later thesis in favor of *mestizaje*" (1992, 52–53).

The figure who Molina Enríquez identifies to carry out that project, indeed, the very embodiment of the radical potential of *mestizaje*, is none other than Mexico's thirty-year dictator, the *mestizo* Porfirio Díaz. Díaz represents the best hope for the resolution of the social tensions diagnosed in Molina Enríquez's *Los grandes problemas nacionales* (1909), which, despite being published on the eve of the Porfiriato's fall, remained influential after the revolution, and is widely considered the sharpest piece of social commentary of the decade (see Brading 1984). At the end of the fifth chapter, "El secreto de la paz porfiriana," Molina Enríquez concludes that Díaz "is a unique man who, in a single nation, has had to govern and has governed wisely, many distinct peoples *[pueblos]* who have lived in different periods of evolution, from the prehistoric to the modern" (1909, 147). The secret to the "paz porfiriana" is Díaz's ability to mediate between the subjects of these "different periods of evolution," reconciling through his talents of *amificación* Mexico's many political and ideological factions, all of which correspond, in Molina Enríquez's schema, to racial designations.[22] Díaz, in short, represents the ascent of "the mestizo" to sovereign power, skillfully giving benefits, offering relief, issuing pardons, and, when necessary, administering punishment. He is the ultimate expression of what Molina Enríquez calls the "*integral* period" of state power and national consolidation (134), representing the conflation of *mestizaje* and nation: faced with the demands of the dynamic and upwardly mobile mestizo middle class, "El Señor Díaz, who saw in them *himself, his race, the nation, the future*, took as his task a pledge to [politically and economically] satisfy them" (138; my emphasis). A year before the whole thing would fall apart, Molina Enríquez saw in *Porfirismo* the necessarily strong state that could realize the positivists' dream, by reason or by force, of articulating Mexico's racial-temporal disjunctures. *Mestizaje* would mediate these processes of articulation, eventually leading to—as they already were under the mediation, integration, and *amificación* of Díaz—a homogeneous nation, a united nation, a historical nation, a mestizo nation. It is under Díaz, then, that *mestizaje* achieves its apotheosis, and becomes the norm of both a hegemonic nationalization of identity and a sovereign institutionalization of state.

6. They Were Not a
Barbarous Tribe

Diez y seis barbaritas, la mayor de edad
de diez años, fueron capturadas por el
valiente general Bernardo Reyes y tuvo a bien
repartirlas entre varias familias para que las
civilicen y eduquen. Trabajo les costará a
esas familias tener á raya á esas niñitas.
—La Libertad, *June 23, 1882*

We have seen that the trajectory of *mestizaje* in nineteenth-century
Mexico speaks less to effective racial reconciliation than to a discourse of nation-state consolidation. The officialist discourse of *mestizaje* crystallized around questions of control and containment, was capable of rhetorically articulating the disjunctures of race, time, and nation, and worked to realize national homogeneity and popular deference to the state. Understood as such, a critique of *mestizaje* need not rest on a reactionary return to something like "purity," but can instead be proposed as an intervention against a hegemonic project, an interrogation of that project's basic concepts. At the same time, the very fact of *mestizaje*'s status as a discursive formation, inextricably linked to multifarious constellations of discursive series—race, nation, time, gender, social class, and so on—makes it a particularly tricky object of critique. Again, I will draw on the influential work of Alan Knight (1990) as an example.

In his widely cited discussion of racism in Mexico (mentioned in chapter 4), Knight clearly and cogently frames *mestizaje* within the discursive parameters of nation-state formation. He also finds "contradictions" there, in that *mestizaje* at once sacralizes and denigrates its indigenous participants. These contradictions, he seems to suggest, could be overcome, or at least mitigated, by paying greater semantic attention to the basic concepts through which social justice is formulated. He notes that "the process of *mestizaje*, sometimes seen as basically racial, is in fact social" (1990, 73); he concludes that the point of differentiation between "mestizo" and "Indian" is "socially, not racially, determined" (74), and bemoans the way that postrevolutionary "political elites habitually resorted to racist shorthand by way of social explanation well into the twentieth century" (88). Ultimately, he seems to suggest that the practice of racism is reducible to the persistence of the concept named "race": "Logically, these theorists [the postrevolutionary *indigenistas*] could have dropped the use of 'race' altogether or at least they could have made clear that for them 'race' denoted a social category. Instead, they remained prisoners of the preceding [liberal-positivist] racist discourse . . . [and] it can be suggested that the perpetuation of this discourse probably helped maintain both the notion of 'race' and, to some degree, the practice of racism" (87). If the problem with racism is its dependence on race, he suggests, then ending—or at least weakening—racism might be achieved by erasing race.[1] On the one hand, Knight is correct in perceptively identifying the ways in which both *mestizaje* and race operate as social relations; and his de-essentialization of biological race is standard critical practice today. But, on the other hand, he underpursues his own inscription of race-as-social-relation within the realm of discourse. His prescription to separate the social from the racial thereby misses the excessively flexible and supplementary qualities of the discursive formation itself, whereby race and social class (like the race-time-nation articulation) are functions of each other that do not need to *name* each other, out loud, in order to work in concert. Judith Friedlander's (1975) indigenous interlocutors who told her that being Indian means being poor, or the popular expression "money whitens," are only two examples of how race and class are *already* articulated in Mexico. It is difficult to imagine how their discursive conflation and/or disentanglement would prevent material discrimination (i.e., racism) against the social-racial category of "the Indian," even if not named as such.

This supplementarity of race and social class in Mexican discourse and society is brilliantly expressed by the nineteenth century's great liberal writer Ignacio Altamirano. His classic novels *Clemencia* (1869) and *El Zarco* (1888; published posthumously in 1901) can be read as allegories of national race relations (Sommer 1991). The protagonist of *Clemencia*, constructed as a patriotic nationalist and "moreno" (1869, 22), is rejected by both of his objects of affection, two white—one Germanic, one Latin—daughters of the liberal bourgeoisie. Both of them in turn fall for the eventual national traitor, identified as Eurocentric, dandy, aristocratic, and white (20). The protagonist exhibits his loyalty and mettle by sacrificing his life for his would-be lover's happiness; she realizes her error too late, as the cunning (French) nature of her love object is exposed. Reading the protagonist as a metaphor for the upwardly mobile Indian, the social commentary is clear: the realization of the *national* benefits of *mestizaje*, as *racial* reconciliation through race mixing, is truncated by *social* conventions of aesthetic taste.[2]

Not once in *Clemencia* does the word *raza* enter into play, and never is the protagonist identified as *indio*. Altamirano's text shows that there is no need: social stasis and racial discrimination are functions of each other. But the critical force of the narrative still operates within the logic of *mestizaje*, even as it displays its failure. The case that Altamirano presents against the Mexican, criollo bourgeoisie is that it is abandoning the national project by not committing itself—owing to the persistence of racist stereotypes of aesthetic beauty (the protagonist's darkness is conflated with his ugliness [e.g., 22])—to *mestizaje* thoroughly enough. The fact that this critique—in the case of *Clemencia*—is leveled during a time when both the president (Juárez) and a leading statesman and writer (Altamirano himself) are "biologically Indian" seems to underscore Altamirano's point. Within the symbolic economy of *mestizaje*, the ambivalence toward the Indian, even an unnamed Indian, still carries a high value in the investment made toward national consolidation. When, in the Porfirian-era *El Zarco* (1901), Altamirano finally does name his Indian, it is with ample conditions attached: Nicolás "was a swarthy young man of well-marked indigenous type, *but* with a tall and slender body, herculean in form, well proportioned, and his intelligent and benevolent physiognomy, of course, worked in his favor . . . It was known that he was an Indian, *but* not an abject and servile Indian, but rather an educated man, embellished by work, and conscious of his force and valor" (1901, 267–68; my emphasis). *Mestizaje*, in Altamirano's novels (where working-class, Indian-looking protagonists are rejected by white, bourgeois women), proposes to eliminate social and racial tensions by *subsuming both* within the project of nation.

A striking example of *mestizaje*'s continued discursive force can be found in a more contemporary document of nation building: Enrique Krauze's ambitious history of modern Mexico, *Mexico: Biography of Power* (1997). This force is notably exerted in a chapter titled "The Triumph of the Mestizo," particularly at the point where Krauze makes an interesting attempt at formulating a structural logic to explain the proliferation of rural uprisings in Mexico. Similar unrest periodically erupts today, but it was regular during the nineteenth century, when the state was beset by scores of such actions.[3] Krauze's explanation is interesting for the rhetorical turns through which it explicitly links hybridity, race, national culture, violence, and representation. These turns emerge as he identifies two types of rebellions.

The first type he calls "social." Short in duration, these actions are linked to specific political grievances, are reconciled through diplomatic solutions, and historically (stretching back to the colonial period) represent the majority of rural uprisings. More significantly, his notion of "social" seems to emerge negatively as the *absence* of a racial or ethnic basis for the tensions: they are not articulated around "ethnicity," but rather around "poverty" (222). Somewhat paradoxically, however, Krauze falls back on the language of ethnocultural typification in order to distinguish these nonethnic rebellions. This happens at the intersecting rhetorics of race and space; that is, their regional contexts—he cites Oaxaca, the eastern sierras, and the central plateau—all show an important similarity: "They had been the scene of intense cultural and ethnic *mestizaje*. And the process of [religious] conversion had been carried out with particular vigor and success" (221). In contrast, a second type of uprising—long, nasty, brutish—also traversed the nineteenth century, again exhibiting a common regional quality. This rare and exceptional region of intransigent rebellion (222) "had two characteristics that ominously distinguished it from the rest of the country. It had only been superficially converted to Christianity; and *mestizaje* was almost nonexistent" (221). Problem spots, then, are pure spots. And they are pure on two counts: they are Indian, and they are fanatic, cauldrons of "the explosive mix of religious passion and ethnic grievance" (222).

Now, let us push Krauze's argument one step forward and demonstrate that it rests on an empirical impossibility. As some of Krauze's own subsequent descriptions suggest, the territories to which he alludes as regions of exception—Chiapas, Yucatán, the northern hinterlands of Sonora—are (and were during the nineteenth century) nothing if not "mixed."[4] More important than the empirical viability of Krauze's model, however, are the symptomatic dimensions of his argument, that is, the way that it illustrates a meticulous recitation of the discursive operations of *mestizaje* within the realm of state ideology. For Krauze's argument to stick, it would need to find support in empirically measurable levels of cultural purity and mixedness. At what point does a region or community become "more mixed" than another? As the long-standing Mexican debate over "when" an Indian becomes a mestizo indicates, many have foundered on the reefs of this question, perhaps none more spectacularly than Manuel Gamio and his attempt to measure the indigenousness of communities through his plan of a "culturally representative census" (1942, 189).[5] Taken together, the critique of the scientific utility and validity of "race" (from Herder to the Human Genome Project) and the critique of the racialization of culture (Hall 1996a; Gilroy 1992; Balibar and Wallerstein 1988, 17–28) have long shown that claims of cultural purity and mixture hold little empirical basis. In short, questions of ethnocultural purity and mixture are not scientific ones to be resolved through empirical objectivity, but rather political propositions that depend on rhetoric and representation (Knight 1990, 74).

Krauze's challenge, then, is a rhetorical one: not simply to identify communities that are "too pure," but to build a convincing case that can make those problematic regions pure: pure Indian, pure fanatic, pure barbarian. Given the rich store of discursive resources that he is tapping into, this is an easy case to make, and one to which he devotes minimal attention; for those resources are maintained precisely by the power move at the heart of *mestizaje*—its dialectical conflation of opposites, its productive contradiction in the service of the nation-state. And it is here that we discover that the purity of non-*mestizaje* is in fact a kind of impurity, a deviation, a heresy; that is, a rejection of Mexican state sovereignty, which is at the same time the same thing as rejecting the *pure mestizaje* that ideologically underwrites projects of hegemonic, national identity formation.[6]

It is not a simple matter of convenience to implicate the basic logic of *mestizaje* in projects of state. As we can see from chapter 5, Krauze's troping of *mestizaje*, in fact, operates within a long discursive trajectory of national consolidation whose modern theorization in Mexico begins not with the postrevolutionary intelligentsia, but with the liberals, positivists, and *Científicos* that dominate the late-nineteenth-century projects of state formation.[7] If, in Molina Enríquez's (and Krauze's) formulation, Díaz represented the mestizo state incarnate—which, of course, is a racialized metaphor for the confluence of Amerindian and European cultures—what function did the Indian half of this social-political contract serve? What was the space of the Indian within the Porfiriato? In short, it was an ancient space, a traditional space, a foundational space, even a sacred space; all of this is another way of saying that it was a space of erasure, abstractly included, concretely excluded. It is not accidental that the necessary confluence of *mestizaje* and *indigenismo* is first deployed systematically in the name of nation-state consolidation under Díaz.[8] It was also the Porfiriato that significantly raised the bar in meeting indigenous resistance with finalizing, modern military "solutions."[9] I mention this quick sketch of the Porfirian Indian policy not only to contextualize Heriberto Frías's *Tomochic* (1906)—the novel to which we are about to turn—but also to draw out an essential link between practices of theorizing hybridity and of colonial discourse: the profound ambivalence that governs their common representation of the colonized other. Despite the fact that Díaz was concerned with "nation," the language of "colonialism" here is not casual, but rather residual: indeed, the association between "development" and "colonization" makes the coloniality of power explicit even in the very title of one of the primary organs of Porfirian state policy, known as the ministry of "fomento, colonización, industria y comercio" (development, colonization, industry, and commerce).[10]

Ultimately, the Porfirian Indian policy reveals that the split that Étienne Balibar identifies between a nationalism "which derives from love (even an excessive love) and the one which derives from hate" (Balibar and Wallerstein 1988, 47) is really the constitutive ambivalence of a single, expansive nationalism. It is a nationalism enabled by a gesture that appropriates while vanquishing, sacralizes while destroying: simultaneously a rescue and an erasure.

It is within the context of this intensification of the inclusive exclusion of competing modernities that Heriberto Frías launches one of the sharpest critiques of the Porfiriato during Díaz's reign, set forth in his serial originally called *¡Tomóchic! Episodios de campaña*. Remembered today simply as *Tomochic*, it novelizes an actual federal crackdown against a popular rebellion in the northern state of Chihuahua.[11] It provides an excellent case study for the increasingly biopolitical stakes of the Porfirian state, and its appropriation of the transforming discourses of *mestizaje*, the Indian, and nation through which the formation of citizens and patriots cedes to, or becomes entangled with, the decision over life itself.[12]

As a narrative in which the ideological and the critical consistently hold sway over the aesthetic, *Tomochic* lends itself to the kind of allegorical reading proposed by Doris Sommer in her study of the nineteenth-century Latin American novel, *Foundational Fictions* (1991). But there is an important difference. The basic structure of the national romances that Sommer has called "foundational fictions" is premised on forgetting: the desire for national bourgeois hegemony is allegorized through reconciliatory (and usually consummated) love stories, whereby racial and social-class tensions are forgotten in favor of the national formation embodied by the protagonists (1991, 6, 19). Frías produces a different kind of foundational narrative, one that emphasizes national disarticulation over reconciliation, and one that is ultimately more faithful to Ernest Renan's maxim: Frías will *ask us to remember* the national crime that has been forgotten, and then at once *assert its necessity* for the process of nation building.[13]

This kind of *foundational disarticulation*, then, allegorizes the nation as profoundly fractured. These narratives are important because they emphasize the basic structure of the coloniality of power, that is, the hidden continuity between colonialism and national consolidation. The healing (or forgetting) agent of that fracture will not be the seduction of romance, but rather the brute force of armed intervention. The project of national consolidation is thus represented as a reconciliation that can only come as a result of the material effacement of challengers to state sovereignty. While the foundational fiction responds to the ideal by representing a nation made whole through race–class reconciliation (ibid., 14), the foundational disarticulation is governed by the real, representing the grim vision of a nation made whole through state-sponsored terror. In the case of the Mexico of Frías's *Tomochic*, it is the tragedy of Ignacio Altamirano's *Clemencia*—a frustrated *mestizaje*—on a massive scale. The basic polemic that arises from Frías's novel is that the foundational moment of the Porfirian state is not the realization, but rather the utter failure—even the abandonment—of an idealized *mestizaje*. This position is insightful, and is what I think endows the novel with the kind of power that Mariano Azuela notes when he calls *Tomochic* (along with Inclán's bandit classic, *Astucia*) one of only two "authentically national" Mexican novels (1947, 659). Beyond the novel itself, a common misreading of its treatment of the discourses of *mestizaje* and the Indian makes it exemplary in a double sense: as a narrative memory of the violence of national consolidation, and as a testament to the referential forgetting established by the ideological triumph of that same process of consolidation.

Tomochic is the account of a state-sponsored massacre. Told in gruesome, naturalist tones, it follows the federal soldier Miguel Mercado as he participates in the government campaign against the village of Tomochic. In a flurry of popular religious enthusiasm that coalesces around a set of federal abuses, Tomochic has taken up arms and declared itself sovereign, responsible only to God.[14] Most of the story focuses on the military campaign against the well-fortified town, and is an extended commentary on the technical and moral bankruptcy of the Porfirian projects of state expansion, modernization, and centralization.

A love story also runs through the novel. Although love interests are typically discarded as irrelevant, distracting, and unconvincing in the commentary on *Tomochic*, Sommer's exposition on foundational fictions—that is, narratives that she proposes as foundational to the bourgeois project of national hegemony—asks us to pay closer attention to them.[15] And indeed, in *Tomochic*, the love story is one of the places where the critique of Díaz becomes frankly ad hominem, and the foundational disarticulation most symbolically realized. Miguel and Julia—a bewitching native of Tomochic—find their mutual affections stymied by Mexico's fragmentation. Julia's repeated declaration "¡Soy de Tomochic!" (I am from Tomochic!) suggests the irreparable disarticulation between the local rebellion and the national project of consolidation in which Miguel participates. The disjuncture is exacerbated by an allusion to Díaz's double, in the figure of Julia's uncle Bernardo, her senior by decades, and an "ogre" who keeps his niece in incestuous domestic bondage (1906, 19–22, 28). The allegorical affinity is clear, especially when we remember that Díaz was not only married to a woman thirty-three years younger than himself (Carmen Romero Rubio, daughter of a former political enemy) but was also previously married to his niece (Delfina).[16] What should be an interregional reconciliation and allegory of national consolidation is instead forcibly sundered, as the civilized capital (Miguel) ends up participating in the murder of the barbarous region (Julia) owing to the greed and perversion of a tyrant (Bernardo), who lords over and manipulates Julia the way that Díaz tightens his "iron grip" around the nation's peripheries (e.g., 1906, 13–16, 143).[17]

As the narrative of a campaign officially framed as civilization's modernist advance against the backwardness of barbarism, Frías's critique hinges on its ability to convincingly reverse the referential targets of those binary signifiers, and, in effect, display the state's project as fundamentally barbaric. This is the critical and thematic thread that ties the narrative together, with Miguel concluding, over and over, that the reality of war, of *this* war, has nothing of the "solemn poetry of war . . . grand, noble, heroic, epic!" (79; see also 143). It is neither a "shadow, nor even a parody," of the epic classics. Even the recent internecine Mexican civil skirmishes, with serious ideological stakes in the balance—the War of Reform that pitted liberals against conservatives—were noble in comparison: Miguel "recognized the tragic barbarism of the catastrophe! The horror of the killing had been as atrocious as defeat . . . !" (ibid.). The entire campaign is shown to be fundamentally misguided, sacrificing young working-class men, conscripts, and petty officers poorly trained by the national academy at Chapultepec to the guns of the Tomoche veterans, who have grown up fighting off bandits and rivals, and whose repeating Winchesters are said to never miss their target (2). Indeed, the federal tactics are displayed as so crude and outdated that their technologically advanced heavy artillery (e.g., "a modern canon" [147]) is effectively neutralized, even mocked, as they have leveled minimal material damage, and no psychological effect whatsoever (138). It is the savage Tomoches, in fact, who display "a marvelous intuition for the modern art of war" (70). They deliver the federal army several stinging defeats, forcing the state to rely on sheer overwhelming force. By the end, the *federales* outnumber the Tomoches ten to one (147). Cowardly federal officers who avoid the fray of battle are juxtaposed against the heroic, if "fanatic," Cruz Chávez, leader of the Tomoches who never hesitates to put himself in harm's way. And even the Tomoches' religious hyperbole is mitigated by the soldiers' decidedly more hollow, if no less fanatical, reverence toward the state. While the Tomoches surge into battle with pledges to "el Gran Poder de Dios" (the great power of God), "María Santísima," "the Santísima Trinidad," and promise death to the sons of "Lucifer," the soldiers less convincingly respond with "¡vivas!" to the "Supreme Government," to "the Mexican Republic," to "the Ninth Battalion," to "General Díaz" (e.g., 56–59), and, ultimately, to the "united Nation" (114).

Drawing an even more damning distinction, we learn that it is the supposedly professional, federal army that consistently violates the normative rules of just war handed down from biblical law and secular scholarly tradition. The Tomoches, meanwhile, exhibit a model respect for the conventional injunctions that govern a just war: restrictions against the abuse of prisoners, the killing of noncombatants, the harming of women and children, and the excessive destruction of other forms of property. On the one hand, the federal soldiers, stymied in their attacks, take up positions in the surrounding hills and fire on any living thing in the town that dares move, busy themselves with reducing the church to rubble, and steal the cattle and other food supply of the Tomoches (85–86). On the other hand, the Tomoches never harm the *soldaderas* who bring food and water to the federal troops: "not once did their marvelous sharpshooters fire on the *soldaderas* . . . The honorable sons of the sierra would not kill women!" (86).

In marked contrast, the federal army, incompetent in battle, defers to a double strategy: first, a policy of scorched earth, burning the church where "the better part of the women of Tomochic had sought refuge," and from whose spire an old woman hurls herself to avoid the flames (115); later, a long siege that yields a final victory over half-dead and starving noncombatants (117–22). Whereas the Tomoches exhibit model treatment of their prisoners (70, 91), returning them, including officers, unharmed, any captured Tomoches are summarily executed by federal firing squad (72, 132, 146–47). In one gripping scene, a group of soldiers heroically pursue a brave Tomoche through daunting terrain, finally bring him down, and cautiously approach the cadaver to find a dead thirteen-year-old boy with a "tranquil expression . . . on his dark, beardless face" that "seems to laugh" at the suddenly less enthusiastic soldiers (97). And, in a devastating parody of militarism, an ironic victory reveille is repeatedly trumpeted throughout the narrative, a kind of leitmotif of unjust war: "And its bellicose, joyful notes suddenly became gloomy in the midst of that field of sadness, of ashes, and of ruin, in that putrid valley of smoking tombs and unburied corpses" (129).

This game of reversals that organizes the critical logic of *Tomochic* rests on a discourse of race, revealing the stakes of the narrative's biopolitical context. It shows the barbarism of a white state that sends its darker young men to die in battles not of national defense, but of conquest. The Tomoches perceive the racialized element of the project, and incorporate it explicitly into their strategy of resistance: "[Cruz Chávez] understood the transcendental importance of eliminating the officers, and he taught his men to recognize them by their white faces and their commanding attitudes" (70).[18]

In short, this vilification of the state, whose military "demolishes an indigenous village" (Monsiváis 2000, 967), is then juxtaposed with a countervailing ennoblement of "those admirable Indians defend[ing] . . . their religion and their lands" (Azuela 1947, 665), of the "Yaqui Indians" assaulted by the Porfiriato (Magaña Esquível 1964, 53), of "the Indians of Tomochic . . . [part of] the Yaqui nation whose tribes refus[ed] to be governed by the central authority and to participate in the process of modernization" (Benítez-Rojo 1996, 479). However, although there certainly is a racialized logic that propels the critical force of *Tomochic*, reading it as a defense of the Indian raises a problem. That problem is the fact that Frías's Tomoches of *Tomochic* are not Indians: "What did they want, concretely, those serranos . . . ? They knew nothing of the *Patria*, ·nor its governors, nor Religion, nor its priests. And the strangest aspect of all was that they were not a barbarous tribe. They were not Indians, but Creoles *[criollos]*. Spanish blood, Arab blood, blood of cruel fanaticism and noble bravery, coursed through that marvelous Tarahumara and Andalusian race . . . Tomochic gave the Mexican Republic the rare spectacle of a village that had gone crazy" (1906, 26).

What can we make of this apparent confusion, where Frías clearly says "not Indian, but mestizo," and yet is widely understood—by readers no less accomplished and perceptive than Monsiváis, Azuela, Magaña Esquível, and Benítez-Rojo—as saying precisely the opposite?[19] I maintain that it speaks loudly to the ideological status of articulating *mestizaje* with Mexican state formation and national consolidation, and, moreover, to the biopolitical function of the Indian in Mexican discourse and society.

Frías's critique, as anti-Porfirian propaganda, is enabled by a racialized discourse, but it is more complex than a simple inversion of the value codes ascribed to a civilized state and a barbaric tribe of Indians. We have just seen how Frías indulges in the classic rhetorical move of reframing his opponent—here, the Porfirian state—as the "real barbarian." But, at the same time, the recodification of the rebels of Tomochic will have greater discursive impact if it can be more nuanced than a simple sublimation, or even civilization, of the noble Indian. Consider the real fears of the metropolitan and largely bourgeois reading public of Porfirian Mexico, the target audience of *Tomochic*, that is, their fears of widespread indigenous revolt.[20] This reading public would have no reason to be enthusiastic about local uprisings that, if contagious, could present a real threat to their material interests.[21] In fact, the Porfirian media machine openly touted its incursions into outlying areas such as Sonora, Chihuahua, Chiapas, and Yucatán as precisely a war against intransigent Indians who insist on frustrating the civilization and modernization of Mexico.[22] A romantic Indian, then, would simply repeat the Porfirian, *indigenista* rhetoric, at best sparking an academic debate over the "good" or "bad" character of the old Indian that, either way, hinders the emergence of a modern Mexico. A Romantic Indian, while perhaps yielding a nostalgic pathos, would likely incite little outrage against the Porfiriato. Hence a sharper critique of the Porfiriato, one that can strike a rhetorical blow, will need to go beyond a romanticization of the Indian. This is precisely the route that Frías takes, as *Tomochic* works not to bring the Indian into the national fold, but rather to *de-Indianize* Tomochic. In other words, Frías's strategy is to show that the Porfirian mission is launched not against *Indians*, as it purports, but rather against *mestizos*. The assault on Tomochic, then, must be represented as an assault on an honorable mestizo community, indeed, against Mexico itself. The action against Tomochic must be a kind of anti-*mestizaje*, deferring to hate over love, destruction over reconciliation. If, as Balibar argues, the nation's articulation to the "racial community has a tendency to represent itself as one big family" (Balibar and Wallerstein 1988, 100), then the racialized mark of that national family identity in late-nineteenth-century Mexico is the mark of *mestizaje*.[23] The crime that Frías must ascribe to the Porfiriato is not the killing of an internal national other, but rather the massacre of a patriotic brother: Díaz's war must be exposed as a perverse excess, a kind of cannibalism, waged against "heroic Mexicans, good and loyal" (104).[24]

Historical context shows that these were in fact the actual terms in play. In a study of the historical (as opposed to literary) uprising and massacre at Tomochic, Paul Vanderwood draws on newspaper editorials and government documents to show the Porfirian state's concerted effort dedicated to Indianizing Tomochic (1998, 135–40, 250–51).[25] Vanderwood's work shows that Frías had objective accuracy on his side: Tomochic was in fact a largely mestizo, though multiethnic, community (51–53, 135). Contrary to the readings of Monsiváis, Azuela, Magaña Esquível, and Benítez-Rojo, the critical edge of *Tomochic* is not a sublimation of the "Indians of Tomochic." Rather, Frías's critique operates within the discursive parameters of *mestizaje*. In other words, it operates within the same system of representation on which the ideological triumph of the Porfirian state rests. With *mestizaje* thus serving as the discursive formation within which the sayable can be said, the common biopolitical premises, where Porfirian Mexico and Frías's anti-Porfirismo meet, clearly emerge. Both recognize the nation embodied in the mestizo. And both assume the material killing and symbolic sublimation of Indians as constitutive of *mestizaje*'s dialectical progress. This is how *mestizaje* exhibits the ambivalence of a colonial discourse. Thus Díaz can at once sublimate old Indian heroes to the status of national icons and tap into a discourse of contemporary Indian savagery as a justification for wars of conquest. At the same time, Frías, too, can speak to the natural sense of honor that Indians exhibit in battle (e.g., 1906, 73, 124–26), while presenting the effacement of their communities as a necessary erasure in the march of progress. This is precisely what happens in *Tomochic*: at one point, as if to underscore the *difference* of the federal incursion against Tomochic, Frías interpolates a short chapter on "the campaign against the Apaches," in which an old soldier recounts to Miguel the costly, even tragic, *but clearly necessary*, war against an "invasive" indigenous savagery (49–51). Later, drunk and swept up in the blind enthusiasm of the Tomochic massacre, Miguel imagines himself in heroic victory, not over the mestizo Tomoches, but over the barbaric Apaches (133). *They were not a barbarous tribe*: clearly, the polemic of *Tomochic* is not leveled at the Porfiriato's genocidal campaign against the Indian, which is tacitly endorsed in the novel. It is leveled at the expansion of that genocide against the Tomoches, "a strong race, deserving to live and to become the root of a robust Mexican people" (136).

It would take nearly two decades after the initial publication of *Tomochic* for Díaz to fall, for Frías's anti-Porfirian politics to morph into official rhetoric, and for the book to be praised as an important, if largely forgotten, precursor to the great "novelas de la Revolución."[26] In the framing of the historical events around Tomochic, however, it seems that the empirical lies of the Porfirian position are in fact a more honest reflection of the discursive truth of biopolitical power. In spite of the revolution and all of its historical revisions, it is Díaz's version of the war against Tomochic that is remembered, when it is remembered at all: the expansive state against recalcitrant Indians.[27] If today modern Mexico remembers "the Indians" as heroes, rather than as a terrifying threat, it is in part owing to the very "success" of the Porfirian

project of pacification,[28] for, as Claude Lévi-Strauss noted in the opening pages of *Tristes Tropiques* (1955), it is only with the removal of that
threat that the former "enemies" of civilization become a source of
"noble and profitable revelations" (33). And it is here, at the notion of
civilization's enemies, that the Porfirian "discovery" of "Indians" at
Tomochic carries an even stronger sense of discursive integrity. The
rebellion at Tomochic was one of several popular religious uprisings
against the Porfirian state. Its inspiration, a mystic, healer, and spirit-
ist known as Santa Teresa de Cabora, had legions of followers across
northern Mexico. These followers were largely drawn from the popular
classes, and her support was especially strong in indigenous communities.[29] The mass appeal of figures such as Teresa de Cabora emerged
from the social sector that was most explicitly brutalized by the dog-
matic positivism and "conservative liberalism" of the Porfiriato.[30] These
largely impoverished masses, while territorially "inside," are excluded
by the nation-state, an inner exteriority always in danger of taking its
allegiance elsewhere. In that sense, Tomochic and the rebel villages
like it—in their very declarations of local sovereignty that thus erodes
national hegemony—perform the discursive function of the Indian. If
they are "mixed," practicing a weird hybrid of popular Catholicisms, it
is the wrong kind of mixture, not *mestizaje*, but a monster.[31] Regardless
of genealogical "race" or traditional "culture," they are "Indian," inauthentic Mexicans, the constitutive erasure in the ambivalent discourse
of *pure mestizaje*.

   With the end of the campaign, the thuggish (and brutal realist) Cas-
torena sarcastically links the fall of Tomochic to that of Tenochtitlan,
as the more sensitive Miguel expresses his "admiration for the heroism
of the extinct Tomoche race" (Frías 1906, 136) that he has just helped
extinguish. Although many have noted that the figure of Miguel is a
stand-in for the author himself (Azuela 1947, 667; Magaña Esquível 1964,
55; Brown 1989, xvi), the narrative voice that communicates the soldier's thoughts is unstable, often rendered as what Bakhtin would call
a double-voiced discourse, at once an affirmation and a criticism of the
war. It is in these final chapters, with the articulation of an increasingly
rigorous homology between sacrifice and the sacred, that the ambivalence of the narrative becomes at once exceedingly intense and politically ambiguous. Miguel, in a dramatic psychological battle with himself,
finally succumbs to state ideology in a way that seems to cast doubt over
all of his previous criticisms. In a paroxysm of newfound nationalism,

he suddenly recognizes himself as a "son of Chapultepec," the site of his military training whose "Aztec name" evokes "an epic song, like a joyful reveille," at once linking him to the "heroism of the epic death of the *niños héroes* of 1847," the "triumphant Netzahualcóyotl," the "pomp of Moctezuma," and the barbarism of Díaz, which now takes on explicitly "Aztec" tones (144). Immediately after Miguel's identification with official indigenism and endorsement of the inclusive exclusion of Mexico's living indigenous past, the biopolitical outcome of Tomochic reaches its eugenic limit: with the Tomoches being executed to the last *man*, it is revealed that this absolute exclusion is to be accompanied by the transfer of the surviving "orphans and widows" to the "leading families of Chihuahua," and hence their inclusion as "seedbeds *[semilleros]*" for future, robust generations of Mexicans. This is to be carried out "for the good of the State [whether this refers to Chihuahua or the nation-state is unclear, and not especially important]" (146). Finally, just before another unsatisfying reveille accompanies the new day's emergence over the ruins of the smoldering town (151), Miguel and his comrades contemplate the heroism of the now sacred, and now dead, Tomoches. All nod in pensive agreement as someone gushes: "It couldn't have been any other way, it couldn't have been!" (147). Whether earnest and ironic, Frías—even *against* Díaz—presents a chilling vision of the foundational disarticulation that rearticulates national consolidation to colonial expansion.

7. *Mestizaje* and Postrevolutionary Malaise: Vasconcelos and Azuela

The year 1925 in Mexico represents one of those historical confluences whose coincidence is too seductive to leave unremarked. First, it is the year Heriberto Frías dies. With his signature work already largely forgotten (Magaña Esquível 1964, 60), both Frías's death and the disappearance of *Tomochic* commemorate the end of a revolutionary cycle. His 1893 critique of the Porfiriato foresaw much of the dictatorship's increasingly repressive tactics, along with the accompanying popular discontent that would eventually lead to its hasty defeat in the revolutionary year of 1911. Frías would go on to actively participate in the reinvention of Mexico, joining *letrados* such as José Vasconcelos at the 1914 Revolutionary Convention of Aguascalientes, where the multiple warring factions attempted to negotiate the installation of a new, legitimate, sovereign government.[1] By 1925, after a series of violent transfers of power, this process had nearly worked itself out, and the contours of a new hegemony were beginning to take shape.

It is also in 1925 that two definitive works of postrevolutionary literary aesthetics either emerge or reemerge in the cultural and political capital of Mexico: first, Vasconcelos's *La raza cósmica*, published in exile in Barcelona, but disseminated quickly throughout Latin America;[2] second, Azuela's *Los de abajo*, originally serialized in an obscure El Paso newspaper in 1915–16, but going largely unnoticed in the Mexican cultural

105

center for the intervening decade (see Ruffinelli 1992, 158–60). Each work participates in producing one of two modes of negotiating a certain postrevolutionary anxiety. This anxiety was symptomatic of a racialized, sociopolitical disjuncture that had reemerged out of the chaos, suggested at first with the fall of Díaz, then later reiterated with the fatal schism—ideological, political, and personal—between Zapata and Madero. Now, it would be questionable, even flatly inaccurate, to characterize the Mexican Revolution as a race war. However, the tumultuous period nevertheless revealed a new kind of consciousness toward a racially demarcated split that had been previously smoothed over, *desarrollado*, with the thirty years of order and progress that defined the *paz porfiriana*. The largely indigenous, peasant army of the Zapatistas that briefly took the streets of Mexico City in 1914 served as a kind of referendum against the liberal-positivist policies of invisibilization, marginalization, and oppression.[3] As Vasconcelos would put it, or rather spin it, the poetic justice of the revolution was that it "made a mockery of the positivist doctrine" with the triumph of a supposedly "irredeemable caste" of Indians, peasants, and workers over Díaz, the patron of the modernization and national consolidation in nineteenth-century Mexico.[4] However, Vasconcelos and the rest of the *maderista* liberals would immediately witness the difficulty in reconciling the metropolitan center with that peripheral, "irredeemable caste," as the negotiations between Madero and Zapata toward a postrevolutionary hegemony first soured and then disintegrated altogether.[5] The revolution was not, then, a race war; rather, it was a war in which all of the "races" participated and thereby asserted new demands upon the postrevolutionary state.

Within this revolutionary trajectory, 1925 is also momentous in that it marks the first full year of the presidency of Plutarco Elías Calles, the caudillo who would succeed in taming, in literally institutionalizing, the war machine known as the Mexican Revolution, eventually reconverting it into a political machine.[6] In short, 1925 marks the year that the Distrito Federal was ready to reappropriate its ongoing revolutionary past. And a crucial question for much of the intelligentsia was the question of the future for, or even the possibility of, an articulate Mexican body politic. The mestizo utopia of Molina Enríquez, after all, had been smashed: Díaz was by now entombed in France. Vasconcelos's theories of racial triumph, and Azuela's themes of racial malaise, offer distinct inflections of this anxiety. Especially interesting for my purposes are the divergent yet compatible ways that they rework, and reproduce, the articulation of race, time, and nation, so fundamental to the generation of positivists that preceded them, and whom they ostensibly write against.

Vasconcelos's formulation of *mestizaje* contained within his basic concept of "the cosmic race" has exhibited a remarkable tenacity, and continues to crop up in all sorts of texts throughout the Americas. He is often credited, usually by way of his famous treatise *La raza cósmica*, as the inspiration for a kind of Mexicanist antiracism. Octavio Paz, for example, claims that "Vasconcelos exhibited no similarity to the caste consciousness *[casticismo]* and traditionalism of the Mexican conservatives" (1950, 184). Gloria Anzaldúa's influential theory of borderland identities leverages Paz's diagnosis of Vasconcelos's tolerance into a "new *mestiza* consciousness," proposing that, "[o]pposite to the theory of the pure Aryan, and to the policy of racial purity that white America practices, his [Vasconcelos's] theory is one of inclusivity" (1987, 77). Richard Rodriguez concurs, calling it a theory of "absorbency," "embod[ied] in blood and soul" by Mexican immigrants to the United States (1991, 48). Joseba Gabilondo maintains that Vasconcelos's aestheticization of Darwinism "reintroduces selection without its imperialist repercussions, in a posteugenic fashion" (1997, 108). And Robert Con Davis-Undiano characterizes Vasconcelos as a kind of friend of the Indian, preoccupied with the "plight of Mexico's native populations" and acting as an early "voice of indigenous cultures and the mestizo perspective" (2000, 120, 138).

At the same time, Carlos Monsiváis has read Vasconcelos as "one of the only Mexicans of this century who knew how to commit himself entirely to the task of mythmaking" (1968, 348). Given the contradictions inherent to myth, perhaps it should come as no surprise, then, to discover, upon reading any number of his texts (including, or especially, *La raza cósmica*), a Vasconcelos much more harried by a kind of racialized paranoia than the preceding citations would suggest. But, despite the quantity of his apologists (which goes well beyond those just mentioned), the highly dubious quality of both his philosophical system and his treatment of race is well known, and widely cited.[7] Thus, the repeated attempts to rescue Vasconcelos as a visionary thinker, especially on the grounds of race, are not a project that I find compelling. Neither, however, does there seem to be much point in yet another condemnation of his failures. If Vasconcelos is interesting today, it is not because he thought about *mestizaje* in a right or wrong, productive or unproductive, way. Rather, it is because his way of formulating it, even in its failure, has entered the realm of ideology. In other words, whatever else he did or didn't do, Vasconcelos articulated the Mexican thematic of hybridity—*mestizaje*—in a way that was especially effective, and readily appropriated, within the context of constructing a postrevolutionary Mexican state, a state that today finds itself, if not "in crisis," then certainly in an intense moment of transition.

The following paragraphs provide nothing like a thorough overview of Vasconcelos's remarkable life, whose basic facts are well known.[8] Nor will I offer a bibliographic review of his oeuvre, which spans more than five decades of constant writing.[9] My reading of Vasconcelos here will be limited to his basic idea of *mestizaje*. I will pursue, through a number of his texts from different periods of his life, how that idea repeats, with or without a difference, the various articulations of race, time, and nation that serve as the organizing problematic of this chapter. I will also offer some comments on what I think his eventual rejection of a cosmic *mestizaje* means for that articulation. Ultimately, I will propose that, though not a wholesale repetition of the positivistic *mestizaje* of the nineteenth century, Vasconcelos's reiteration serves much of the same function: an effective articulation of race and time that helps to reconcile the hegemony of the nation with the sovereignty of the state. I read Vasconcelos, then, as an idealist confronted with the limits of his own project: the consolidation of nation and state that can at once appropriate his work, yet ultimately symbolize its universal impossibility. Reading Azuela's text, and its own incorporation into the state's cultural institutions, alongside the Vasconcelian discourse of *mestizaje* will highlight this paradoxically successful failure.

La raza cósmica is the standard point of reference when noting Vasconcelos's contribution to theories of identity in Latin America, and is sometimes cited as the moment when he makes a kind of turn to race. Critics have nevertheless pointed out several preludes to Vasconcelos's later ideas on race, dating as far back as his dissertation in law school.[10] However, a 1916 speech delivered in Peru is the earliest elaboration of the basic theses that will govern *La raza cósmica*, later to be developed more fully in the less famous collection of speeches and essays called *Indología* (1926).

The key pivot in "El movimiento intelectual contemporáneo de

México" (1916), which marks it as an anticipation of *La raza cósmica*, happens when Vasconcelos invokes a kind of classical Greek *mestizaje*. He describes a post-Peloponnesian War meeting at the "Ilión," a reunion of "all the tribes . . . in a common effort to bring together their heterogeneous virtues and knowledges." In their wisdom, the Greeks went as far as to include in the meeting "the contributions of the precious genius and culture of the vanquished, the refined but expired Trojans." Together, the Greeks were able to subsume individual identities to the greater task of elaborating a "national spirit" (1916, 20). Over the next paragraphs, in what will later become the political message of *La raza cósmica*, he hypothesizes that Latin America is in an analogous situation, and needs to come together as a "future great race."[11] This will require "the integration of the new ethnic unities," and hence a nationalism that is expansive, not reductive: a "double love for nationalism and for a continental dream" (22). This dream will rise as a "*patria*, the work of mestizos, formed of two or three races by blood, and of all cultures by spirit" (ibid.). The realization of this dream will entail that "upon mixing with the Indian, the Spaniard will be separated from his trunk and the Indian will abandon his" (23).

This is all pretty familiar after the positivists, who, from Barreda to Molina Enríquez, consistently pointed to *mestizaje* as the dynamic motor of the nation. It is interesting, then, to note that this text, like nearly all of Vasconcelos's early writings, is framed as a critique of positivism. Even if Vasconcelos went beyond many of the positivists by looking past national boundaries, this move does not transcend, but instead repeats, in another register, the supplementary articulation of race and nation that we saw in postivist discourse. Indeed, it exemplifies what Balibar identifies as the basic structure of panracial ideologies, such as Aryanism, Zionism, Hegelian universal idealism, or cultural imperialism, in that it couples the internationalist elitism of a "superior" or "chosen race" (the mestizo) to the nationalist populism of a "unified nation" (Mexico, America, etc.) (Balibar and Wallerstein 1988, 62). This is an important point, because it helps to understand Vasconcelos's racism, sometimes construed as emerging only in his later work, as a constitutive element not only in his own thinking, but within the Western philosophical tradition in which he operates. In other words, his racism, far from exceptional, is quite conventional, and speaks to the difficulty of extricating oneself from one's discursive parameters. It would be a challenge, in fact, to find a significantly less problematic thinker on race—by today's standards—in 1920. At the same time, this constitutive racism requires that the critic exercise restraint and consider the implications of framing Vasconcelos as a progressive thinker on the question of race in Latin America, still a surprisingly common practice, especially among critics writing from the perspective of the allegedly purist binarism of North American race relations.

The place where the legacies of positivism exercise their greatest tenacity in the work of Vasconcelos is around metaphors of time; or, more specifically, at the confluence of evolution and history that Vasconcelos consistently attacks, and then proceeds to reproduce with a different vocabulary.[12] In discussing the mestizo in the Peru speech, he concludes that "we have no past, our *patria* and our empire are the future" (1916, 23).[13] With Hegel, then, Vasconcelos perceives a continent-in-progress, what he calls at one point a "confusion of messages" still waiting to be deciphered (1926, 118). His first step in cracking the code is to look for the very origins of the "New World." He quickly finds a paradox: decadent "new" cultures conquered by an ascendant "old" one. He notes in *Indología* that it "is truly curious to observe that this continent, which we have taken to be so new, is in reality so old" (ibid., 116).[14] He thus proposes the conquest as a youthful invigoration (117–18), and in that sense does nothing to go beyond Barreda, who spoke of the modern "germ" of progress that infected the conquistadors and was transmitted to the new, mestizo race. And, as with the positivists, the Indian becomes both a "sometimes coauthor of a great [new] culture" and a necessary erasure within that same project: "On our continent, the material conquest was accompanied by the destruction of the indigenous ideology; but that destroyed ideology was replaced, and I doubt that anybody would deny, seriously, that such a replacement is anything but an improvement" (144–45). Where he does go beyond Barreda, and most of the positivists, however, is with his elaboration of a fantastic historical schema that theorizes not just a series of civilizational "levels" through which Mexico will ascend, but rather a conflation of Latin America with the end of universal history itself, a future event that depends explicitly on a discourse of race. For Vasconcelos, the end of history will require the end of race.

Vasconcelos's turn to race, then, meets many theorists of hybridity, from Molina Enríquez to García Canclini, at the pivotal site of temporality. Indeed, the central preoccupations of his major works on *mestizaje*, namely, *La raza cósmica* and *Indología*, are related to time: What is

Latin America's historical relevance? And what fate awaits its future? The basic thesis that accompanies these questions is that Mexico's history is *cosmic*, and that it *should have* considerable glory ahead of it.[15] The answers to these questions, and the proof behind Vasconcelos's theses, are worked out through an explicitly racialized temporality. Beyond the biological and spiritual mixing associated with his notion of *mestizaje*, it is in fact a kind of multitemporal heterogeneity that enables his hybridological framework, articulating its various components. Vasconcelos's idea of a "cosmic race" prophecies the eventual and necessary fusion of "all races" (following Kant, he identifies four) into a universal fifth race.[16] But as much as this project rests on questions of biology (1926, 68–74), geography (63–67), and Spirit (74–76), it also outlines a carefully constructed historicism.

The problem, for Vasconcelos, is not just the existence of different races, but the relation of those races to temporalized historical consciousness. Each color-coded race—black, red, yellow, and white—having passed through an age of glory, is now old, decadent, degenerate. Latin America, then, is composed of various levels of intermixed "oldness." Whiteness, or Europe, has witnessed two waves of ascendancy, first Luso-Hispanic, then Anglo-Dutch, both of which are now languishing (49). And even though Anglo America emits an energy that gives it a blush of the new, this industrial mirage is merely the extension of Old Europe, Hegel's "historical lumber-room" (1837, 86), its fate sealed in its genocidal and segregationist social politics that leaves it (as Kant tried to theorize against) destined to something like inbreeding (1797, 57). In Latin America, confronting this doomed industrial modernism is the even heavier oldness of the remnants of indigenous civilizations (e.g., 1925, 56; 1926, 116) and the descendants of African slaves (1925, 79). But this multitemporal heterogeneity, these layered times, these ethnic histories do something very important: they mix. And through that *mestizaje*, Mexico's multiple oldness is renovated, becoming not only new, but also *future*, even *cosmic*: "Thus will be engendered the synthesized [racial] type, bringing together all of the treasures of History, and giving expression to the entire world's desire" (58). Mexico, or more expansively, Latin America, represents the beginnings of the final phase of humanity's mission: "The so-called Latin peoples, by virtue of having been more faithful to the divine mission of America, are called to consummate it" (ibid.). Latin America's role in that mission is universal ("cosmic"), and will lead to the founding of "Universopolis" (not, incidentally, located in Mexico, but in Brazil) whose hybrid glow will encircle the globe via "armies [he also mentions an air force] of wisdom, life, and love" (ibid., 65). The age of Universopolis will be an age of what Vasconcelos calls "aesthetic eugenics" (70). This new mode of life, in which only the beautiful will reproduce, will enable the emergence of a final race that will include elements of all races (61–62). He also emphasizes that one of the clear benefits of this project will be the "evolution" of the "sleeping" Indian (72, 56), and the "redemption," or eventual "disappearance," indeed, the "voluntary extinction," of the "recessive negro" (72).

Aesthetic eugenics: Given that programs of eugenics are *always* aesthetic projects, the adjective seems excessive. It also renders somewhat perplexing Gabilondo's claim, in a prominent afterword to the bilingual version of *La raza cósmica*, that Vasconcelos is "posteugenic" (1997, 108). While Gabilondo is correct to point out that Vasconcelos is writing in a kind of Darwinian (or better, Spencerian) moment, we should note that Darwin himself regretted his invocation of "natural selection," and that many others, not least Franz Boas (already in the 1890s), had begun to throw Spencerian social selection into question. Although Vasconcelos could at times certainly prove himself a vigorous critic of imperialism, his turn to *mestizaje*, far from overcoming racism, seems equally capable of taking racist discourse to its moment of greatest intensity. Indeed, his theory of "aesthetic eugenics" fits comfortably within what Balibar calls the "racist ideal": "This ideal connects up both with the first man (nondegenerate [Vasconcelos's conquistador]) and the man of the future (the superman [Vasconcelos's mestizo "Totínem" or "todo hombre"]) . . . The aestheticization of social relations is a crucial contribution of racism to the constitution of the projective field of politics" (Balibar and Wallerstein 1988, 58).

Latin America, often theorized as degenerate and outside of History in the philosophical traditions of positivism, Aryanism, and race science that Vasconcelos is writing against, is reconfigured as anything but. Not satisfied with simply reinscribing Latin America into the universal flow of history, Vasconcelos makes it the quintessence of that flow: central not only in its past as the beginning of history's end, but also framed as man's only hope for a *future*, to be ushered in with the "Totínem" or "todo hombre" (1926, 93). *Latin* America represents an invigoration of, and commitment to, Europe's pretensions to universality, in that it actively, willingly, and literally incorporates its others, delivering them up from "mindlessness" to a new, universal, aesthetic monism.[17] For Vasconcelos, Latin America is a marriage, spanning time, with a historical mandate on the future to consolidate the conflictive many into a spiritual One.

In writing *La raza cósmica*, even though in exile, Vasconcelos still rides the heady wave of the cultural renaissance that accompanied the revolution, a rebirth in which he cut a charismatic figure, often finding himself at the center of things. Mariano Azuela, as a doctor with Julián Medina's forces who never experienced significant political dividends, saw the revolution from a perspective that was at once inside yet peripheral. At the risk of overpsychologizing, I think that this peripherality reemerges in his articulation of race and the destiny of the Mexican *pueblo*, which, to put it lightly, is much more sober than that of Vasconcelos. The work's status as *the* "novel of the revolution" makes it worth attending to, especially given the countervailing treatment—vis-à-vis the 1920s Vasconcelos—that it lends to the articulation of race, time, and nation at the heart of *mestizaje*.

Los de abajo is Azuela's portrait of the Mexican Revolution, told from the perspective of an unruly band of soldiers allied with Pancho Villa's famous División del Norte. As a "novel of the revolution," it is widely regarded to be the genre's masterpiece. It sets an appropriate tone of postrevolutionary malaise that would be repeated in many literary accounts of the contradictions between revolutionary ideals, the often petty violence of the revolution, and the conversion of the revolution into a new vehicle for political ambition. In a way, it is even visionary, given its composition in the mid-1910s. Writing at a time when dramatic violence was still accompanied by an optimism for social change, Azuela would anticipate the more widespread artistic disillusionment with the revolution that would run through Martín Luis Guzmán and Orozco, and culminate in Rodolfo Usigli's theatrical reduction of the entire project to the very literal terms of a masquerade.[18] This is part of the irony of the genre, and Azuela's novel is exemplary in that regard: what is taken as "of the revolution" is in fact antirevolutionary. Not *counter*-revolutionary, which might imply a reactionary return to something like the Porfiriato, but rather antirevolutionary in the sense of being highly skeptical of the revolution as a project, and critical of its consolidation as an institution. In short, there is nothing "patriotic" or redemptive about *Los de abajo*, nothing that the revolution should feel good about.

Its title evokes this perspective, and has been poorly translated into English as *The Underdogs*. The translation is inadequate in that it implies a story of the downtrodden who attempt to better their situation through revolutionary activity: in short, *underdog* implies something like the "little guy," in a desperate fight that the reader might expect to sympathize with. Indeed, this is how the novel is often read, but it is a misreading. *Los de abajo* gives us nothing of the idealized heroism of the underdog, representing "those from below" as an all-too-human lot, participating in the revolution not out of ideals of social change, but for adventure, lust, hyperbolic revenge, or even for no reason at all. "Those from above" are worse, war profiteers cynically speaking of the lofty goals of revolution while jockeying to reap the dividends of the political and economic fallout. It is a story whose protagonists are decidedly antiheroic. It stands in contrast to *Tomochic* (with which it has been compared), in that Frías aims his critique specifically at the power elite, while ennobling (if ambivalently) the Tomoches and representing the federal soldiers as manipulated victims.[19] Azuela, on the other hand, only allows the slightest of opportunities for readerly sympathy. The tragedy of the protagonist, Demetrio Macías, is that his social condition has led him inevitably to a life of violence from which he can barely consider, or even desire, escape. The revolution is simply one more scene in Demetrio's fatal trajectory. *Los de abjajo*, then, is a foundational disarticulation on a grand scale, written at a time when caudillos were still on the move, and when revolutionary peace had not yet materialized. It is a hard, even harsh, novel of the periphery, told in the reticent language of the Mexican North, and punctuated by coarse, colloquial dialogue. It took a long time to make it to the capital, and only became something of a hit when Francisco Monterde unveiled it in 1925, in order to offer an affirmative answer to Julio Jiménez Rueda's question of whether there was, in fact, a "virile Mexican literature" (see Ruffinelli 1992, 158–59).

For Azuela, the problem of racial, temporal, and national articulation is unresolvable through the standard routes of a biological, aesthetic, or cultural *mestizaje*. Instead, that same *mestizaje* signals the incommensurability that repetitively disarticulates the very idea of Mexico as an integral body politic. If there is a thesis in the disjointed, episodic structure of *Los de abajo*, it is that the violence that is the revolution is a violence whose only end is violence. But, unlike Octavio Paz, who, in a famous interpretation of the 1968 massacre at the Plaza de las Tres Culturas, would describe the eruption of state violence by resorting to the cliché of "the [Aztec] past which we thought was buried" (1970, 236), Azuela draws no explicit link between the trope of indigenous blood sacrifice and the excesses of the revolution. Rather, we find ourselves again facing a problem of multitemporal heterogeneity. As always, the Indian is old, as old as the land: mountain faces become "Aztec idols" (Azuela 1915, 160), and the only actor in the novel identified as *indio*, beyond the protagonist himself, is the aged, federalist spy that Demetrio executes (131). The most sinister figures, representing the morally vapid nature of modernity, are consistently white: Cervantes, the cynical *letrado*; *el güero* Margarito, the sociopath; the reactionary federalist *jefe* (127). In the antiheroic figures of the mestizo rebels—Demetrio Macías and his men—these two temporalities are continually portrayed as irreconcilable, mixed but inarticulate.[20]

This disconnect is expressed in the various comedies of inverted opposites that Azuela constructs as the rebels conquer and occupy rural towns. The rebels become something like the new savages, misinterpreting the grammar of civilization as they reduce all signs and fetishes of civility and culture to the most base levels of use-value and exchange value: an imported divan becomes a horse's trough (158); a once luxurious, now manure-spangled, salon (158, 164) becomes a flophouse, those piles of manure serving as beds (137); a typewriter, sign of *letrado* learnedness and modernity, becomes a burden, eventually condemned to the rocks, smashed by a looter who quickly tires of its excessive weight, small exchange value, and general uselessness (137). No Caliban, much less Ariel, appears to urge a salvation of the books as a source of power: colorful pictures are torn out (152), and the texts burn along with the mansion and its inhabitants (164). Demetrio Macías himself embodies this disarticulation, appropriating the ideological sophistication of a *cause* that Luis Cervantes lends to his battles, and then eventually confessing that he *has no cause* when confronted by a general and asked to make a conscientious, political choice between warring caudillos: "Demetrio, quite perplexed, brought his hands to his head and scratched a little. 'Look, don't ask me questions, I'm not really a schoolboy . . . The officers' stripes *[la aguilita]* on my sombrero, well, you gave them to me . . . I mean, you know, all you have to do is tell me, "do this and this . . ." and that's it, that's the end of the story!'" (192). It is a revolution without mediation, inarticulate, with fighters who cannot even articulate their own participation.[21]

Finally, in a sort of apotheosis of the various metaphors of mixed times that we have seen throughout these chapters, Azuela beautifully expresses the materiality of multitemporal heterogeneity that seems to weigh on the Mexican intellectual's psyche. Azuela's take on mixed times seems to reject the possibility of their mixedness, displaying them as riven in a very literal way: "Demetrio takes out his [spoils, a] jewel-encrusted watch and asks Anastasio Montañés the time. Anastasio looks at the watch, then he sticks his head out a small window and, looking at the starry sky, says: 'Taurus is pretty low, compadre; the sun will be up soon'" (149).

Azuela does not offer a vision of a degenerate race, stuck in time like Vasconcelos's *indios*, or "insane" like the "anarchic" Mexico that the positivists would seek to "cure." Nor does he offer the romance of the standard reading of the old Zapatistas, whose failed revolution tends to be framed as an impossible return to a primitivist "tradition," someplace before modernity.[22] Rather, Azuela sketches a race condemned, one that literally *cannot tell time*, out of step with the modern world: modern, but not modernized. Decades before Paz would argue something similar, Azuela portrays his mestizo Mexico as a kind of mask: "[the] grimace . . . of an unredeemable race," in the words of Solís, another disillusioned *letrado*. And decades before García Márquez would erase Macondo from the face of the earth, Azuela's revolution is the ultimate—unending and repetitive—expression of this condemnation, announced by that same *letrado* as "the hurricane, and the man who gives himself to it is no longer that man, but a miserable dry leaf at the mercy of the storm" (135). If there is a comment on *mestizaje* in *Los de abajo*, it is a pessimistic ode to its very impossibility, its sterility, its unproductivity. Luis Cervantes, still idealistic about the revolution, gazes at the battlefield smoke in the distance. Alberto Solís, long since descended into cynicism, follows his gaze toward an epiphany: "And he thought he had discovered a symbol of the revolution in those clouds of smoke and dust that ascended fraternally, embraced, mingled, and then dissolved into nothing" (144). He raises his hand, ejaculates an inarticulate "¡Ah... ahora sí!" and promptly takes a bullet to the stomach.

Vasconcelos would eventually reach similarly dire conclusions about his once cosmic race, but in a much less reflective, and more harrowing, way. By 1937 his *mestizaje* had become a nightmare. This dark vision was expressed in a short, dystopic essay by Vasconcelos titled "México en 1950." It would be rewritten, with minor changes, in 1955 as "México en 1980." Certainly a farce in part, Vasconcelos's compulsion to repeat suggests that it also reflected the author's durable anxieties. The vignette opens with a militaristic state procession in honor of "His Excellency Netzahualcóyotl Rosenberg, president of the United Soviet States of Mexico," who is accompanied by "Colonel Huichilobos Pershing" and blandishes the presidential sash that honors "Plutarco Elías Calles, exterminator of the Gentiles" (1937, 133). What was once cosmic has returned as monstrous, the paranoid vision of a cabal of evil geniuses—bloodthirsty Aztecs, national traitors, Bolsheviks, imperialists, atheists, Wall Street bankers, Jews—all rolled into one. *Mestizaje*, for Vasconelos, had spun out of control, and into a strategy for a cunning alliance premised on "the mixture of native blood with the new Hebrew immigrants" in the service of "Anglo-Saxon hegemony" (137).[23] Later still, shortly before his death in 1959, the dream that Vasconcelos once predicted would emerge as the triumph of love, the rise of aesthetics, and the end of violence was reconverted, no longer a cosmic fusion, but now a radical and fiery fission: the H-bomb, a fate that Vasconcelos welcomes as a liberating holocaust from the threat of a "world of slavery and cruelty like the one founded by the Soviets" (1957, 225).

This morbid paranoia in the face of the totalizing binarism of Cold War politics, its accompanying move toward a Hispano-Catholic fascism, and the increasingly overt racism of Vasconcelos's discourse tend to be explained as the latter of the "two Vasconceloses," with the division placed at his debilitating electoral defrauding, his unanswered call for revolutionary action, and his subsequent exile. This biographical division, however, loses some of its explanatory force when confronted with the theories of Hispanist racial superiority that emerge even in Vasconcelos's earliest work. Recall the tone and word choice of his 1916 formulation of a politics of *mestizaje*. Although, contrary to the Porfirian positivists, he seems to place equal weight on the transformation of *both* cultures, it is clearly the Indian who can rejoice in the change. "[T]he Spaniard *will be separated*"—perhaps with regret, surely with violence— "from his [civilizational] trunk." Conversely, "the Indian *will abandon* his" (1916, 23).

Vasconcelos's theory of "the cosmic race" was never about multiple hybridizations in the plural, but rather a universal hybridity in the singular; not *la raza* as an articulate heterogeneity of races and cultures, but *mi raza* as one homogeneous race; not, in fact, a sustainable hybridity at all, but rather the sign of a new and total purity, one that takes hybridity as its prior condition and constitutive opposite.[24]

But rather than sully Vasconcelos's already tarnished legacy any further, we could equally read him as a tragic, even postcolonial, figure, whose crowning vision, the cosmic race, is itself tinged with a kind of malaise, the acknowledgment of futility. The last lines of *La raza cósmica* are telling in this regard, for they speak of a failure, both material and metaphysical. He concludes by noting the national allegories that he had once ordered carved in the Palacio de la Educación Pública during his remarkable tenure as its secretary, underneath which *"should have been raised* four grand statues, [representing] the four great contemporary races . . . to indicate that America is home to all and needs them all." He adds that "a monument *should have been erected . . .* to indicate that . . . in America we shall arrive . . . at the creation of a . . . final race, a cosmic race" (1925, 80).[25] But this new symbology would only come to pass as precisely that: symbols that prop up dogma.

The disillusionment of the tragic Vasconcelos is the malaise that inflicts all idealists when confronted by the insatiable appropriation of revolutionary ideals that accompanies the hybridization of nation and state.[26] This intersecting of hegemony and sovereignty at the site of the nation-state, for Vasconcelos, presents an impasse. Vasconcelos's monist fantasies, as Zea has pointed out, are consistently put forth in terms of "all or nothing" (1943, 30). But this totalizing obsession runs counter to what Gilles Deleuze and Félix Guattari have called the law of the state: "The law of the State is not the law of All or Nothing . . . but that of interior and exterior. The State is sovereignty. But sovereignty only reigns over what it is capable of internalizing, of appropriating locally" (1980, 360). Thus, although perhaps Vasconcelos saw in the postrevolutionary education project a *practical* vehicle, as Monsiváis has argued, for appropriating the local masses into a project of *state* (1981, 35), his *ideal* is the revolutionary homogeneity that drives the passions toward *nation*, a *pueblo mestizo* that would eventually span a universal scale. It is a conservative gesture, a millenial futurism premised on a backward gaze toward a totalizing Hispanism, an imperial past that dreamed of a limitless nation.[27] The state, on the other hand, is the modernist gesture of politics, of negotiating limits, and represents the ultimate victory of the Porfirian model: *amificación*, interiorization, appropriating what it can (e.g., the Indian) and exteriorizing what it cannot (e.g., indigenous communities). The ten-year delay in the revival of Azuela's novel can be chalked up to the chaos of the revolution, and *La raza cósmica*'s publication in exile can be called a historical accident. But if those gaps in time and space represent anything at all, they represent the necessary historical lag during which revolution becomes indistinguishable from state, an institutionalized revolution strong enough to hold up as "of the revolution" a novel that is profoundly *antirevolutionary*, and capable enough to incorporate as *its* ideology a cosmic race on whose annulment it depends, brokered in the schism between Mexico and Morelos, and sealed in the blood sacrifice of Zapata, which represents something like the assassination of revolution itself. It is this latter figure, of course, always understood (and likely understanding himself) as a kind of purist, who in fact offers the closest thing to a *critical* and *radical hybridity*: Nahua and Spanish, orality and literacy, memory and legality, community and property; together they swirl and hybridize into the shape of an alternative modernity. It is this kind of radically critical, even subversive, mixture that asks precisely the questions that hybridologists tend to avoid, or cannot even confront.

In chapters 4 to 7 we have seen some of the mechanisms through which the Mexican discourse of *mestizaje*, while ostensibly speaking to the mixing of genes and cultures, has been historically invoked as a gesture of nation-state consolidation on the behalf of an ascendant power elite. Although there are many variations of the invocation of *mestizaje*, a persistent discursive function that it serves is the ideological articulation of race, time, and nation. This was the case with the nineteenth-century liberals and positivists—such as Mora, Barreda, and Molina Enríquez—and continued to be the case for their opponents in spite of various polemics against and critiques of the positivist doctrine: in Frías, Vasconcelos, even Azuela. Each, in his own way, transforms *mestizaje* into a historical metaphor for the articulation of the nation with its others; each, in other words, strives to recodify the Indian as a national participant. The Indian participant in the process of *mestizaje*, as we saw, is always an old participant, a prehistorical foundation to be overcome by History's appointment of a mestizo future. In other words, it is precisely *not* the active, political participation of real, living indigenous communities. What is at stake, today, in this long trajectory of constructing the oldness of the Indian? One of its effects is to naturalize the Indian as existing outside of modernity. This ahistorical positioning has, of course, at times been effectively appropriated by indigenous groups themselves as a strategy for reclaiming the lands with which they have a "timeless" relationship. At the same time, however, that same appropriation of an essentialized identity can play into the hands of the imposer, who now attempts to undermine indigenous claims by debunking the always-already bunk ahistorical status of indigenous communities. In other words, the task of the new corporate or state technocrat becomes one of exposing indigenous claims as not pertaining to transcendent Indians, but rather to immanent mestizos, always already participants in the nation, and hence deserving of no "special treatment" (i.e., justice). Hence, in the very flimsiness of its historical reification of a pre- or extramodern Indian, the discourse of *mestizaje* again emerges as a power play.

Operating within the coloniality of power, *mestizaje* is structured around the ambivalence of colonial discourse, simultaneously constructing a participatory, symbolic Indian as coauthor and effacing indigenous communities from the future nation-space. We also saw something like *mestizaje*'s alternative in writers whose objective is not to reconcile the disjunctures of nation-state consolidation, but rather to criticize that consolidation as a project. These narratives of foundational disarticulation also run through *mestizaje*, speaking to its ideological status as an inescapable point of reference. For Frías, *mestizaje* configures the discursive boundaries of critique, such that his attack on the Porfiriato finds its limit—or its point of agreement—in the figure of the Indian and that figure's necessarily violent erasure. Finally, in *Los de abajo*, Azuela rejects the articulate mestizo nation altogether, representing it as of the same order of fantasy as revolutionary idealism.

Despite the occasional references to impregnation, inoculation, and reproduction, a kind of chastity, and almost Puritan politeness, runs through the Mexican discourses of *mestizaje* that have just been examined. All of these appropriations, modifications, or rejections of Mexican *mestizaje* are articulated in a relatively abstract mode, often deferring to questions of race, time, history, nation, and spirit, with only occasional, and usually oblique, reference to the heterosexual, reproductive matrix that enables hybridity in the first place. Indeed, this matrix is sometimes simply absent, discarded in favor of the fleeting, homoerotic utopia of warrior brothers that one can sense in Azuela's reference to the "fraternal embrace" that marks the "perfect symbol" of the revolution. And although gendered metaphors abound, the active role of women in hybridity, especially Indian women, is consistently downplayed, with the boom of Malintzín, or La Malinche, still years away. However, there were theorists of hybridity in late-nineteenth- and early-twentieth-century Latin America who took a much more explicit approach to the mechanics of *mestizaje*. It is to the relationship between those mechanisms and the coloniality of power that we now turn, to Brazil and the work of Gilberto Freyre.

Part III
Brazil

The most productive feature of slave property
is the generative belly.

> —Joaquim Nabuco, quoting and criticiz-
> ing a "manifesto issued by slaveholding
> planters," 1883 (cited in Freyre 1933)

Brazil

I have been arguing that the ambivalence at the heart of hybridity theory stems from and plays on hybridity's stake in race. It is this stake that most explicitly reveals hybridity's basic and necessary relationship to the coloniality of power. Just as the various instantiations and permutations of colonial discourse—from the *Requerimiento* to the civilizing mission—construct the colonized other as a racially marked inner exteriority to be simultaneously rescued and erased, incorporated and expelled, so do the various Latin Americanist theories of national or regional hybridity depend on a simultaneous sublimation and effacement of a similarly marked, marginal subject.[1] This common gesture—whether announced as an irresolvable ambivalence or a dialectical sublation—does not *merely* hover at the rhetorical level of representation: it flags the hidden complicity between projects of colonial expansion and national consolidation. We saw this gesture emerge as the paradigmatic movement of *mestizaje* in the Mexican inflection of hybridity. In these final three chapters, our national frame shifts to Brazil.

Although these chapters build and depend on the themes established in Part II, and although *mestizaje* (now *mestiçagem*) as a theory of hybridity will still receive much attention, my goal is not to offer a rerun or an alternative version of that discussion. Rather, I consider the theorization of hybridity not only within a different national context, but also by adding another discursive variable. Perhaps "discursive variable" is too weak: I would like to flesh out a *constitutive element* within hybridity that has heretofore only lurked as a notable absence. Continuing this silence would be an error: hybridity's stake in race is gendered. Theories of hybridity are theories of (re)production. Fundamentally, as we saw in the comments that opened Part I, hybridity theory is a discourse on the biopolitical implications of the practice and consequences of the sexual reproduction that occurs between differently constructed "races." In hybridity theory, then, discourses of race are inextricable from discourses of gender.

The gendered configuration of hybridity coalesces in literary narratives at the site of what I will be referring to as the "national family." I will dwell on this theme momentarily, but I want to stress from the outset what I am attempting to get at—and not to get at—through this term. First, despite a reliance on a number of concepts—such as ambivalence and disavowal—whose critical currency is traceable to Freudian psychoanalysis, the national family that I invoke is not an implicit reference to Freud's Oedipal conflict harbored in the "family romance." Although Part III will involve many scenes of "romance" (in both the narrative and courtship sense), "castration," "seduction," "desire," and other metaphors central to psychoanalysis, and although the inherent ambivalence of the Oedipal structure could certainly yield a host of insights on the texts that I will be handling, that structure is not the explicit route that I will take in my dialogue with them. Second, despite the centrality of the concept of the nation throughout this book, the national family that I invoke is not a pseudonym for the construction of an imagined community, in Benedict Anderson's sense of the term (1983). Again, this is not to say that reading these texts through and against Anderson would be uneventful; it is simply not the reading that informs my analysis. Third, I cannot emphasize enough that I am not proposing that "nations" *really do* operate as "families"; in other words, I am not proposing metaphorical transparency between "family" and "nation." Rather than let the metaphor do the explaining, I hope to explain the workings of the metaphor, that is, analyze the way in which the discourse called "national family" is deployed in texts and how this deployment relates to the institutional maintenance of ideological authority. Achieving this effect will entail a de-emphasis, if not total rejection, of thinking about the national family in strictly metaphorical terms.

Positively speaking, what I *will* attempt to pursue through the notion of the national family is the formation of a *normative discourse*. The normative discourse, as I use it here, signals the articulation of a set of representational strategies whose supposed grounding in a material referent conceals the tautological participation of that same articulation in the standardization, normalization, and concretization of that same referent. I ultimately defer to the discursive over the merely representational because of the emphasis on materiality—of both particular statements and the "enunciative function" in general—that the Foucauldian concept emphasizes (Foucault 1969, 105). The implication that arises from the articulation of (even contradictory) authoritative statements and representations—in this case, on or of the national family—is that the normative becomes the natural. Thus, insofar as the normative discourse of what I am calling the national family *conceals* the consolidation of a specific set of relations of power, it does so by *naturalizing* those relations: paradoxically, by making the natural status of those relations obvious, or self-evident. These are the terms within which Hannah Arendt perceived the nation–family relation, and which I follow here (1958, 28–37, 256–57). What is the naturalized outcome of the national family's entry into discourse? Without mincing words, it is a political legitimation of eugenics. I invoke eugenics here in both its inflammatory and technical senses: inflammatory in the very real sense in which it is linked to projects of genocide and ethnocide; technical in the sense that it is put forth within hygienic projects of national population that turn on theories and practices of "good breeding." *Both* of these senses, I argue, are naturalized in the texts I read here through the formation of a normative discourse of national family.

What does this Brazilian national family look like? How are its racialized and gendered coordinates produced within canonical texts? And, most important, how does it articulate with, inform, and enable theories and narratives of hybridity today? These are the general questions to which Part III attempts to respond.

More specifically, I frame this part as a reconsideration and critique of the narrative of hybridity that emerges from the work of Brazil's most important theorist on that topic, Gilberto Freyre. The bulk of Part III is a discourse analysis of his most famous text, *Casa-grande e senzala* (1933). Although my reading depends on two forays into key texts by an important predecessor and an insightful descendant, the conclusions that I reach should be understood as pertaining primarily to the hybridological discourse that plays out in *Casa-grande e senzala*. I would argue that these conclusions attain a wider relevance for Brazilian literary studies, Brazilianist cultural criticism, and contemporary Brazilian public culture in general, if for no other reason than Freyre's tremendous—and still explicit—influence in each of those domains.[2] I simply want to signal that this is not a sociological study of race and gender relations in Brazil, even though I need to speak somewhat sociologically of race and gender relations in Brazil in order to proceed. Nor is it a panoramic survey of hybridity within Brazilian literatures. Nor still is it a study of Freyre's thought and how it changed in work subsequent to *Casa-grande e senzala*. In short, this is a reading of hybridity and its relation to race, gender, reproduction, and nation within Freyre's greatest work.

Two central objectives govern my reading of that text.

First, I maintain that the generally accepted and orthodox critique of Brazilian "racial democracy," especially in its association with *Casa-grande e senzala*, has been misarticulated. By "misarticulated" I do not mean that it is "wrong," but rather that it could be sharpened in the name of a fuller assessment of *Casa-grande e senzala*, a text that is regrettably underrepresented in discussions of twentieth-century Latin American literary and intellectual production. I make this argument neither as an apology for nor a case for the recuperation of Gilberto Freyre. Rather, I do so in order to subsequently propose what I hope is a more effective approach to reading *Casa-grande e senzala*. By "effective" I mean that I would like to take account of the discursive force that it exerted at its historical moment of enunciation, and confront that force with whatever potential *Casa-grande e senzala* may exhibit for speaking to us today, if it can do so at all. I do not propose this contextualized reassessment of the racism and sexism of *Casa-grande e senzala* in the name of cordoning it off, sanitizing it, or pacifying it in order to show how far we have progressed in our contemporary ideas on race and other matters. Rather, I am interested in a more open, and less reductive, reading of *Casa-grande e senzala* (less reductive, that is, than the standard references to the text that dot the contemporary critical landscape), because I think it is worth allowing it to speak to us anew. Why? Because Freyre's most audacious challenge is that which has faced many writers since 1933, and which still poses an epistemological and conceptual problem today: the construction of a (trans)national identity without resorting to the language and science of race. He will fail in this attempt. Is his failure indicative of a larger failure of hybridity, one that speaks to the current impasse in theorizing hybridity that I sketched in chapter 1? I think that it is, and this is why I bother with attempting to draw forth his innovations alongside his many shortcomings. These themes—after chapter 8's introduction to the confluence of race, gender, family, and nation in Latin America—round out chapters 9 and 10. Ultimately, the central claim will be that Freyre's deployment of hybridity in *Casa-grande e senzala* does not move toward the construction of a convivial racial democracy, but rather toward a naturalization of the eugenic discourse embedded within colonial plutocracy.

Second, Part III attempts to trace the unfolding of Freyre's inflection of hybridity through a careful reading of the dynamics of gender, race, reproduction, and colonial historiography as they interact in *Casagrande e senzala*. In order to enable my interpretation of and dialogue with Freyre on these themes, I will interpolate two texts into the conversation: Silviano Santiago's famous essay "O Entre-lugar do Discurso Latino-americano" (1971) and José de Alencar's Romantic classic *Iracema* (1865). These texts help me consider the organizing problem of this book—that is, the relations between the coloniality of power and contemporary theories of hybridity—within the specific context of Brazil. I am not interested in the ways in which these texts relay a concept of mixture that I am generalizing as "hybridity," the one to the other. Rather, I am interested in how the discourse of hybridity helps them navigate the dialectics of repetition and differentiation that mediate their respective treatments of race, gender, reproduction, and nation, as they each ultimately construct a naturalized, and *essentially* critical, space called "Brazil."

8. The Brazilian Family

Let us begin with an unextravagant premise: the territory that defines
the nation-space—whether imagined by a community of readers, a
classroom of students, or a national viewing audience—is often metaphorically represented as a woman. Indeed, this feminization of space
is codified as such even when future nations are still being dreamed up,
materialized in a thousand images of (neo)colonial invitation, conquest,
penetration, and rescue. The America that beckons a nervous Vespucci
in the famous Galle engraving is a cannibalistic naked woman. The
Cuba of 1898 that hails Uncle Sam in numerous North American political cartoons is a damsel in distress. The ongoing U.S.-led military
operation that is framed as reintegrating Afghanistan into the family
of nations gains moral force by representing itself as the "liberation"
of veiled women. When Oswald de Andrade updates the nation-space,
at once satirizing the conquest and formulating a project of modernist
recuperation, he rewrites Pero Vaz de Caminha's indigenous maidens as
"Train Station Girls" ("As meninas da gare"): "They were three or four
young ladies, very ladylike and very elegant / With very black hair down
to their shoulders / And their shame so high and so insatiable / That to
look closely upon them we had no shame" (Andrade 1922, 69–70).[1]

This masculine gaze that equates space with woman is of course well
known, indeed, a discursive constant in Western culture (Jardine 1985,

24–25).[2] The transformation of a desirable, objectified territory into the patriarchy of *patria*, however, requires a recodification of masculine privilege that moves beyond the descriptive conquests that serve as the companions to imperial projects; that is, the conversion of *conquered territory* into *sovereign nation* must transcend mere "seduction" and embark upon the institutionalization and regulation of procreation. As Étienne Balibar has pointed out, the ideal of racial community and the "naturalization of belonging" produce national essence insofar as it is consistently represented in its "'normal' or 'natural'" state as "one big family" (Balibar and Wallerstein 1988, 96, 100).

It is at the naturalization of this big national family, through narratives that assert and reassert the production and reproduction of normative family units, that discourses of gender, sexuality, and race articulate with considerable intensity. Race, of course, has always been formulated alongside and within the biopolitics of sexual reproduction: its regulation, its proliferation, its restrictions, and its social implications. The historical construction of race relations is inseparable from the construction of gender relations. The relationship between racism and sexism, then, is not one of analogy, but rather of mutual dependency. It turns around and through a matrix of heterosexual reproduction, and rests on the discursive formation and material deployment of what Abdul JanMohamed has called a "racialized sexuality" (1992, 94).[3] Gilles Deleuze and Félix Guattari put it quite succinctly when they declare that "bastard and mixed-blood are the true names of race," positing that race only emerges as "the impurity conferred upon [a minority group] by a system of domination" (1980, 379). However, as in the exemplary case of Mexico, many of the nation-states that constitute Latin America alter Deleuze and Guattari's statement on impurities. As *pueblos mestizos*, the "mixed-blood" figure, as we saw earlier, is reconverted into the normative embodiment of the nation, with the objectified "pure" other—*el indio, el negro*—occupying the space of immediate or potential scandal: the "pure" becomes stagnant or even degenerate, to be uplifted through its contamination by the other. In its most explicitly racialized form, this discourse is often summarized as "whitening" *(emblanquecimento, blanqueamiento)*. Many Latin American narratives of *forjando patria*, then, construct a normative national family that presupposes a timeless foundation in interracial romance. Latin American racial-national normalization does not always rest on theories and practices of *explicit* segregation that resist, at all costs, the production of "bastard and mixed-blood." Rather, that normalizing process draws on the discursive and material regulation of the sexual equation through which *mestizaje* is effected. In short, national narratives that assert a family normativity are often interracial romances built around a confluence of specifically performed genders and races effected through the continuation of colonial relations of power. Ever since Cortés and Malintzín, the foundational romance of Latin America has been represented as the consummation of passions that both constitute and correspond to specifically racialized and gendered coordinates of desire: masculine Europe and feminine America.[4]

The iterative and regular quality of this racialized configuration of the colonial family shows up throughout Western colonial discourse, but is especially diffuse in Latin America, running from the early colonial Iberian endorsements of marriage between conquistadors and indigenous women to today's *telenovelas* that so often represent love stories between a white aristocrat (male) and a brown peasant (female). It is not insignificant, in this regard, that the erotics between the white, male, speaking subject and the "train station girls" in Oswald's poem are reiterated—ironically, to be sure—at a moment when a surge of triumphalist modernism was claiming the cultural rediscovery of Brazil: the "we" *(nós)* of Oswald denotes a nationalized, masculine subject (we Brazilians) that replaces the conquering "we" of Caminha (we Portuguese).

More striking, however, are the evasions that surround the "other" relationships, those between white women and black or brown men. The many tables, charts, and illustrations of race mixture that constituted the architecture of the obsessive *régimen de castas* of the late-colonial period in Spanish America provide a nomenclature of race mixing between blacks, whites, and Indians that can surpass two dozen designations. While *blancos* or *españoles* (white men) proliferate and miscegenate with *indias, negras,* and so on, *blancas* or *españolas* (white women) rarely appear on the chart at all. When they do, they are paired with "mestizos," *mulatos,* or *castizos,* but never *negros* or *indios.*[5] The famous poem by Nicolás Guillén "El abuelo" (1934), whose form replicates the classic, courtly homage to an expected pure, Eurocentric, feminine beauty, catches the reader in a surprise ending that reveals "the sweet dark shadow of the grandfather who flees / the one who forever curled your golden hair" (1979, 68). Guillén seems to suggest that the African male, having through his very appearance destabilized the racialized norms of both colonial courtship and courtly poetry, is left with only one alternative: flight, *al monte*, to the nation's margins.

This discursive struggle to fix—and to problematize—the coordinates of race, gender, and sexual reproduction within the paradigm of the national family is always, of course, largely ineffectual if we take as our standard the sexual practices of everyday life. The national family is a normative discourse of prescription and proscription, constantly beset by the open secret that the massive (forced) migration of labor and (primitive) accumulation of resources that accompanies projects of colonization and modernization brings women and men of all races and cultures into intimate contact with each other.[6] The interesting point for a study of Latin American literatures and cultures, then, is not to "expose" the normalizing, discursive formations of nation, race, gender, and sexuality as a kind of lie. Rather, it is to ask after the strategies through which those formations are not only maintained, but succeed in converting the normative discourse of the national family into a self-evident, naturalized configuration of social relations. One of those strategies is the theorization of hybridity.

Thus far I have merely suggested some of the ways in which hybridity is bound up with discourses on gender and sexuality. Although theories of hybridity respond to many social and cultural themes, they emerge, as we saw in Part I, as a specific mode of both naming and producing the concept of interracial reproduction. My interest now is to determine the ways in which the stereotypical relation of colonial power and reproduction that I have been outlining is reified as a sign of national identity. In other words, my object of analysis is the representational process through which a multiplicity of racialized and gendered coordinates—or, a heterogeneity of hybridities—is transformed into and reified as a single, normative discourse that couples white men to brown women. Through what representational strategies does this colonial configuration become naturalized as *the* national narrative of hybridity? Empirical questions of "who was really having sex with whom," though not unimportant, are not something that I can address in this endeavor. This is not to evade the social and material implications of the national family; it is simply to acknowledge the analytical limits of this book. The material referents of the statements and enunciations that form the normative discourse of the national family must be inferred by analyzing what a set of textual narratives permit and prohibit, what they claim and deny, where they speak and where they remain silent. Thus my critique is directed toward the means by which one particular representational norm—racialized, gendered, heterosexualized—among many at once produces and enters into a discourse of nationness.

The national text that centers my reading is Freyre's *Casa-grande e senzala*. Brazil and Freyre are obvious choices for thinking about hybridity's relationship to the discursive confluence of race, nation, and gender. Brazil is exemplary because of what is often stereotypically perceived as its exceptional qualities of tolerance, fluidity, and openness around issues of racial and sexual relations (e.g., Candido 1951, 293). Freyre is a key figure in the popularization of that image. Not only was he a public intellectual of the first order, but he was also very public about his sexual appetites, namely, his fetish for *mulata* women and his bisexuality, both of which he would inscribe as identifying marks of Brazilianness.[7] Nevertheless, it is precisely the effective promulgation of these stereotypes of "racial democracy" and "sexual anarchy," often associated with Freyre's work, that make his vision of Brazil a compelling case study of the coloniality of power that underwrites national theories of hybridity. I will not attempt to prove these democratic and anarchic images as somehow "false." Rather, I am interested in pursuing the power relations that both persist within, and enable their very conceptualization. In short, I will attempt to problematize the critical limits of the self-evident, national hybridity that Freyre meticulously constructs in *Casa-grande e senzala*. The ultimate expression of those critical limits is its reification of a normative discourse of national family that is at once racialized and gendered.

The protagonists of this national family, progenitors of a mestizo nation, are normalized through constructions of a masculinized whiteness and a feminized brownness. This configuration goes hand in hand with European colonialism in general. It is often received as an uncritical assumption, even appearing in the work of Frantz Fanon as an "unproblematical given," as Robert Young puts it (1995, 202). Young himself, however, in his brilliant discussion of hybridity and race in *Colonial Desire* (1995), seems to reaffirm the self-evidence of this configuration by lending comparatively little consideration to the fanatical treatment of the inverse relationship—brown men, white women—that recurs throughout colonial discourse and race science. Young thus misses a key nuance in an otherwise sharp reading of Gobineau's nineteenth-century

treatise on racial hierarchy. His objective is to trace the logic of hybridity's ambivalence, whereby Gobineau "articulates a horror of racial mixing while at the same time proposing the sexual desire of the white races
for the brown and the yellow as the basis of civilization itself" (115).
Young then concludes that Gobineau posits that "the same *mélange* of
races [that produces cultural advances] also brings about the decay of
civilization" (112). But it is precisely not the same. For Gobineau, as
Young shows, the engine of productive hybridity stems from the explicitly gendered desire of the male of "strong races" (Europeans) to "mix"
with the females of "weak races" (colonized peoples). Only at the reversal of this equation does decadence become a problem: "the children of
a *mulatto and white woman* . . . cannot really understand anything better
than a hybrid [for Gobineau: mixed, artificial, unproductive] culture"
(Gobineau [1853], cited in Young 1995, 114; my emphasis). The horror
of racial mixing, for Gobineau and many race theorists, turns out to
be a specifically gendered horror, as degenerate hybridity is specifically
denoted as the product of brown *men* and white *women*.[8]

   This articulation of race and gender at the site of hybridity estab-
lishes the horizons of representation out of which will coalesce the normative discourse of the national family. That discourse unfolds through
a kind of race-relations dialectic of mediation and containment that derives from the nation's colonial conditions of possibility. The violence
inherent to colonial discourse is often "softened" through the presence
of a mediating figure. That figure tends to be a woman. But not just any
woman: specifically, the mediation between colonizer and colonized,
and between precolonial, colonial, and postcolonial society, is embodied
by a woman of the colonized culture (Franco 1992). This sublimation
of woman as mediator within colonial discourse is well known, thanks
mainly to the post-Lévi-Straussian interventions on the part of numerous feminist critics.[9] But, unlike the "traffic in women" that Lévi-
Strauss identified through his studies on the structures of primitive kinship, and that Gayle Rubin famously revised, the national family model
that I will be working with here does not move toward anything along
the lines of "cementing the bonds of men with men" (Sedgwick 1985,
25). Rather, it strives to cement the unequal power relations of one class
of men on a constellation of racialized and gendered others.

   Thus enters mediation's dialectical opposite: containment. Two key
objects of that containment are apparent in the normative discourse of
the national family. First is the potentially transgressive agency of the

gendered other—the white, or colonizing, woman—whose exchange value within a patriarchal system is carefully regulated along race and class lines, and whose role within the discourse of *national* family is often limited. Second, and more important for my analysis, is the masculinity of the racialized other—the brown, or colonized, man—which is ascribed no space within the normative discourse of national family at all. More specifically, the masculine, colonized other is discursively stripped of any procreative agency; the masculinity of the colonized other is effaced from the nation space. Although my analysis here is limited to the discursive, that discourse was often carried out in slavocratic Brazil through very material practices: in *Casa-grande e senzala*, Freyre notes that it was common for slaves accused of engaging in sexual relations with their white mistresses to be castrated before being executed.

I will attempt to complicate the blunt, color-coded schematicism of this nationalist model (the white male's intercourse with brown women at the expense of white women and brown men) as I move into the texts themselves, but it is the general structure from which my analysis embarks. Moreover, it signals two points that will be important for my reading of hybridity as it is deployed in *Casa-grande e senzala*. First, all of the identifying coordinates of the normative national family circulate in relation to the classical subject of colonial discourse, that is, the European (or Eurocentric), white, colonizing (or settled) male. This is the subject position from which Freyre speaks, and, although he will modify it in sometimes interesting ways, it is the position of colonial privilege that his narrative strives to naturalize.

Second, the discursive companion in this endeavor—that is, in the normalization of a national family—is not the *other* group of men as in the "traffic in women" theory, but rather the colonized woman. In other words, in the specifically Latin American discourse of the national family, the symbolic colonized woman, though exploited and victimized, can still (even as a potential threat: a witch, a cannibal) play a heroically (re)productive role. To be sure, she is commodified as a natural resource to be harvested and exchanged. Nevertheless, she often occupies a productive position, *within the normative discourse of national family*, as one who decides. More than a mere vessel, she is repetitively interpellated as a *subject* within narratives of hybridity. She is a "subject" in both senses: insofar as she is subjectified as an agent, and insofar as she is subjugated by a system of patriarchy. To posit the colonized woman as a subject within hybridological discourse is not the same as framing the colonial project as some kind of rescue mission that subjectifies formerly abject women. It is, in fact, something like the opposite. It is to question the discursive function of the symbolic centrality of *woman* for the production of a normalized national family that reflects not some sort of objective reality, but rather the reification and naturalization of particular power relations.

Theories of hybridity are theories of (re)production. As Gayatri Spivak has wisely concluded, the fact of childbirth obligates the reader to consider the implications of reading women and the domestic as sites of social and economic production. Brazil, in many ways, makes an obvious case study for the confluence of racism and reproduction. Brazil's first tentative steps toward abolition, after all, were articulated around the Law of the Free Womb.[10] In narratives of hybridity, woman *always* figures as a site of (re)production. It is with the production of children— slave children, free children, *national* children—that the situation of colonized women enters nationalist discourse, recodified as partners in a liberating marriage, as opposed to victims of an ethnocidal violation. In chapter 10's analysis of Freyre's rewriting of José de Alencar's novel of national foundations, *Iracema* (1865), I will show one of the ways that this discursive trajectory has played out in Brazil.

To reiterate: the problematic task for hybridity as it emerges through the normalization of the national family is how to contain the masculinity of the racialized other, and how to regulate the sexuality of the gendered other. This is one of the problems that *Casa-grande e senzala* addresses, and through which it emerges as a thorough, profound, and influential articulation of the Brazilian inflection of hybridity. Moreover, it is at this site of discursive production that it readily displays the necessary relationship between gender and race. How does Freyre accomplish this nationalist reconversion of colonial hybridity? How does *Casa-grande e senzala* seize upon hybridity and recodify its status within the articulation of the coloniality of power to national discourse? The text weaves a deceptively complex, and even contradictory narrative, and hence the answers to these questions are multiple. However, I will assert up front that Freyre's articulation of hybridity is not *merely* a nostalgic lament for, and reformulation of, colonial relations of power (though it is, in part, that). It is, moreover, both an appropriation of, and a critical reflection upon, the hybridity that mediates and regulates colonial and neocolonial constructions of race relations. Besides its redeployment of the normative discourse of national family, *Casa-grande e senzala* also blazes a political, critical, and analytical path for both the study of culture in general and the cultural singularity of Brazil (and Brazilian identity). Before examining it as a document that attests to the tenacity of the coloniality of power, let us take some time to ask how it operates equally importantly as a critical moment in the trajectory of Latin American nationalist intellectual production.

9. On the Myth of Racial Democracy

Gilberto Freyre probably exerted the most profound impact on Brazilian national identity of any public intellectual during the twentieth century.[1] He inspired generations of disciples and incited legions of critics, and holds the distinction of having effectively synthesized a set of emergent, yet still inchoate, ideas on "Brazilianness." His vast writings on questions of race, culture, family, history, national character, academic production, and interdisciplinarity were articulated so powerfully, and with such excellent timing, that much of his conceptual apparatus has moved into the realm of "myth." Contemporary critics recognize this fact nearly every time they mention "racial democracy," the concept most often associated with his work. This recognition happens through the near-automatic qualification of racial democracy with tags such as "myth of" or "ideology of," and the subsequent citation of Freyre as the author of the concept. This relegation (or sublimation) of Freyre to the role of mythmaker is a way of signaling all of the unsavory implications that accompany Brazilian racial democracy, and whose basic outlines were elegantly sketched in his monumental opus, *Casagrande e senzala*.

Although the critique of racial democracy is well honed, dating back at least to the early-1950s work of Guerreiro Ramos (Skidmore 1974, 282), there is a dangerous recoil that follows the constant association between racial democracy, myth, and Freyre. That recoil is an almost total disengagement in contemporary studies on Brazilian race relations with the objectified text from whence racial democracy allegedly emerges, *Casa-grande e senzala*.[2] Moreover, that disengagement is typically justified by quickly listing the empirical failures of what is essentially a literary text. It has simply become too easy to say, "That was the-myth-of-racial-democracy book," and move on.[3] There are good historical, analytical, and theoretical reasons for thinking about hybridity and race in Brazil through a return to Freyre's text itself, if nothing else than for the bare fact that it radically altered (which is not to say "improved") the dominant Brazilian discourse on race and national identity. The point that I want to make here is a delicate one, so let me be as clear as possible. I am not attempting to deny the general validity of the critique, insofar as it takes as its object the ways in which racial democracy coalesces as an ideology within Brazilian society, and how it serves as the often negated unconscious (precisely by being qualified as "myth") of what Michael Hanchard calls Brazil's "racial exceptionalism" (1994b; see also Fernandes 1965, 194–210). Rather, I am asking for a rereading of racial democracy as it emerges in the text *Casa-grande e senzala*. I am, then, attempting to take seriously the contested (and contestatory) nature of the text (in the broad, deconstructive sense) as a producer of meaning whose appropriation is an essentially political act (Mowitt 1992, 10; Bhabha 1994, 110). Ultimately, this rereading may have repercussions on how we think about the discursive construction and material transformation of the articulation of ideas of race and gender in Brazilian society over the past century.

Why is it important to think and write against this generalized critique? That is, why rethink the standard critical gesture that quickly glosses *Casa-grande e senzala* as the origin of the myth of racial democracy and then leaves the text itself to one side?

Briefly, I would argue that the constantly repeated qualification of racial democracy as "myth" has been a largely ineffective strategy against the tenacity of institutional racism in Brazil. The structural articulation of race and class in Brazilian society, in which nonwhites of all shades carry a grossly disproportionate burden of poverty-related maladies, has changed over the past century with the emergence of various affirmative-action policies, but only painstakingly and often with negligible social effect.[4] This is despite the fact that, as Hanchard points out, the refutation of the truth of racial democracy has been widely accepted "even [or especially] by white elites at the level of the state and in civil society" (1994b, 44), and that laws against "practicing racism" in Brazil have existed at least symbolically for several decades (Rodrigues 1995, 18; see also Htun 2004; and Hanchard 1994a).[5] Currently, national debates on race-based quotas in the university system and federal agencies, as well as on the media representation of blacks, are active and regularly reported. And even the sentimental racism, which Hanchard identifies as the "most damaging consequence" of racial democracy, seems to have been brought into the public consciousness. Although, for Hanchard, racial democracy produces "the inability of many Brazilian citizens to identify problems of race at all, and the lack of recognition that particular problems of racial discrimination, violence, and inequality exist in Brazil" (ibid., 47), a poll released subsequent to the Hanchard citation shows that 89 percent of Brazilians do in fact recognize racial discrimination as a problem in Brazil (Rodrigues 1995, 11). Again, however, this recognition of a pervasive "cordial racism" that persists as the taint of racial democracy has done little to overturn the material consequences of long-standing sentiments, practices, and institutions that produce race-specific marginalization (Htun 2004, 62, 84).

Within this context—where everybody recognizes the mythic nature of racial democracy, yet everybody still draws on the power of its discursive truth—the incessant reminder of the dangers of racial democracy by way of qualifying it as "myth" and/or "ideology" itself contains an element of risk. The risk is the way in which "myth," when issued as a skeptical qualification against a cultural norm (in this case, racial democracy), becomes a way of saying something like "not truth," and ideology something like "false consciousness." This connotation reduces racial democracy to a lie, something that should be punished by submitting it to its opposite, that is, "the truth." This approach, however, rests on a naive notion of the complex sociological and psychological workings of myth, which, as Roland Barthes has proposed, is not a "lie" at all, but rather a kind of representational "inflexion" that works by converting "history into nature" (1957, 129). Given that myths are the very elements through which we construct a multiplicity of social "truths" (e.g., free labor, survival of the fittest, universal rights, equality before the law), and given that ideology, as the old saying goes, has no outside, it is unsurprising that the reduction to "myth" has made less headway than one might hope against the materiality of racism in Brazil. The task, then, is not—or not only—one of exposing the lie draped in truth, but rather one of *denaturalizing* history. Although Freyre has been rigorously read in the light of the former's logic of contradiction, the latter task has gone largely unpursued vis-à-vis his work; for the recognition of the material effects that accompany the inflective conversion that Barthes identifies as "myth" is precisely the point where the binaristic rhetorics of truth and lie yield to the more complex articulations and enunciations, often thriving within contradiction, of the Foucauldian notion of discourse (cf. Hasenbalg 1996, 237). In short, even though widely reduced to the category of "myth," Brazilian readers still readily see themselves within Freyre's text.[6]

The danger is that the constant critique of racial democracy that hinges on calling it a "myth" ends up participating, by surprise, in the very same "exceptionalism" that secures Brazil's identification as a relatively harmonious space of race relations. It does so by turning racial democracy into the example against which that exceptionalism rests. Racial democracy becomes the example of Brazil's delusions of racial paradise, and Freyre the exemplary author of that exemplification. Via the cunning "logic of the example," that exemplary status itself becomes exceptional: such a blindingly clear example that other beneficiaries from the system of "cordial racism," which racial democracy obscures, find their own participation in that system mitigated.[7] Racial democracy becomes a mistake ascribed to the past, from which we (Brazilians and/or students of Brazilian culture) learned, and which we now recognize as mere mythmaking, a project in which we no longer participate. It thus becomes very easy for individuals belonging to the sector that Hanchard calls the "white elites" to recognize past errors and contemporary problems, and then go about their business in a racist social structure—no longer democratic, but still comparatively exceptional—in which the vast majority of material benefits accrue to their subject position. As Hayden White puts it, "[t]he unmasking of . . . myths . . . has not always been followed by the banishment of their component concepts, but rather their interiorization" (1978, 153). The reduction to myth, then, becomes a tired simplification of what amounts to Freyre's singular participation in a much more complex Brazilian discourse of race. As part of a discourse—which readily accepts contradictory rhetorics, languages, practices, and modes of representation, from myth to science—Freyre's text is not based on a simple set of assertions that can be effectively combated by being empirically disproved (which they have been, methodically).[8] Rather, the discursive power of, and continued popular

fascination with, *Casa-grande e senzala*, radiate from its profound contradictions: that is, its fundamental ambivalence.[9] Taken seriously, it is
thus a difficult text to convincingly "refute." A better approach, in my
view, would be to read not for empirical errors that can be refuted, but
rather with an attentiveness to the strategies of political and social reification and naturalization that emerge out of its discursive operations.

The task at hand, then, before moving into a more thorough critique
of hybridity as it is theorized by Freyre, is to account for racial democracy as it emerges in *Casa-grande e senzala*. A striking fact that a careful
perusal of the text yields is the surprise that racial democracy does not
emerge at all; that is, although Freyre makes two or three comments on
the "democratic" aspects of Brazilian society (more common descrip-
tors include "patriarchal," "aristocratic," "authoritarian," "anarchistic,"
and "sadomasochistic"), nowhere in the text does he explicitly announce
Brazil's status as a *"racial* democracy." Let me immediately acknowledge
the banality of this point, and its general irrelevance for a discourse
analysis. Before prosecuting my critique on grounds of the absence of
the actual word, I could just as quickly disqualify my own framework of
"hybridity" by holding it to the same standard: hybridity too, after a notable appearance in the title of the first chapter of *Casa-grande e senzala*,
only reappears in the text through other codes. At the same time, even
in its banality the absence of the words "a democracia racial" is suggestive; for it is precisely this absence that incites the reconsideration of
the constant relation drawn between racial democracy and *Casa-grande
e senzala*. What will be found upon thinking through that relationship
is that Freyre's text and the orthodox critique of it do not exactly line
up. What I am suggesting is that a responsible reading of *Casa-grande e
senzala* requires the work of thinking against its dominant opposition.

If Freyre, in 1933, was not yet specifically talking about racial democracy, it would be helpful to ask what racial democracy means at all, especially in relation to *Casa-grande e senzala*. The first thing that one must
note is that racial democracy is not really about "democracy" in any
kind of systemic political sense. What critics mean by racial democracy
as used in the context of Brazilian race politics has flourished under
regimes of monarchy and dictatorship, and does not imply anything like
the institutionalization of "rule by the people," free elections of political representatives, collective bargaining between various constituencies,
or equal access—racial or otherwise—to the benefits of an economic or

juridical system. It is not, in short, a democracy in the socialist sense of the word (see Fernandes 1965, 204–5). Rather, racial democracy is very much a liberal concept, and tends to be invoked sentimentally, as a kind of *feeling* that ostensibly translates into positive institutional and material effects. As Hanchard puts it succinctly, it is the perception "of racial equality in a society where there [is] none" (1994b, 32). In this sense, Hanchard continues, it operates discursively along lines similar to the "American exceptionalism" that imagines a society free of class consciousness (174). Racial democracy therefore implies the notion of a heterogeneous population that interacts within a mobile civil society that throws up no, or at least few, segregating, institutional barriers against interracial social intercourse (Fernandes 1965, 199).

Underscoring the sentimental anchor that grounds this alleged socio-racial flexibility, critics often sum up racial democracy by deferring to the *tolerance* that is supposed to define Brazilian race relations (Candido 1951, 293; Fernandes 1965, 194; Hanchard 1994b, 32; Marx 1998, 167). This tolerance, in turn, has been linked to a specific colonial history, the (now entirely debunked) idea that there was something essential about what Freyre would call the "Portuguese type" that lent a "more humane" element to Portugal's global expansion and practices of slavery (Hanchard 1994b, 44; Fernandes 1965, 197)—more humane, that is, than the colonialism and slavery of the English, Dutch, French, and Spanish. *Tolerant* thereby becomes synonymous with not only *humane*, but semantically proliferates into *friendly* and *respectful* (Marx 1998, 30). This historical construction of a "friendly" colonialism has contemporary implications. Thus Hanchard, on Brazil's belated 1888 abolition: "[Twentieth-century] [e]lites justified the long delay in unchaining the enslaved [by arguing] that Brazilian slavery was actually less harsh than the working conditions of [European] peasants and wage laborers . . . and that slaves were actually spared the horrors of savage Africa by being transported to the more civilized and enlightened Brazil. This justification, buttressed by purported cultural differences between Portuguese and other European civilizations underpinned the now well-known myth of racial democracy (Freyre 1946 *[Casa-grande e senzala]*)" (1994a, 171).

Even though they were slave drivers and even though slavery was "bad," the Portuguese talent for intercultural relations, according to elite nationalist dogma, led to a colonial system that was "less bad" than elsewhere. In a word, the Portuguese were *tolerant* of cultural difference, and this led to a different kind of colonialism, premised on paternalistic incorporation rather than exclusionary exploitation. The tolerance thesis is the essence of the historical misrepresentation that undergirds the myth of racial democracy; for in fact, Portuguese colonialism was anything but tolerant, if by that is meant less exploitative and genocidal than other colonialisms.[10]

Almost all of these points can be cobbled together from *Casa-grande e senzala*. Freyre bluntly states that the Portuguese was "the European colonizer who best succeeded in fraternizing with the so-called inferior races . . . [and] the least cruel in his relations with his slaves" (189/185).[11] What is interesting about Freyre's rhetoric, however, is that in that very same passage he replaces, without ironic intent, "Portuguese" with "terrible slave-driver *[escravocrata terrível]*" and notes the genocidal inhumanity of the slave trade (ibid.). For the bulk of Freyre's critics, the racism of a racial democracy that argues for the "tolerance" of Portuguese colonialism is that it denies the material exploitation of their colonized and enslaved others, and constructs a world of colonial conviviality.[12] But this is not the "tolerance," nor the racism, of *Casa-grande e senzala*. For Freyre, tolerance does not morph into conviviality, equality, or even interracial friendliness. Besides "terrible slave-driver," the other key word in the just-cited passage is "fraternize *[confraternizou]*": by that, Freyre means to say "engage in sexual relations with" (cf. 1946, xxix). The "tolerance" that appears throughout *Casa-grande e senzala* is one of the ways that he refers to what he often calls the "miscibility" *(miscibilidade)* of the Portuguese: the fact that their particular national history had left them, as it were, ready to miscegenate (1933, 250). Not a tolerance that implies respect and equality, Freyre's Portuguese colonizer and slave driver exhibits a "tolerance" for intimate domestic and sexual relations with *his* colonized other. This sexuality—gendered and racialized—is the essence of the Luso-Brazilian exceptionalism that Freyre constructs, here for Brazil, expanded in later work as applicable for the entirety of the Portuguese empire (in America, Africa, and Asia). Tolerance, then, in *Casa-grande e senzala*, becomes synonymous with voracity: the willingness to *consume* just about anything (or better, anyone).[13]

The racism of *Casa-grande e senzala*, then, does not work in the direction that Freyre's critics almost universally propose, that is, through a rhetoric of tolerance that is synonymous with a racial democracy that hides exploitation. Rather, and this is a substantive distinction, the racism of *Casa-grande e senzala* is the *naturalization* of that exploitation: not a case for democracy, but a discourse that makes colonial hierarchy and plutocracy so obvious and deterministic as to appear inevitable. What emerges is a plutocratic hierarchy that spins into a normative discourse of national family that naturalizes colonial (sexual) relations along specifically gendered and racialized lines. And the naturalization of that hierarchy is not a discourse of democratic, procreative "freedom." Despite his insistence to the contrary (196), it is in fact a discourse of eugenics: "There is, in short, [in the Portuguese colonial state] a great *tolerance* for any sort of union that results in the increase of the population" (246/254; my emphasis), by which he means to say a "tolerance" for (i.e., policy of) genetically (and generatively) expanding the empire. In the colonial Brazil that Freyre constructs as his national unconscious, however, as I will show (in chapter 10), this "any sort of union" becomes a eugenic sort of union, ossified along specifically colonial, racialized, and gendered coordinates.

One of the most striking aspects of *Casa-grande e senzala* that emerges within and against its naturalizing discourse is Freyre's nearly constant, and often quite devastating, moral critique of both the Portuguese colonial project and the genocidal practices of the individual Portuguese colonizer, missionary, and slave owner. The gloss that Freyre is often accused of placing on Brazil's history of racial conflict is a reading that the text itself—including illustrations of the torture of black slaves—goes great lengths to resist. This "other side" of Freyre's treatment of Brazilian history is rarely admitted into the discussion. Upon reading *Casa-grande e senzala* against its contemporary critics, one gets the feeling that half of the work is being forgotten. This, I argue, attests to the profound ambivalence that undergirds theories of hybridity, and—as a discourse reducible to a theory of hybridity—Freyre's *mestiçagem*. It is a hybridological discourse that, like colonial discourse as theorized by Bhabha, moves simultaneously in two directions. On the one hand, it moves toward closure, realized through his frequent self-congratulatory statements on Brazil's creation of the first "modern society formed in the tropics with national characteristics and qualities of permanence" (12/17), by which he basically means the allegedly precocious implementation of settler colonialism, and the *mestiçagem* that emerged out of it.[14] Underneath this nationalist gesture that conflates the "success story" of colonization with national essence, Freyre is much more ambivalent, both in his treatment of the racialized heterogeneity of colonized subjects and of the colonial project as such. In fact, embedded within his famous theme of "resolving antagonisms," which I will consider momentarily, is the persistent frustration and contradiction of an unresolvable dialectic of love and hate, attraction and repulsion, the very definition of classical ambivalence (Freud 1913, 830).

Chapter 10 is dedicated to Freyre's ambivalence toward the colonized other, but I want to linger for a moment here on the contradictory moves that systematically structure the narrative organization of *Casa-grande e senzala*. Far from an unselfconscious embrace of colonialism as ultimately "good," Freyre in fact couches nearly every "positive" element of the colonial project in a recognition of the fundamental decadence and inhumanity that that project represents. Thus, many of the myths—or better, dubious representations—are there, implying the colonial invasion of Brazil as the establishment of an agrarian economy whose dependency on slavery was comparatively less cruel than elsewhere, with well-fed slaves and a permeable family structure that constituted an interracial, paternalistic system of social relations. Yet at every turn we find him desecrating this idyllic pastoral. Jesuit priests are interpreted as having "contributed greatly to the degradation of the [indigenous] race it was supposed to save" (154/174), and the portrait that emerges of the Brazilian slave owner is that of a sadist who, as a child, had "them pull out the teeth of the Negro [playmate] who had stolen his sugar-cane" (51/76), and as an adult "vented furious passions upon [his] victims" (50/75). Structuring his rhetoric, then, is a kind of tension that always goes unresolved. Even the literal closure of the book resists resolution. In the second of two chapters dedicated to "the negro slave," the protagonists of his drama of national foundations, Freyre has just furnished historical evidence for his proposal that the African slave "gave to household life in Brazil its cheerful note" (462/472). This thesis on the allegedly happy slave, however, is immediately undercut by an entire catalog of the hardships of slave life that provoked a high level of suicides, depression, and madness (464). And as if to signal the corrosive effects at the very heart of the system, Freyre ends the five-hundred-page work with a list of diseases suffered disproportionately by the slaves. The literal last word in the book is claimed by neither a summary nor a celebration, but by a quote from a nineteenth-century public-health report on slaves in Rio de Janeiro: "Worms, especially the tapeworm and lumbricoid roundworms, are to be found in great abundance" (464/475). The end. It is as if the unresolvable dialectic of discursive closure and disclosure that structures Bhabha's theory of colonial discourse (1994, 110) were here laid bare for all to see.[15]

But perhaps a question persists: *So what?* In other words, why does this nuance matter, if, after all, Freyre's text is still a highly problematic foundation for Brazilian race relations, and ultimately exemplifies the specificity of "Brazilian racism"? To this reasonable skepticism I would respond with another set of questions: What is it that we are trying to forget by writing off Freyre's dystopic digressions that weigh against his more famous nostalgic idealism, and that amount to roughly half of *Casa-grande e senzala*? Of what is this elision symptomatic? Is it merely an error, or is it in some way a motivated forgetfulness? I would suggest that it is, in fact, very much an *active* forgetting. As one representative example, witness that *against* Freyre's thesis that the nature of the Portuguese "type" led him to mix with his darker others, the normally careful Hanchard (1994b, 48–50) puts forth an entire list of deterministic factors (mate scarcity, political backwardness, economic underdevelopment) that, rather than contradict Freyre, in fact simply repeat and reaffirm many of his central theses.[16] The forgetting is active, then, in the sense that Freyre's own hesitations and misgivings that circulate around and through the discourse of tolerance that would later be called "racial democracy" that emerge from *Casa-grande e senzala* are systematically ignored by its critics. The text is then represented as a set of simple assertions that can be refuted, one after another. This contemporary othering of *Casa-grande e senzala* again exhibits something of the logic of the example. Within the racist system in which academic knowledge continues to be produced, *Casa-grande e senzala* becomes such a strong example of a peculiar Brazilian racism that it is converted into a kind of exception, a failed antiracism against which we can say, "Now we know better." Freyre is thus placed in quarantine, sanitized, and held up to the glare of the contemporary critique of race. In effect, his text is made safe, its ambivalence discarded, and its project univocal.

Safe: the impossibility of his project is delinked from the vertiginous impossibility of our own. What is that impossibility? I think it is the impasse at the heart of hybridity's ambivalence: the impossible desire to think a world without race. Although aporias are always daunting, it is worth remembering, with Derrida (1990), that their impossibility is also productive, and that their attempted passage (or, the undecidable decisions that they provoke) is the essence of effective critique. Freyre, steeped in enthusiasm for the Boasian critique of race in anthropology, seeks to erase race; that is, his motivation is to eliminate the category of *race* in favor of *culture*. He fails utterly in this attempt in that the more he strives to explain cultural specificity, the more he derives his authority from the scientific discourses of genre—taxonomy, typification, categorization, essentialization—that enable and underwrite race science. He thus arrives at all kinds of sophisms, such as his demand to think of the "Negro" not as essentially "Negro" but as "slave," but then immediately essentializes the "slave" as "Negro" (e.g., 315); or the thesis that Portuguese anti-Semitism was not racism, but religious fundamentalism, as if there were no relation between the two (e.g., 226).

Nevertheless, just as we today refute the liberal racism of Freyre's discourse, so did Freyre apply the same kind of refutation to his conservative opponents. What Freyre seemed to miss about race is the way in which race sticks to culture (Hall 1996a; Balibar and Wallerstein 1988; Gilroy 1992). What we seem to be missing about Freyre is the fact that the anthropological notion of culture that is still dominant today was on the cutting edge of antiracist discourse in 1933, and was thought to hold considerable promise as the necessary escape hatch from the essentialisms of the production of racial difference that enable racism. None of this mitigates the racism that persists—indeed, flourishes—within Freyre's culturalism. I am arguing, rather, that if Freyre is to be made an example of, we should do so at the risk of exposing his discourse to ours. To do so, I hope, means to take seriously the ways in which race sticks to culture, in which gender sticks to race, and in which all of these discourses so easily reintegrate in new configurations that naturalize old relations of power. What I am suggesting is the need for a more comprehensive treatment of *Casa-grande e senzala* as a document whose racism emerges from a desire for antiracism. Such a reading of *Casa-grande e senzala* should not forget the targets against which Freyre's critique was launched. Three are worth mentioning, not in the name of recuperation nor even approbation, but rather responsible reading.

First, against the Aryanist doctrine of whitening as Brazil's peculiar institution of civilizational development, Freyre made the case for a process of "darkening."[17] By turning race science and racist bias back on themselves, largely through a series of ingenious reversals, he effectively closed the door on the long trajectory of the fantastic discourse of a "white Brazil" (see esp. 294–97). His tendency is to argue that it was, in fact, the Europeans who had been improved in Brazil through miscegenation with their darker others.[18] Radicalizing the pioneering work of Roquette Pinto and Franz Boas, he made the long-disparaged African slave the protagonist in the evolution of Brazilian national culture, a minority position that he self-consciously acknowledged would be received as "extravagant" (284). He proposed that the slaves were the "real colonizers" of Brazil (he means this as a compliment, i.e., that they were the "strong" element), and that any "Europeanization" of the country was almost entirely disseminated by acculturated Africans (284).[19] He ranked the *senzala* alongside, and sometimes above, the *casa-grande* as exerting the greatest influence on Brazilian culture, effectively decentering the colonial project in a way that was ahead of its time.[20] He argued that the most dynamic of contributions to what would become the national culture were "donated" by the Africans. He asserted the cultural superiority—from literacy to diet to hygiene to artistic production—that the Africans often wielded over a rude confederacy of decadent landowners to whom a cruel historical irony had left them enslaved.[21] And finally, he asserted that the cultural openness that produced the success of the Portuguese colonial project stemmed from its own cultural status as a bridge between continents, a hybrid society, European in form but infused with centuries of contact with and domination by the Moors: Portugal essentially arose from "the cultural past of a people existing indeterminately between Europe and Africa and belonging uncompromisingly to neither one nor the other of the two continents . . . with the hot and oleous air of Africa mitigating the Germanic harshness of institutions and cultural forms, corrupting the doctrinal and moral rigidity of the medieval Church, drawing the bones from Christianity . . . , Latin . . . , and the very character of the people. It was Europe reigning without governing: it was Africa that governed" (5/5).[22] Portugal, in short, was prepared, at an essential level, to partner with the Africans who were already "in their blood" as it were. As colonizers, for all their civilizing attempts, the singular legacy that is attributable *exclusively* to the Portuguese efforts—that is, effected *against* as opposed to *with* their colonized others—was the "syphilization" of Brazil (47). This thesis, paired with other graphic interpretations of the sex lives of a colonial elite that was the genealogical origin of the contemporary national elite, created, in 1933, nothing short of a scandal.

None of this "valorization of the Negro," of course, is incommensurable with coloniality of power. Nor am I unaware of the stereotyping involved in Freyre's hierarchical flip-flop that, in many instances, ends with the African id suddenly—and unsurprisingly—dominating the European superego. I am simply trying to point out that what today appear as easy banalities were in 1933 some of the earliest systematic attempts to put a positive value on the African contributions to Brazilian culture. Whatever its motivation, it hit a nerve, even inciting threats against Freyre's life.

Second, both in and after *Casa-grande e senzala*, Freyre is not uncritical of real race relations—not just the fading rants of the aging Brazilian Aryanists—within Brazil itself. As is well known, with *Casa-grande e senzala* Freyre had made a case for Brazil as the first modern civilization in the tropics, a civilization whose highest achievement is having renegotiated a harsh legacy of slavery into one of the most dynamic and fluid frameworks of race relations to be found anywhere in the world, a truly multicultural and hybrid society that, moreover, recognized itself as such. This thesis had a strong appeal, not just for progressive Brazilians, but for progressive antiracists everywhere. The influence of Freyre's portrait of a relative race-relations success story was compelling enough to attract, in the early 1950s, a UNESCO group commissioned with studying how others might imitate Brazil's success (Wagley 1952, 14). Brazil, the studies went on to claim, has effectively abolished the problem of "race relations," subordinating them to more appropriate questions of "human and social values" (ibid.). Despite espousing a model that admirably articulated race and class (9), the limitations of these studies would be almost immediately called into question, and their optimistic socioracial panorama beset by systematic and anecdotal counterstudies showing that "the darker a Brazilian the more likely he was to be found at the bottom of the socio-economic scale by every indicator" (Skidmore 1974, 216). Ultimately, the UNESCO studies symbolize the end of the "racial democracy" that Charles Wagley (the director of the UNESCO group) so confidently proposes as Brazil's universally recognized trait (Wagley 1952, 7), and the beginning of its replacement by the "myth of racial democracy." By the early 1970s, Wagley himself would admit as much: "It is curious that although these UNESCO studies were motivated by showing a positive view of race relations in one part of the world (i.e. Brazil) from which it was thought that the rest of the world might learn something, they actually modified the world's view of race relations in Brazil" (cited in Skidmore 1974, 282).

The presumed father of racial democracy himself, however, was explicitly articulating the same line of critique years earlier. Indeed, one can find it in the pages of *Casa-grande e senzala*. It is important to remember that the racial democracy that Freyre is alleged to have popularized emerges from the cultural reciprocity that plays out between and around *Casa-grande e senzala*: between the big house and the slave barracks, between masters and slaves. In other words, Freyre reads the formation of modern Brazil through the explicitly material, economic, and social conditions of colonialism that define the origins of Brazilian civilization:

monoculturalist agrarian production, slavery, and, most important, the patriarchal authoritarianism of the extended family that traces the circuit between *casa-grande* and *senzala*. This is not an accidental framing on Freyre's part. Thus, although he often slides into a celebration of the idealized vision of contemporary Brazilian society, he is also self-critical, articulating many of the same conclusions that would later come as an unexpected disappointment to the UNESCO researchers (Skidmore 1974, 216). Five years before the UNESCO project, in a 1945 preface to the first English translation of *Casa-grande e senzala*, Freyre, though not retracting "the democratizing factors of a society that otherwise would have remained divided into two irreconcilable groups," extenuates those same factors by pointing to the symbolic rancor contained within the organizing "complex" of his work: "The two expressions that make up the title—the Portuguese *casa-grande* . . . and the African *senzala*—have here a symbolic intention, the purpose being to suggest a cultural antagonism and social distance between masters and slaves, whites and blacks, Europeans and Africans, as marked by the residence of each group in Brazil from the sixteenth to nineteenth century. An antagonism and a distance that conditioned the evolvement of the patriarchal-agrarian or, simply, the feudal complex in Portuguese America" (1946, xvi). This qualification is key for reading Freyre: tolerance, antagonism, domestic intimacy, and social distance are not mutually exclusive terms.

The third aspect of Freyre's critique that must be recognized is that its celebration of a multicultural national character is articulated at a historical moment when the West appeared increasingly dedicated to theories and practices of repressive segregationism and enforced purity. Against the institutionalized racism of the Jim Crow–era United States, and the rise of fascism in Europe, Freyre put forth a cultural model of national character that attempted to reject the dominant notions of racial purity by theorizing a biological desegregation as Brazil's origin. This move, especially against the United States, itself reveals an obviously affirmative, nationalistic gesture. This regional competition for political and cultural influence, however, is not of the same order as that which we saw with Vasconcelos. An important difference is the fact that Freyre's attitude toward the United States, as opposed to Vasconcelos's, is not consumed by hostility. He studied and taught there on multiple occasions and often credited many of his insights to his anthropological training at Columbia (alongside Ruth Benedict, Zora Neale Hurston, Robert Lowey, and Margaret Mead, among others), especially his early

1920s work under the tutelage of Franz Boas (xlvii).[23] And he drew on his travels in and knowledge of the American South as inspiration for his study on Brazilian society (xlvi–vii, 376), anticipating many of the revisionist regional models of analysis—Benítez-Rojo's "repeating island," Gilroy's "black Atlantic"—that have reemerged on the contemporary, postcolonial scene.[24]

Yet in spite of this cordial relationship with his neighbor to the north, there is a clearly ethical edge to Freyre's project that he explicitly invokes in the many comparisons *against* U.S. society. One of those comparisons is powerfully told in the publication of his diary entries, collected under the title *Tempo morto e outros tempos* (1975). In a 1919 passage from when he was studying at Baylor—he would have been eighteen or nineteen years old—he recounts the smell of burning flesh as he entered the small town of Waxahaxie, Texas. He was informed of its source: "'It's a nigger *[negro]* that the *boys* [English in original] just burned!' . . . I never thought that such horrors were possible today in the United States. But they are. Here they still lynch, kill and burn blacks. This wasn't an isolated case. It happened several times" (1975, 33).[25] Like many Brazilians, Freyre was baffled by the barbarism of the "land of the free," and was determined to write against its hypocrisy.

The Brazilian difference that Freyre held up against his hemispheric other was hybridity. Where the United States would segregate itself into a host of social problems, Brazil would mix, achieving what he perceives as the quintessential Brazilian trait: "The strength, or better, the potentiality of Brazilian culture appears to me to lie wholly in a wealth of balanced antagonisms *[antagonismos equilibrados]*" (335/348). The fulcrum of that balancing act, whose effects would ripple through all aspects of Brazilian culture and society, was interracial, sexual reproduction: *mestiçagem*. Again, Freyre is not only in dialogue with a foreign power on this point, but with Brazil itself. And although he was not, as we will see, anything like Brazil's first advocate of racial or cultural hybridity, his valorization of *mestiçagem* came at a time when the social ramifications of race mixing were still a topic of vigorous debate. In one of the many prefaces to *Casa-grande e senzala*, dated 1946, he remembers that decades earlier, as a student in New York, he had once "caught sight of a group of Brazilian seamen—mulattoes and *cafusos*—crossing the Brooklyn Bridge . . . [T]hey impressed me as being caricatures of men, and there came to mind a phrase from a book on Brazil written by an American traveler: 'the fearfully mongrel aspect of the population.'

That was the sort of thing to which miscegenation led."[26] As he puts it succinctly, "of all the problems confronting Brazil there was none that gave me so much anxiety as that of miscegenation" (1946, xxvi). The setting clarifies the national, and social class, stakes of this anxiety-provoking event: the apotheosis of modernity that is the Brooklyn Bridge, and the "caricatures of men" that seem to mock Brazil's entry into that modern world, condemning Freyre's class (note the social distance implied in "caught sight") to an eternity of backwardness.[27]

It is this mark of backwardness—*mestiçagem*—that Freyre helped transform into the symbol of Brazil's strength, the unifying essence that links its modern present to a prehistoric past, and that propels it into an exemplary future. Significantly, he did so without resorting to the whitening that helped to soothe the anxieties of the Brazilian elite, and that so impressed Teddy Roosevelt. The symbolic strength of Brazilian *mestiçagem* was that it embodied, for Freyre, Brazil's remarkable talent for "balancing antagonisms." *Mestiçagem*, then, represented the mediation, and Brazil itself embodied the productive, feminized, in-between space of the tense conflicts through which national identity would construct and reproduce itself: "Between the opposing mysticisms, that of Order and that of Liberty, that of Authority and that of Democracy, our political life after we had precociously emerged from the regime of master and slave has ever sought a balance. The truth is that the balance continues to lie between certain traditional and profound realities: sadists and masochists; masters and slaves; *letrados* and illiterates; individuals of a culture that is predominantly European and others whose culture is chiefly African and Amerindian" (52/77; translation altered). More important, Brazil's ability to negotiate these tensions, witnessed by its immeasurable racial diversity, provided Freyre with living evidence that he could show to a world in which theories and practices of segregation as social policy, and racial purity as national legitimacy, seemed to be on the rise, and whose proponents were not exactly rejected in Brazil.[28]

None of the foregoing review of the innovative and critical elements of *Casa-grande e senzala* is meant as an apology for Freyre. Rather, it is a way of framing a reading strategy on Freyre's most famous text; for it is precisely at his strongest and most important of moves, the transformation of hybridity from biopolitical deficit into a cultural asset, that Freyre's critical project is revealed as a decidedly *affirmative* critique of the legacies of colonial history. It is not that the history that he tells magically

On the Myth of Racial Democracy ◄ 157

becomes democratic. On the contrary, it is explicitly undemocratic: a forceful and authoritarian process consecrated through an originary invasion of a continent and governed by the subsequent foundation of a society of masters and slaves. The key move that Freyre makes, and hence the most direct point of critical dialogue with his work, is not to declare a racial democracy where there is none. His move, instead, is to *naturalize* and reify a nondemocratic power relation, rooted in colonialism, slavery, and genocide, as the normative organization of contemporary Brazilian social life. Brazil's negotiation of its antagonistic clashes through the production of *mestiçagem* at the uterine in-between space is at once Freyre's choice of critical strategy, his country's example to the world, the foundation of its exceptionalism, and the means by which he naturalizes a colonial, slavocratic past. His "valorization" of colonial others, which there is no textual evidence to suggest as insincere, also valorizes a discourse of eugenics in a new way. Thus, like Kant's affirmative criticism, Freyre submits his opponents—the Aryanists and race scientists—to a critique that never really destabilizes the disciplinary foundations through which both they and he construct the inclusive exclusion that maintains specific orders of privilege as a sign of Brazilian national identity. Although the racists are now "wrong," even after Freyre their position of privilege remains static, state-sponsored, and, ultimately, natural.[29] Dialectically, his theory of hybridity becomes the synthetic resolution that effects a racialized and gendered sublation, reconciling Brazil's colonial past, moving beyond it, and raising it up to the higher unity of a contemporary present. Freyre's triumph, like that of Vasconcelos, is to rewrite, both compellingly and forcefully, this narrative of national essence. Unlike Vasconcelos, Freyre's greater dexterity as a writer, and greater patience as a thinker, would help him in making the triumph of hybridity stick in a way that Vasconcelos could not: by endowing it with an eloquent scientificity.[30]

Writing between the muse and the scientific method—a self-acknowledged novelistic style backed up with an archive of historical documents and scientific references—Freyre weaves an old set of colonial truths into a new national narrative. This literary appeal is in part responsible for the continued popularity of *Casa-grande e senzala*.[31] The appeal has proven tenacious, even though most of the central "facts" of the work have since been proven false, including its basic organizing premise, the system of the extended patriarchal family.[32] They are "false," however, like literary narrative; or, for that matter, "false" like race. Not so much false, then, as fictive. In other words, his openly hybrid form that blends literary narrative technique with scientific claims is the ideal method for filling in the "prehistoric" (his term) blank of national origins, and a sometimes very real blanking out of history in general.[33] It is through this harmonious confluence of hybridity as both form and content that Freyre delivers the decisive blow against the race scientists, but he does so without radically upsetting the status quo. There are no drastic calls for racial reparations in *Casa-grande e senzala*, and certainly nothing approaching social revolution, or even justice. His ambivalence again becomes visible as he praises the 1835 slave uprising in Bahia as a legitimately "political" revolution, and then links that political legitimacy to the fear that would have stricken his slave-owning ancestors: "they did not commit robberies nor slay their masters secretly" (299). In this he is very much true to his class, whose stakes are nicely articulated by Anthony Marx: "Brazil had directly experienced this threat [to 'social order'] during its long history of slave revolts, more extensive than those in the United States. With a state and a culture fixated on the idea of unity and stability, it is not surprising that they chose to suppress [both the memory and reemergence of] such conflict" (1998, 165). Freyre's hybridity as antiracism, then, though not exactly "suppressing conflict," reaches its limits before promoting any revolutionary transformation of colonial race relations.

Most of the attention directed toward Freyre revolves around his often pathbreaking studies of Afro-Brazilian culture, and the sexual (and other) relations between (white) masters and (black) slaves. One of the passages that most clearly lends itself to his narrativization, nationalization, and naturalization of colonial relations, however, is his rewriting of the Edenic origins of Brazil's national family. It is this "national prehistory," more than any other, that calls for Freyre's skills as a storyteller. He characterizes this period as a timeless half century of haphazard, unsystematic proto-colonialism, "fora mesmo da civilização." This first meeting between Europeans and Indians on Brazilian soil, he asserts, while leaving the "vestiges of hereditary stigmata," has not left an adequate archive of historical documents (19).[34] It is here that Freyre's literary imagination most insistently fills in the historical gaps by drawing on anthropological discourse as the scientific method that, in its recording of cultural singularities, precisely speaks to the timelessness of humanity, its essential regularity that spans cultural differences. Let us turn our attention, then, to Freyre's narration of the "national pre-history": the early colonial society forged between Portuguese coloniz-ers and Brazil's indigenous communities. It is an extremely important gap for Freyre because it represents the origins of the heterosexual and interracial reproductive matrix that coalesces as his quintessential sign of the Brazilian nation.

10. The Iracema Effect in *Casa-grande e senzala*

Luso-tropical *mestiçagem,* for Gilberto Freyre, is the natural force that propels Brazil's critical hybridity. By "critical," I mean that it challenged, and opened avenues for rethinking, some of the dominant stereotypes of its time. Freyre's theory of hybridity rested on a rhetoric of racially coded sexuality that attempted to offer a Brazilian alternative to, and point to exits from, Western racism. How does Freyre invoke *mestiçagem* as the key to Brazil's national identity in *Casa-grande e senzala*? In attempting to answer this question, let us consider Freyre's deployment of race, gender, and sexual reproduction in his narration of national origins.

In so doing, I would like to introduce and discuss what I call the "Iracema effect" as it expresses itself in *Casa-grande e senzala*. By the Iracema effect, I mean the conversion of a foundational national romance—precisely José de Alencar's Romantic novel of national origins, *Iracema* (1865)—into another discursive order.[1] I ask: How, and to what ends, does *Casa-grande e senzala*—as a social-anthropological study of national foundations—rewrite, transform, and perhaps even transgress the discursive parameters of the classic, Brazilian indigenist novel? This is not a question of transparent "influence." In other words, I am not asking "How was Freyre influenced by the writers who preceded him?" For answers to that question, we could easily turn to Freyre himself, who writes widely on the topic.[2] The standard that governs my evaluation of *Casa-grande e senzala* is not its faithfulness to a perceived model, but rather its navigation of the tension between repetition and difference. Or, more precisely, I am interested in exploring the critical limits of the dialectics of repetition and differentiation within the context of Freyre's account of national origins.

This reading strategy is informed by the influential work of Silviano Santiago, but with a critical difference of my own. Let me first explain Santiago's position.

In an important 1971 essay, Santiago introduces his notion of the "space-in-between" *(o entre-lugar)*, which he proposes as the location of Latin American discursive production. The *entre-lugar* is the metaphorical, interstitial space that names the condition of inner exteriority of Latin America vis-à-vis the "universal culture" of Western Europe and the United States.[3] To arrive at this point, Santiago rearticulates and, to some extent, radicalizes Roland Barthes's theory of the *texte scriptible* by relocating it in the peripheral domain of what he calls "Latin American literature" (1971, 28). As I will show momentarily, he effects this move not so much through a transformation of Barthes's idea as through an emphasis on its radical potential. The implications of this gesture have been suggested by Malcolm McNee, who, in order to signal Santiago's eccentric appropriation of Barthes's concept, astutely deviates from Richard Miller's now standard English translation of *texte scriptible* as "writerly text." Instead, McNee renders the *texte scriptible*—or, for Santiago, the *texto escrevível*—more literally as a "writable text" (2001, 200). He thereby highlights the emphasis that Santiago's appropriation gives to the often ignored referential—and ultimately political—qualities of Barthes's theory.

In the widely cited exemplification of semiological practice, *S/Z* (1970), Barthes makes it clear that the "writerly text *[texte scriptible]* is not a thing" (1970, 5) but a conceptualization of action that provides "access to the magic of the signifier, to the pleasure of writing" (4), and, most important, to the polysemous and ambivalent qualities of all texts. The writerly text is the text decommodified, opened up to a complex process not unlike the Bakhtinian notion of hybridization that would reverberate in Bhabha's theory of hybridity.[4] Reading as such becomes a *productive*, not passive, activity. Reading is like writing; or better, reading becomes a *kind of* writing. Thus Barthes problematizes the reduction of reading to consumption, and the concomitant deification of writing.[5] "Writerly" names this dialectical conflation of reading/writing. All texts, then, in their objectified form ("works"), are readerly (Barthes names no writerly text, and in fact denies its very existence [4–5]); "writerly" is the method through which the reader-writer opens up the text's semantic multiplicity.[6] The act of (re)reading is inextricable from an act of (re)writing, a *productive* practice that seeks to "obtain . . . not the *real* text, but the plural text: the same and new" (16). All of this is well known, and can be summarized as nothing less than Barthes's stamp on poststructuralism.

As John Mowitt has indicated, a political project is embedded within Barthes's theory of the text: Barthes's pluralization "of the text . . . has less to do with some bland notion of multiple meanings, than with an empowerment that enables our constructions to be ceaselessly challenged— not merely contested at the level of conclusions, but subverted at the level of disciplinary legitimation . . . Through the concept of the text it may become possible to articulate in a fairly direct way the struggle over interpretation with the struggle to change the world of disciplinary power" (1992, 46).[7] With this reading of Barthes in mind, it is easy to understand the appeal of the writerly for a critic in Santiago's position. In 1971, the year that he introduced his theory of the *entre-lugar,* he formed part of a generation of Latin American writers that was explicitly attempting to extricate itself from a disciplinary model premised on the conflation of cultural and economic production, reducing both to questions of debt and dependency. That critical discourse, he asserts, "does not, in its essence, present any difference from neocolonialist discourse: both speak of deficit economies" (1971, 20). The actors that constitute these "economies" would be, to paraphrase Naipaul, forever destined to consume the inventions of a metropolitan center, or, at best, produce cheap copies for mass export. Barthes, by rethinking originality as a question of contingency, and interpretation as a question of political power, destabilizes this model, insisting instead on the more democratic "plurality of codes" that writing produces: "Only writing, by assuming the largest possible plural in its own task, can oppose without appeal to force the imperialism of each language" (1970, 206).

The move to the writerly, and the rejection of "force," is only a partial solution, however, as the brute, social fact of neocolonial imperialism remains. For Santiago, the very condition of neocolonial society is governed by an inescapable exportation of raw materials that *always* return as a particular kind of consumption: that of outdated products and outdated ideas (1971, 17). The neocolonial relations that govern Latin

American cultural production complicate any quick escape from the tyranny of the commodity, the thing, the work, the master text: it is the culture of the center that *produces* the cultural backwardness of the periphery.[8] Thus emerges a subtle, but crucial, difference in Santiago's rewriting of Barthes. Where Barthes aligns the digression of writerly reading with the slowness of decomposition (1970, 12–13), Santiago characterizes it as that which can *"accelerate* the process of expressing [the writer's] own experience" of (neo)colonialism (1971, 22; my emphasis). And it is here that Santiago's emphasis on the material remainder of the writable *is* a kind of opposition that, contrary to Barthes, does in fact "appeal to force" (Barthes, 1970, 206).[9] The theory of the writable text is thus appropriated and redeployed as an *act upon and against* a model text—a "real" text—a move that speaks to the cultural imbalance between center and periphery. For the Latin American writer, "To speak and to write mean: to speak against, to write against" (Santiago 1971, 19). In the hands of the Latin American writer, then, for whom the distant "classic text"—the work—is always at least slightly *fora de lugar,* writerly practice (reading as writing) is less precisely characterized as play than as vandalism. Santiago's *writable* text *(texte scriptible, texto escrevível)* reasserts the materiality of practice as praxis, an act of literally *writing on the text* (see esp. 22–23).

The writable text, in Santiago's version, is unambiguously commodified. Reading in the periphery—in "one culture dominated by another"—becomes "the search for a writable text, a text that incites [writers] to work and serves as a model for organizing their own writing" (22).[10] This "search," however, is not reducible to imitation, re-presentation, and innovation, but rather connotes a kind of appropriation, digestion, and differentiation. The Western tradition and legacy of great works is thus transformed, approached by the Latin American writer no longer as canon to be admired, but now as canvas to be painted upon, or, better, as a monumental wall that tempts the graffito. Through this practice of persistently writing upon and hence opening, decentering, and rewriting the master text, the situation of the Latin American writer becomes— like Freyre's Brazil—the *entre-lugar,* the space-in-between "prison and transgression" and between "submission and aggression" (28): not a docile practice of imitation, but amphibiously "in between" mere imitation and an aggressive, even transgressive, repetition with a difference.[11] "Duplication," which, for Santiago, is imposed on the colony as "the only valid rule of civilization" (17), becomes denaturalized, as Western culture in the periphery is submitted to a different kind of consumption, a practice of cannibalism (28).[12]

As evidence of this practice of differentiation, Santiago draws on two moments that, through his own critical sleight of hand, will become something like the same moment. One (which in the chronology of the essay is the second) is the emergence of a Latin American textual experimentality exemplified in two avant-garde narratives by Cortázar and Borges. This is not too surprising, as Borges and Cortázar are often cited as particularly good examples of the writerly tendencies in post–World War II Latin American fiction. The second moment is the very formation of America itself. Specifically, it is the emergence within Latin America, and especially Brazil, of a "sociedade mestiça" (17). How is this originary *mestiçagem* linked to Borges and Cortázar, two cosmopolitan writers associated with a nation (Argentina) whose fictive ethnicity is that of the "most European" (i.e., "least mestizo") of Latin America? For Santiago, it is through the critical practice common to both Borges's rewriting of the *Quixote* and the Brazilian Indian's historically partial, yet excessive, assimilation—sometimes too material, sometimes too symbolic—of European religious practices (14–15). Both Borges and the Indian suggest an imitation that slides into differentiation, a mimicry always in danger of converting into mockery.[13] As Bhabha puts it, "almost the same, but not quite . . . almost the same but not white" (1994, 86, 89).

Santiago's critical genealogy—from the Indians to Borges—is enabled by a historical gap. That gap marks, if not a contradiction, then a space for problematization in Santiago's essay. One of the stated goals of his critique is to articulate the referential play of the signifier with the *action* of reading, a practice that mirrors the work of cultural production and liberation (1971, 28). The writable text has the ability to incite us to participate in this task, by fomenting a writing praxis that throws up the system—writing itself—as an object of critique and potential transformation (23). This is what the *modernistas* understood so well, as they cannibalized their own colonial archive in exuberantly refashioning Brazilian cultural identity.[14] Writing becomes a reflection upon its own limits and conditions of possibility as they relate to the social, a potentially radical move in societies where access to writing is drastically uneven. However, Santiago precisely glosses his own prescription to work, and to take seriously the polysemy of the signifier, when he produces Latin America—or, more specifically, Brazil—as the fixed, essential, and naturalized in-between space of this writerly transgression. Brazil becomes, a priori, a naturally critical force, as opposed to a fiction, a made object, a discursive effect. This happens through the sublimation of *mestiçagem*—embodied in the formation of a "sociedade mestiça"—to an essential doubleness that perverts the Eurocentric standards of purity and unicity (17–18). *Mestiçagem*, then, imposes "subtle metamorphoses" and "strange corruptions" that, in Santiago's wonderful phrase, "transform the integrity of Europe: its Bible, its Dictionary, its Grammar" (18).[15] I will resist the temptation to pause at this point in order to consider whether or not purity and unicity were in fact standards of the Portuguese colonial project; many, including Freyre (and, more recently, Gruzinski [1999]), have suggested that they were not (but cf. Marx 1998, 29). Regardless of historical accuracy, it is important to emphasize that the *mestiçagem* to which Santiago explicitly refers is the one that happens at the early moments of conquest, between "Indians" (that is, the exclusive inhabitants of Brazil prior to 1500) and Europeans.

On this point Santiago draws on a range of ethnographers—from colonial Jesuits, to the Huguenot Jean de Léry, to Claude Lévi-Strauss—and offers some impressive exegeses on the unforeseen cultural destabilization that *mestiçagem* exerted on the colonial project, as indigenous peoples confronted an expansive, Christian Europe with something like a differential universality. He clearly articulates the ambivalence of colonial discourse, noting the European gesture of founding a "new world" that is premised on the erasure of that world's newly "discovered" cultural foundations (16). Too quickly, however, Santiago then declares the mestizo synthesis—the "progressive infiltration effected by the savage mind"—that emerges from this invasion as "the only possible road that can lead to decolonization" (17), ostensibly "destroying" the "unicity and purity" of Europe and becoming the "greatest contribution of Latin America to Western culture" (18). Now, I am aware of the immediacy of the center–periphery debate (19) that lends to Santiago's tone a somewhat polemical edge. Nevertheless, it is worth looking past the bright light of his assertion, which can blind the reader to the way that Santiago turns away from modern Brazil's own rewriting, and reappropriation, of that same, colonial "sociedade mestiça"; for the ideological (and material) conversion of the Indian into the mestizo—in Brazil as in Mexico—is not so quickly reducible to a kind of critical move against "unicity," or an infiltration against "purity." Rather, it is an intellectual project of national consolidation that, *in and of itself,* produces a new kind of totality. Moreover, it is a project that serves, along with French poststructuralism and critical ethnography, as Santiago's own writable text: it is precisely the national model that he is engaged in rewriting, transforming it from cordial conviviality to dangerous transgression. As we saw in chapter 1, this is a difficult move to execute well, for his "transgression" simultaneously marks, and to some extent reaffirms, the "law" (or "code") that he hopes to subvert, ultimately running the risk of becoming an integral part of that law. This point could not be clearer in his rewriting of Freyre, in that he attempts to convert Freyre's law of "balanced antagonisms"—"between Europeans and Amerindians"— into a less comfortable space from which to issue a challenge against the Eurocentrism of cultural dependency.

It was the Romantic *indigenistas,* such as Alencar, and later their critics, such as Sílvio Romero, who first took the discursive responsibility of rewriting the constitutive actors of Santiago's colonial drama.[16] The nineteenth century, in other words, witnessed the symbolic conversion of the savage Indian into the national *mestiço.* It is precisely this trajectory—whose literary apotheosis is Alencar, and whose modernization is Freyre—that Santiago leaves to one side as a potential producer of writable texts. This turning away happens very literally. There is a moment in the essay where Santiago touches upon the figure of the modern Indian. He notes that whereas for the European Romantics the Indian symbolized a desire for expansion and the exotic, for the Americans the Indian became a politicized symbol of identification, "a symbol of nationalism" (25). He thus quickly traces the transition, or tension, between competing discourses, two modes of primitive accumulation: one imperial (external colonialism), the other national (internal colonialism). He concludes: "And if among the Europeans [the Indian] expresses a desire for expansion, among the Americans its translation marks the will *[vontade]* to establish the limits of the new *patria,* a form of contraction" (ibid.). But, as we will see with Alencar, it is precisely *mestiçagem*—the very basis of Santiago's critical apparatus—that marks the realization of that contraction, and hence the consolidation of a new discourse of national normativity.[17] This is not to suggest that the national cannot be critical: the critical force of Brazilian *modernismo* is, after all, couched largely in nationalist terms. It *is* to suggest that the national, as much postcolonial criticism has shown, is a risky context for self-reflexive critique. It is precisely here, on the cusp of the dialectical negative whose realization might push his thinking in new and challenging directions, that Santiago literally "stops" . . . and turns to Borges (ibid.).[18]

I want to stress that my point here is not to level any kind of "charges" against Santiago based on what he could not do in a twenty-page essay. Nor is my objective to imply—as Roberto Schwarz has done in a famous 1986 essay on Brazilian nationalism (1992, 7)—a dehistoricized irrelevance in Santiago's critique.[19] I am simply noting a curious, but loud, silence; for if the mark of Latin American discourse is its occupancy of a cannibalistic, hybrid, in-between space, then one of its hallmarks, especially in Brazil, has been the obsessive cannibalization of its own national archive. My dialogue with Santiago, then, does not insist "should have," but rather asks "what if?" If the national classic is a writable text, how is it rewritten? What kind of difference is produced? What are the critical limits of that differentiation?[20]

These are the questions that I want to consider as I reread the national narrative of *mestiçagem* through Freyre's rewriting of Alencar. Critically, I am willing to provisionally accept Santiago's formulation of the writable text as enabling a transgressive gesture that moves from the *entre-lugar* against the "master code." Here, however, I am interested in pursuing the way in which those same modes of critique—the writable text, the *entre-lugar*, and, most of all, hybridity—are not only deployed toward opening the road toward decolonization, but also tread a well-worn gendered, racialized, and sexualized path that leads from colonial discourse to national narrative without ever abandoning the coloniality of power.[21] This will entail a consideration of gender and race, which, as everybody knows, are problematic in Freyre. The point is not to put Freyre on trial, yet again, but rather to ask *how* those problems both repeat—with or without a difference—and mark the limits of his own, and perhaps Santiago's, critical project.

Freyre's account of Brazil's hybrid foundations exhibits the trajectory of his critical and rhetorical logic in general. This logic draws upon, in a national context, what I, via Quijano, have been calling the coloniality of power. Ambivlent like Bhabha's colonial discourse, it is simultaneoulsy a discourse of inclusion and exclusion, at once tolerant and reactionary. It is the organizing logic of *Casa-grande e senzala*, and rests, not without fissures and exceptions, on a relatively consistent play of reversals and reassertions. Let me explain.

Like any social anthropologist or historian of his time, Freyre wrote within (and, in his case, against) a long-standing discourse (still in consistent use today) on the victims of colonialism that, in Latin America, has traditionally been summarized as the binary tension between "civilization and barbarism." Often associated with nineteenth-century narratives of centralized and expansive state power vis-à-vis the inhabitants of the national hinterlands, the discourse has a history as durable and malleable as Eurocentrism itself.[22] There is an important distinction, however, between generalized, Eurocentric models of center–periphery and the specific articulation of civilization and barbarism within Latin American nationalist discourse. In colonial moments, the border dividing center from periphery is usually synonymous with that dividing the colonizing culture from the colonized culture; in neo- or postcolonial contexts, the border may be rearticulated—as we just saw with Santiago—as falling between what used to be called the "First" and "Third" Worlds. The discourse of civilization and barbarism represents the installation of this Eurocentric perspective *within* Latin America, reproducing its binary ossification of cultural and epistemological multiplicity in a process of internal colonialism: specifically, Latin American, metropolitan centers of modernizing ("civilized") political power vis-à-vis the marginalized ("barbarous") communities largely denied access to national forms of political agency and action.[23]

Freyre's approach to this discourse could be described as something like a truncated deconstruction. This critical move is carried out by way of two key steps. First, in Montaignian fashion, he reverses the terms of the binary. He thus shows that the qualities ascribed to the "barbarians" are, in actuality, mere transferences of the qualities that the "civilized" refuse to examine within their own social norms. For example, following this strategy of reversal, the Western obsession with barbaric anthropophagy would become a psychological mechanism deployed to cope with and justify the civilized "cannibalism" of invasion and conquest. The civilized are hence exposed as the "real" barbarians. In Freyre, however, the potentially radical force of this deconstructive move is undercut by a second. Now reversed, the binary "civilization and barbarism" is not displaced or decentered, as it would be were the deconstructive gesture carried through (Spivak 1976). Instead, its organizing logic—or allegorical economy—is reasserted.[24] This reassertion happens as the value attached to civilization and barbarism is shifted along with its referents. Thus, in the cannibal example, once cannibalism is identified as the barbarism interior to civilization, cannibalism itself would elude its potential reinscription within the immortal catalog of national crimes, and transform into the natural virtue of domination; *for it is the strong, the civilized, that are willed by the scientific laws of nature to consume the culture, if not the literal flesh, of the barbaric, the meek.* And so on.

This naturalizing gesture is a dominant trope of evolutionist race science, and a foundation of the Eurocentric justification of projects of genocide carried out against the indigenous peoples of the Americas. Despite his implacable critique of that science, it is a gesture that Freyre repeats. And it is through that gesture that Freyre's critique of colonialism becomes at the same time a naturalization of colonial relations of power, that is, an affirmative critique. As I mentioned, Freyre's achievement is to simultaneously write against race science and yet still lend the racist, colonial natural order of things an aura of scientificity. In this, he draws extensively on the science dedicated to "the nature of mankind," that is, the discourse of anthropology. It is this discourse, dedicated to the scientific description of "other cultures," and the categorical segregation of barbarians (primitive cultures) and the civilized (advanced cultures), that governs his narration of national origins. Freyre's account of the early colonial intercultural relations between indigenous Brazilians and Portuguese colonizers, then, draws on anthropological discourse in a way that is both critical of the colonial gaze and a reassertion of the natural status of colonial relations: *Iracema* dressed up in the language of science. This portrait of original Brazil is indicative of the ambivalence of his antiracism, or what is often referred to as his "tolerance" for, and celebration of, his country's multicultural character.

Let us begin with the basis of his critique. In the aptly titled second chapter of *Casa-grande e senzala*, dedicated to "The Native in the Formation of the Brazilian Family," Freyre attacks the Eurocentric objectification of the indigenous civilizations of Brazil. His point of attack is what he perceives as a misreading of indigenous sexuality, and the accompanying construction of the supposedly insatiable sexual appetite of the Indian. He notes the mixture of "amazement" and "horror" (101) with which the early chroniclers, such as Soares and Anchieta, described what they understood as indiscriminate incest. Such allegations of the savage's "failure" to discriminate, as René Jara points out, are a classic strategy of Eurocentric othering.[25] This is the point that Freyre attacks, producing a 1500 letter from Vespucci to Lorenzo de' Medici as his most graphic piece of evidence. The Indians, Vespucci reports, "take as many wives as they like, and the son has intercourse with the mother, and the brother with the sister, and the male cousin with the female cousin, and the one who is out walking with the first woman whom he meets" (101/96).

Freyre challenges this stereotypical image of a lustful Caliban, completely out of control, by submitting it to science. In other words, he rereads the colonial chroniclers in the light of contemporary anthropological knowledge. While conceding that there is valuable descriptive evidence to be gained by the early ethnographers, in general Freyre disqualifies their interpretations as stemming from the superficial imposition of one moral code upon another: the chroniclers, in short, did not understand what they were seeing. Drawing on the explosion of Boasian anthropological research of the 1920s and 1930s, Freyre maintains that "laxity of this sort, sexual license and libertinism, are not to be met with among *any* primitive people" (101/97; my emphasis). The natives of Brazil in fact exhibited a complex system of prohibitions and taboo. Thus, "what tends to disfigure these customs is the evil *[má]* interpretation that has been put upon them by superficial observers" (102/97).

Beyond the disconnect between moral codes, Freyre also suggests a psychic phenomenon of transference at play in the construction of savage licentiousness, or what he often calls "priapism." He refutes this priapic thesis by replacing it with a new one: the *truly* licentious element, the "savage" sexuality in the foundational romance of Brazil was, in fact, the Portuguese male. He offers a host of factors to support this claim, not least of which is the centuries-long contact between Christians and Moors in the Iberian Peninsula, which, in Freyre's view, had rendered a Portuguese male "addicted *[afeiçoados]* to polygamy" (100/94). But the most important factors, for Freyre, always stem from the economic determinations of the colonial project itself: there were few white women on hand; the first colonizers were separated from the restraining effects of family; the "outstanding problem" of the colonial project, that of population, "led to the attenuation among us of scruples concerning irregularities in moral and sexual conduct" (443/446); and, of central importance, the idea that the colonizers themselves represented an unusually strong-sexed sample of the larger population. This last thesis, again, stems from the fortuitous confluence of specific colonial policy and historical accident. To arrive at it, Freyre cobbles together archival evidence on the Portuguese Inquisition's tendency to exaggerate "slight or imaginary misdemeanors . . . into heinous offenses," and Brazil's colonial status as a refuge for criminals and the accused (20–21/29). With this information, Freyre offers the conjecture that the colonial project had a de facto eugenic policy: "It is possible that, with the genetic interests of the population in view, certain individuals were deliberately sent to Brazil whom we know to have been expatriated for irregularities or excesses in their sexual life: for hugging and kissing, for employing witchcraft to induce love or hatred, for bestiality, for effeminacy, procuring, and the like" (20/29). It is a savage sexuality—"perversions" reducible to an overcharged libido—now ascribed to Europe that would enable the genesis of Brazil, constitutive of what he calls the "racial heterogeneity" of the "national prehistory" (19): "To the wilderness, so underpopulated, with a bare sprinkling of whites, came these oversexed ones, there to give extraordinarily free reign to their passions . . . Unbridled stallions is what they were . . . Europeans all of them, in the prime of life and in the best of health, young and full of masculine vigor, 'adventurous and arduous youth, brimming with strength'" (21/29–30; at the end of this passage Freyre is citing Paulo Prado's *Retrato do Brazil* [1928]).

The question of the discursive normalization of a national *family*, however, still remains: How to effect the originary *mestiçagem* with all of the indigenous restrictions surrounding sexual relations? In other words, how to establish the family constellation of a "prehistoric Brazil," centered on the indigenous female? For it is the production of Brazil through this particular family unit that serves as Freyre's thesis on the topic of the indigenous contributions to Brazilian culture: "Hybrid from the beginning, Brazilian society is . . . [a] society . . . that was Christian in superstructure, with the recently baptized native woman as wife and mother of the family" (91/83–84; see also 17). Freyre solves this potential impasse—between libidinous colonizers and frigid Indians—by hypothesizing that indigenous sexual norms must have taken a toll on indigenous women, who, like the Portuguese colonizers, also happen to exhibit a strong sexual impulse. The foundational romance, before it could be curbed by the intervention of Jesuit missionaries (92–93, 101), comes into focus as a kind of foundational orgy of "sexual intoxication" (93), in which "young stallions" find themselves surrounded by a "host of nude women" (21): "No sooner had the European leaped ashore than he found his feet slipping among the naked Indian women, and the very fathers of the Society of Jesus had to take care not to sink into the carnal mire . . . The women were the first to offer themselves to the whites, the more ardent ones going to rub themselves against the legs of these beings whom they supposed to be gods. They would give themselves to the European for a comb or a broken mirror" (93/85). Although all of this, from Freyre's perspective, written in the wake of the sexual revolution of the 1920s, has a decidedly utopian (as in unplaceable) metaphorics to it, it is ultimately *not* metaphorical, but literal—not, of course, in the exaggerated and highly dubious portrait of indigenous female sexuality, but rather in its biopolitical and eugenic implications. As Freyre explains, the scene serves powerful reasons of state: the need to populate the empire. This "miscibility" is the signature of Portuguese colonialism, and it is thus that mestizo Brazil is born (9).

But Brazil, in this sense, turns out to be less exceptional than Freyre implies. For one, the gendered code of the reproductive family unit that he sketches transports to a postcolonial, nationalist context the structure of what Foucault later called the emergence of "class sexualities" that accompanied the historical rise of the bourgeoisie, and whereby that bourgeoisie "endowed itself, in an arrogant political affirmation, with a garrulous sexuality" (1978, 127). Freyre's unapologetic racialization of this discourse through the thesis that the excessive sexual desire of the female Indian stemmed from an excess of domesticity (101) is also an old move, and effects an operation familiar to what Foucault identifies as the sexualization of the so-called "idle woman . . . [who] was assigned a new destiny charged with conjugal and parental obligations" (1978, 121) as a project of state. But this gendered configuration is a hallmark of colonial discourse and speaks to the particular sexual "agency" of colonized women in general: the fact that they choose, of their own accord, white men. This "fact" is certainly not objectively "false": the agency of women mobilizing their own bodies in the name of social ascent is an ancient, oft-told (often in misogynistic terms) history.[26] Building on that bibliography, however, is not my concern at this point. Of concern here is the way in which that agency of women installs itself as a key element of the normalizing discourse of national family that is powerful enough for even contemporary critics of the colonial legacies of race relations to draw uncritically on its truth. For example, in his pathbreaking study of race and racism in Brazil, Thomas Skidmore concludes that Brazilian discourses of "whitening" or "Aryanization" succeeded in producing a conforming "social reality" because "females, wherever possible, had powerful conditioning to choose lighter partners than themselves" (1974, 46). That this conditioning becomes a generalized material practice and a social reality, however, would be a difficult thesis to prove, and does not seem to rest on any convincing empirical evidence.[27] Either way, the repeated pronouncement that dark females are attracted to lighter men is not unique to Brazilian national discourse, and its effect is to endow the racist normalization of pigmentocratic society with a pseudoscientific, deterministic behaviorism. This assumption in Latin America finds its popular expression in the well-known, vulgar homage to eugenics: "mejorar la raza" (to improve the race).

The explicit language that Freyre applied to colonial heroes certainly scandalized some conservative sectarians, who dubbed him "the pornographer of Recife" (Skidmore 1974, 275). This attack, however, obscures the paradoxical political commonality that Freyre shares with his conservative opponents, as it misses the authoritative move contained within his thesis of colonial, sexual anarchy (an authoritarianism that would become more explicit with Freyre's turn to the political right in the 1960s); for the anarchy that Freyre described was not anarchic at all, but rather hierarchic. And his discourse of sexual openness and tolerance does not necessarily translate to a commitment to liberate individuals and communities. Rather, like Foucault's comment on Freud, it rests on "a new impetus to the secular injunction to study [the colonial experience of] sex and transform it into discourse," to discipline the productivity of its truth (Foucault 1978, 159). Freyre's configuration of the originary, Brazilian sexual economy, in fact, simply reconfirms the gendered narrative of colonization that marries white men to brown women. It was an easy story to sell, and one with which Brazilians were already quite familiar.

Iracema (1865) is José de Alencar's memorable indigenist narrative of interracial romance. It is remembered as the love story between Martim, a "white warrior" (1865, 9) and devout Christian (23) who has gone native in early colonial Brazil (13), and Iracema, an Indian "maiden with lips of honey" (11) who represents precolonial America itself. It is perhaps the most well known story in Brazil.[28]

The trajectory of the novel's central love story is standard, Romantic tragedy: Martim and Iracema are immediately attracted to each other; after the requisite complications, they consummate their mutual affections; Iracema gives birth to a son; Iracema dies. For an intertextual reading with *Casa-grande e senzala*, it is important to note the ways in which the obvious allegory of conquest plays out. As with Freyre's "nude women" who accosted the Portuguese conquistadors, Iracema exhibits an agency that defies her self-declared condition as Martim's "slave" (73). In fact, it is Iracema who seems to enslave Martim, and who acts as the primary agent at almost all the key turns in the narrative's action. Throughout their courtship, it is Iracema who consistently takes the romantic initiative, and she intervenes to save Martim's life on multiple occasions (40, 54, 58). Even the amorous culmination of their tortured passions frames Iracema in the position of active subject. During Martim's escape (orchestrated by Iracema) from hostile forces, he orders Iracema to return home, at which point she reveals that she is now his wife (68–69). This information both surprises and dismays Martim. Upon learning that he has had sexual relations with the erstwhile maiden, "The Christian hid his face from the light. 'God!' . . . he exclaimed tremulously" (69). As it turns out, Martim had been too hallucinatory to even know what he was doing when they finally made love: he had been drugged by Iracema (61, 69).[29] Iracema, then, is both enslaved and enslaving, the embodiment of a kind of natural wealth that Martim, the white warrior—thousands of miles from the "chaste affections" of the "blonde maiden" of his homeland (59)—is mercilessly compelled to take as his own, in Camõesian fashion, "aquela cativa que me tem cativo."[30]

The romance, however, becomes more complicated, as *Iracema* tells not one love story but two. The secondary love story, which equals the primary in terms of allegorical significance, unfolds with the arrival of Martim's "Indian brother," the warrior chief Poti. The pivotal figure in the triangulation of desire that ensues, however, is not the alluring Iracema, but rather Martim himself.[31] Indeed, Poti's first appearance in the novel—in which he comes to rescue Martim from jealous and vengeful forces that have gathered in Iracema's tribe—spells out the possibility of an amorous conflict. Attempting to coax him from hiding, Iracema hails Poti by declaring that she "comes to you, because the foreigner [Martim] loves you [Poti], and she [Iracema] loves the foreigner" (51). These dual affirmations of love—between, on the one hand, Martim and Iracema, and, on the other, Martim and Poti—recur throughout the novel (77, 94–95, 97–98). When Martim and Iracema make love, the reader is reminded of Poti's presence (e.g., 95). When Iracema advises Martim of her pregnancy, Poti is there (93–94).

Although the friendship between Martim and Poti remains platonic throughout the novel, its development is governed by a thinly veiled metaphorics of homoeroticism. It is, in many ways, the narrative anchor of the story. The stabilizing function of that narrative is how unproblematic the relationship is when compared to the complications that surround the relations between Martim and Iracema. Martim is fraught with indecision and guilt, feeling that he has betrayed the hospitality of his hosts by eloping with Iracema (e.g., 68). Iracema, for her part, constantly worries that she will lose Martim, either to battle (100), to his Portuguese fiancée (61), or to Poti.[32] Thus Martim's relationship with Iracema is marked by a persistent ambivalence, with either political or romantic tension surrounding their every meeting. This tension stands in marked contrast to the frequent embraces, unambiguous declarations of love, and warrior camaraderie that defines Martim's relations with Poti. In the transitional chapters that narrate Martim's escape from Iracema's village, repeated affirmations of his love for Poti are accompanied by confessions of his fear of Iracema.[33] Upon the establishment of Martim and Iracema's conjugal home on an isolated shore, Poti— despite being a tribal chief—sticks around, apparently cohabitating with them, and frequently counseling Martim on matters of the heart.[34] The source of this knowledge, however, is a general kind of indigenous wisdom, as Poti exhibits not a single hint of overt heterosexual desire or experience. Alongside his discourses on the passions and his legendary reputation as a warrior chief, there is no mention of a wife, a family, or a love interest (beyond Martim) in Poti's life, an odd—and, I think, significant—elision in the Romantic novelistic genre.[35]

In the end, the intersecting love stories, like the novel in which they reside, are transcultural narratives of contact and exchange. What Alencar brought to Brazilian literature was a sublimation of the Brazilian language: a Portuguese "softened," as Freyre puts it, with an indigenous lexicon and African-influenced colloquial phrasings, all wrapped up in an eloquent, Romantic lyricism—a softening that for Freyre, not insignificantly, is associated with the feminine (1955, 31). But, like the rise of print capitalism that was redefining the nature of storytelling and language itself in nineteenth-century Brazil, there is an implicit power relation in the transcultural dynamics that play out between Martim and his Indian companions.

Martim will be "influenced" by the Indians, adopting their language through extensive contact (13), their culture through formal ceremonies (96–98), their women through love, and their men through warrior bonding. Ultimately, however, it is the Indians who accept Martim's seed, and their own colonial fate, without resistance: at one point, Iracema remembers "her *pátria*" that has been "erased *[apagada]* by love," a fact that she "does not regret" (105–6). Both romances, then, represent two important conversions from savage tribalism to civilized nation.[36] Iracema represents the racial and territorial conversion: after giving birth to "the first son that the blood of the white race begot in this land of liberty" (116), she dies;[37] that is, original *America* dies. The cultural tragedy that marks the forging of mestizo Brazil is inscribed in the son's name, Moacyr, which, Iracema explains, means "born of my suffering" (117). Iracema, meanwhile, merges with the land itself, receding into nature as her grave is watched over not by a cross or a carved stone, but by a palm and a bird (127, 130). Poti, on the other hand, represents the religious conversion. In spite of drawing Martim into indigenous culture with a formal naming ceremony (96–98), in the final chapter Poti turns to the path of monotheism. With Martim's return from overseas, accompanied by a priest and "many warriors of his race" (129), Poti is the first to kneel before the cross. Whether or not he was coerced is not entirely clear, but the results are explicit: "he would no longer allow anything to separate him from his white brother. They should share a single God, as they shared a single heart" (ibid.). With the new God come a new name, a new king, and a new language: "his fame increased, and even today he is the pride of the land where he was born" (ibid.). But even despite Martim's successful penetration, with the "word of the true God germinated in the savage land" and in the heart of Poti, Martim cannot shake his longing for the reincarnation of Iracema (ibid.). The novel ends, as Sommer has noted, with that sweet sadness so often associated with Brazil, the "tragi-paradox" (1991, 170) of a foundational erasure, the permanent homesickness of nonbelonging, a cultural upheaval that cannot be undone, an essential *saudade* inspired by the inevitable with the novel's closure: "Tudo passa sôbre a terra" (130).

Freyre's rewriting of the romance between Iracema and Martim is clear enough. The Iracema figure could serve as a metonym for Freyre's more generalized "indigenous woman." Even in her eventual fading from the scene of the normative national family, Freyre repeats much of Alencar's gendered construction of the Indian. Whereas Alencar's Iracema cannot lactate sufficiently, and thus cannot fulfill her domestic role as caregiver to the colonial family (126), Freyre notes that "Indian women did not make such good domestic slaves," yielding to the "African ones . . .

as cooks and nurses of the young" (96/89). He goes on to state that their only contribution in terms of animal husbandry was their use of "honey-making bees" and "domesticated birds" (98), each of which are associated with Iracema in the novel. But, for Freyre, as for Alencar, she is nonetheless the maternal source of national essence: "The native woman must be regarded not merely as the physical basis of the Brazilian family, upon whom, drawing strength from her and multiplying itself, rested the energy of a limited number of settlers; she must also be considered a worth-while cultural element . . . in the formation of Brazilian society" (94/87). After listing an inventory of cultural contributions, most of which also appear in *Iracema* (most notably the hammock and practices of "tropical hygiene"), he concludes that "The Brazilian of today, a lover of the bath and always with a comb and mirror in his pocket . . . is reflecting the influence of his remote grandmothers" (ibid.). And if Freyre's Portuguese colonizer is considerably less pious and more roguish than Martim, they share the common role of fathering the nation.

There is nothing surprising or scandalous in the fact that Freyre would repeat, and even literally draw from, Alencar. As Antonio Candido has hypothesized, the lack of an institutional infrastructure of scientific investigation has always led "the best" Brazilian thinkers—sociologists, anthropologists, historians, philosophers—to ultimately and openly embrace literary discourse (1950, 152). Alencar is a classic example of the novelist-scientist, blending observations of his own surroundings, philological innovations, and an extensive knowledge of the colonial chroniclers into a national narrative of natural foundations (Sommer 1991, 144, 148, 154). Freyre, working on the same project at a different historical moment, will, of course, not be able to, and indeed does not desire to, make a clean break with that discursive past. At stake, then, is not *whether* he rewrites, but *how* he rewrites *Iracema*, and at what point that repetition becomes a differentiation.

How, then, does this rewriting play out around the figure of Poti, the indigenous male? Here again we find a gesture common to both Freyre and Alencar. In terms of the normative discourse of the national family, however, it is a gesture not of inscription, but of expulsion. Both writers, in the end, effect a rhetorical containment by way of exteriorization, and neutralization, of indigenous masculinity as a potentially (re)productive agent in the normative discourse of the national family, which, it is important to reassert, is essentially a eugenic discourse.[38]

For Freyre, the primary colonial function of the indigenous male is that of a warrior brother. Ineffective as a plantation slave, the Indian, like Poti, "made up for his uselessness . . . by his brilliance and heroism as a soldier, not only in connection with the invasion of the backlands, but in defending the colony against the Spanish, against enemy tribes of the Portuguese, against corsairs" (94–95/88; translation altered). Freyre naturalizes this function by linking it to the nomadic qualities of indigenous civilization that never "permit him [the Indian] . . . to settle down to a life of patient and rewarding labor" (95/88). But this restive precolonial life, with its constant activity of hunting, warring, and cannibalizing, has led to an imbalance in Freyre's theory of the domestic configuration among the Brazilian Indians. As we saw, that domestic scene featured, according to Freyre, a strongly sexed female component. Now, despite, or perhaps because of, its forcefulness, this is not one of Freyre's best arguments, as he posits a *lack* of domesticity as the reason for indigenous women's "failure" as house slaves, and an *abundance* of domesticity as the reason behind their "priapism." Regardless of logical consistency, the discursive effect of this configuration is to leave the Indian male with a sexual problem vis-à-vis his "highly sexed" companion: "absorbed by the necessities of competition before [his 'animal ardor'] could be sexualized, [h]e did not possess that surplus of leisure and of food which Adlez from the biological and Thomas from the sociological point of view see as bound up with the development of the sexual system in man" (100–101/95–96).[39]

This scientific evidence leads Freyre to conclude that it was around this "relatively weak sexual impulse" of indigenous masculinity (102) that the complex systems of indigenous taboo and prohibition turned. As we saw, he accuses the chroniclers of completely misunderstanding this dynamic, constructing a savage sexual monster as a flimsy substitute for their own colonial desires. This misreading, he suggests, is being corrected by carefully gathered empirical evidence, namely, the science of anthropology. Citing Soares's sixteenth-century contribution to the long-standing Western fascination with ritual phallic enlargement, Freyre notes the Tupinambá practice that reportedly "leaves the organ so huge and misshapen that the women are not able to endure it" (102/97). Based on these accounts, conclusions were drawn that the Tupinambá are "exceedingly libidnous" (ibid.). Freyre's exhaustive reading of the contemporary anthropological literature, however, leads him to determine that precisely the opposite is the case: the practice of phallic enlargement "indicates the necessity that the natives felt of making up for a physical or psychic deficiency with regard to the generative function, rather than dissoluteness or sadistic masochism" (102/97–98). In relation to whom or what this sensed "physical or psychic deficiency" would have developed is not a question that Freyre entertains. But in terms of its colonial truth, the thesis is nicely consistent with the discourse of civilization and barbarism, and exemplifies the truncated deconstruction that he assiduously applies to that discourse. What was once perceived as an uncontrollable passion, the light of modern science has shown to be, like "orgiastic practices" among primitives in general, a kind of "compensation" (102). For? "[F]or the difficulty they experienced in achieving, without that aphrodisiac oil provided by the sweat of lascivious dances, a state of excitation and erection such as is readily accomplished by the civilized. The latter are always ready for coitus; savages practice it only when pricked by sexual hunger" (102/98).[40] This should not surprise us, he concludes, because "[i]t is indeed a known fact that among primitive peoples the sexual organs are generally less developed than among the civilized" (ibid.).[41]

Freyre thus updates, modernizes, the containment of the indigenous male, once a lugubrious Caliban, now the mere shell of a man. In desavaging the savage—no longer a sexual monster, but actually, like Poti, quite tractable—the formerly savage sexuality has suddenly converted into a sign of civilization. The conquest, again, is naturalized, as is the white man's superior position within its hierarchy, as the underdevelopment of Brazil's indigenous civilization ("one of the most backward populations on the continent" [89/81]) merges with the underdevelopment of the primitive's genitals.

In what sense, then, does Freyre's narrative of foundations rewrite *Iracema*? The scientificity with which it reconstructs the reproductive pact between Martim and Iracema is, of course, obvious. Moreover, it repeats the naturalization—and nationalization—of a colonial discourse in which the entirety of the conquered culture is at once feminized and infantilized.[42] Freyre can be explicit on this point, in one turn configuring the child, the woman, and the slave as each at once a "helpless victim of the male's domination or abuse," which is "linked naturally with the economic circumstances that shaped our patriarchal society" (51/76). Yet, at the same time, "feminize" is not the precise rhetorical move here. Besides yielding an unwanted recoil that implies the tired, anticolonial "solution" in a remasculinization of colonized men, it must be remembered that Freyre is very specific and consistently laudatory about the productive role of the feminine within the normative discourse of national family. The male Indian is not so much "feminized," then, as desexualized: erased as a procreative agent within the eugenic discourse of hybridity; not reproductive like women, but completely unproductive, or at best prepubescent, underdeveloped, like children. Indeed, harnessed to the developmentalist theories that dominated his generation, Freyre sees the natives of colonial Brazil as "bands of grown-up children . . . a culture that was still cutting its first teeth" (82).

The Iracema effect in *Casa-grande e senzala* thus serves a double purpose. First, invasion is recodified as a gender- and race-specific discourse of national family. Second, genocide is softened—like Alencar's Brazilian language—even euphemized, as the infantile, asexual, indigenous male is subtracted, as a matter of natural course, from that family equation.[43] The mechanism of containing the masculinity of the other is different. The statist discourse that governs *Iracema* is predominantly a religious one, through which the sexually neutral warrior brother accepts the seed of Martim's faith and develops up from a chaste paganism to a chaste Christianity. In *Casa-grande e senzala*, religious discourse is usurped by an anthropological discourse with scientific credentials that nonetheless traces a regular trajectory, as indigenous cultures develop, by way of the "cleansing" effects of "mestizo culture" (103), toward civilization and away from the barbarous, impotent underdevelopment of the pure Indian's phallus. In this sense, the materiality of the eugenic discourse that underwrites *Casa-grande e senzala* remains as less a rewriting than a reaffirmation of Alencar's simultaneous nationalization and naturalization of colonial relations. With Freyre's foundational *mestiçagem* we find ourselves, to paraphrase Gayatri Spivak, confronted with yet another permutation of white men heroically rescuing brown women from the clutches of brown men (Spivak 1988, 92)—not, in this case, with the arrival of civil liberties and a lifting of the veil, but with the exuberance of sexual liberation. Again, Freyre is unambiguous: "So far as the aborigine's culture was concerned, it was, so to speak, the feminine part that was to be saved [*se salvaria*]" (159/180). As much as a rescue, this process is also a harvest and an investment, a primitive accumulation of organic goods that mirrors the colonial plunder of the jungle itself. For Freyre, the Brazilian Indian is reducible to a jungle plant, "vegetable in his mode of aggression, little more than an auxiliary of the forest" (90/82). Alencar's Iracema, in turn, is like "the palm" (24), "the vanilla plant" (32), "the rice plant" (45), "the Easter lily" (58), "the plant" (66), "the rosy cactus" (67), "the flower" (85), "the sweet potato" (126), and so on.

We have seen how Freyre's *Casa-grande e senzala* not only rewrites, but also reasserts, the normative discourse of national family embedded within Alencar's Romantic best-seller, *Iracema.* However, a question remains: In what sense, if at all, does that repetition of that discourse articulate a differentiation? To what extent, in other words, does Freyre appropriate and transform his writable text in the manner theorized by Santiago? Two important examples of the difference within Freyre's repetition are worth noting. The critical possibilities of both, however, are limited by the ambivalence that governs the hybridity that articulates *casa-grande* to *senzala.*

First is the reinterpretation of the colonial project as such. As we have seen, Freyre's hybridist inscription of colonized others into the national narrative exhibits the same kind of ambivalence that governs the colonial discourse that he is attempting to rewrite. If Freyre reasserts the indigenous communities of precolonial Brazil as a foundation of national identity, this reappropriation comes at a price: their metaphorical relegation to an irretrievable, prehistoric memory, a cultural trace that occasionally reminds Brazilians of their "indigenous grandmothers." This is the same logic that we receive from Alencar (and that we saw in chapters 5–7). However, Freyre is ambivalent not only in his rescue of the colonized other, but also in his treatment of the colonial project itself. Despite the common critical reduction of Freyre's work to an unabashed and unproblematic case for the benefits of colonialism, the ambivalent position of *Casa-grande e senzala* often digresses into an open critique of the conquest of Brazil in a way that *Iracema* does not: "As we consider, in this essay, the clash of the two cultures . . . from the point of view of the social formation of the Brazilian family . . . let us not forget, meanwhile, to note the effect of this contact upon the native from the point of view of his own culture. That contact was dissolvent in effect . . . The history of the contact of the so-called 'superior' races with those looked upon as 'inferior' is always the same. Extermination and degradation" (108/106–7). He continues with a highly critical treatment of the Jesuit occupation of indigenous land, and their "protection" of the Indians from the slavery of the colonists, which in the end became a parallel form of slavery in the Jesuit *aldeias* (109, 157). Seen as "heroism" on the part of the Catholic church, Freyre argues that the transculturative actions of the Jesuits' pedagogical pretensions must be seen from a multiplicity of perspectives: "Judging them, however, by another criterion . . . we must conclude that their influence was a harmful one" (110/109).[44] Above and beyond the pernicious influence of the missions, he goes on to assert the genocidal effects of the colonial economy in general: "Sugar killed the Indian" (157).

Out of *Casa-grande e senzala*, then, we can extract a critique of civilization and barbarism that, in 1933, had not yet become standard practice in the rediscovery of colonial relations that was all the rage in the Brazil of Freyre's era.[45] Nevertheless, the stereotype of cultural superiority of the Portuguese over the indigenous is only slightly disturbed, and the exploitative gestures of primitive accumulation are frankly naturalized. Thus, when Freyre writes of the enslavement of the Indians during the early colonial period that literally reduced people to a form of currency, he frames it as the effect of "a quasi-biological differentiation of the Portuguese toward slavery," a conclusion that he supports by drawing a comparison to parasitic "slave-making ants" studied by Darwin (156/177). The Portuguese colonizers, while compared to parasites, are simultaneously naturalized, because they can now be understood as simply following their instincts. And although he criticizes the Jesuits for seeking "to castrate every virile expression of religious or artistic culture" (109/107) of the Indians, Freyre participates in the same kind of neutralization by literally writing out of Brazilian history the possibility of the indigenous male as a reproductive agent. Thus, although he celebrates the transcultural give-and-take of *mestiçagem*, Freyre's narrative is simultaneously a reiteration of the gendered discourse of colonial rape whereby indigenous communities are "penetrated" by a new, dynamic culture, while their own culture bends and breaks under the weight of capitalist slavery and Jesuit indoctrination (109, 156). Ultimately, then, the cultural transformation of the early Brazilian landscape is, in Freyre's interpretation, a natural process of acculturation whose end result will be more of "the same drama: the backward cultures disintegrating beneath the yoke or pressure of the more advanced ones" (159/181). Although both cultures suffer a "degradation" (ibid.), it is the Indians who will, in the end, cede to the invaders, eventually being swallowed up by the new dominant order (ibid.). And there is room, with Freyre, for celebration in the process: "Although a perfect intercommunication between its cultural extremes has not been achieved in Brazil . . . none the less we may congratulate ourselves upon an adjustment of traditions and tendencies that is rare among peoples whose social formation has taken place under the same circumstances of modern imperialist colonization in the tropics" (159–60/181). Hybridity, then, exhibits its material effects: while indigenous cultures "adjust" out of their precolonial social fabric, they will provide a foundational part of the "lubricating oil of a deep *mestiçagem*" (160). Thus Freyre's hybrid society includes a space for an elemental indigenous contribution to contemporary national life. This same offer, however, is conditioned by a theory of hybridity that might agitate civilization and barbarism, but that never really empties the categories of their implications. The indigenous contribution to hybrid Brazil, though perhaps making "itself felt in the living, useful, active . . . presence of elements that have a creative effect upon the national development" (160/181), remains a material substrate buried within the exceptional case of Brazilian *mestiçagem*; buried at the edge of the forest, with Iracema, brown mother to a new world in the tropics.

The second difference that Freyre exerts in his rewriting of Iracema is the inscription of the African within his narrative of national foundations.[46] Although it has not been the focus here, this valorization of Afro-Brazilian culture is often what Freyre is remembered for. Alencar made the African nearly invisible in his extensive writings.[47] But in *Casa-grande e senzala*, the African slave becomes a "partner," even the driving force, in the cultural transformation of Brazil. Here again, however, the narrative of African participation is constructed as a heterosexual romance, with "Africa" as a whole playing the female part. The figures that dominate the two chapters of *Casa-grande e senzala* dedicated to the African are either women or play a stereotypically feminine role: the "masochistic" black or *mulata* slave who receives the "sadistic" advances of the white master (e.g., 51, 379); the "young Negro playmate" who receives the same treatment from the slave owner's son (e.g., 336); the black nanny who nurses the infant through childhood (e.g., 283, 335–36). The dominant tendency is to naturalize this relationship alongside the consistent recognition of the cruelty of Portuguese slavery (e.g., 252). Any potential for reproductive, masculine sexuality of the colonized other is once again effaced. And this effacement is facilitated with a turn to scientific evidence.

Despite the African's exemplary civilizing role in the formation of the nation, in Freyre's libidinous hierarchy of colonial Brazil, the African, "[c]ontrary to the general impression," was, in fact, "sexually the weakest of the three elements that united to form our country" (100/95). More precisely, he means to say African men. Freyre, again, draws this conclusion from the most contemporary anthropological research and its inverse correlation between sexual rites and sexual potency, which ascertains that among the Africans "erotic dances were more frequent and more ardent than among the Amerindians and the Portuguese, and this would appear to indicate a weaker degree of sexuality," in other words, the need for excessive stimulation (ibid.).[48] He extends this argument in his chapters on the black slave, where he paints an image of the colonial "harem" that revolved around a Portuguese *fazendeiro* (plantation owner) whose slothful life had left him with "[a] woman's hands [and] a child's feet, [while] the sexual organ alone was arrogantly virile" (429/428). This virility stands "in contrast to the Negroes; for so many of those enormous giants had the penis of a small boy" (ibid.). On this point he cites evidence from an old *Manual do Fazendeiro* (plantation owner's manual) (468).

As for productive cultural contributions to the Brazilian national identity, the African, like the Indian, is almost exclusively exerted in the domain of the stereotypically feminine. With most of the men working in the fields, it is the black nannies and *mulata* lovers who take the responsibility of Africanizing Brazil, both through the production of children and through their contributions to the slave owners' domestic life. When African men participate in these domains of the *casa-grande*, their "masculinity" is always thrown into doubt, like "the great [black] chiefs of colonial times" who "were always very effeminate *[amaricados]*" (454/460). In rare moments when black masculine participation in the reproductive process is acknowledged, it is only under very specific circumstances. One is the obvious question of breeding more slaves (429), although the white master's participation in that endeavor is what tends to draw the attention of Freyre's hybridological thesis (e.g., 317, 378). The other is the case of backland communities of escaped slaves: "Women of their own color being scarce among the fugitives, they would have had recourse, in supplying the lack, 'to the rape *[ao rapto]* of Indian women' or the *caboclas* of the nearest towns and settlements" (46/69). The wording here speaks loudly to the rhetorics of Freyre's construction of Brazilian masculinity. On the one hand, what distinguishes the Portuguese and African male is the intensity of their "sexual impulse," which is strong in the former, weak in the latter. On the other hand, the "sadism" of the Portuguese is never once articulated as an act of "rape" *(rapto)*. Although cruel, degrading, and demoralizing, it is the natural outcome of a more generalized system of degradation: the slave economy that was necessary to the development of colonial Brazil (e.g., 283–84, 317, 320).[49] Moreover, Portuguese or *fazendeiro* sadism was received and mitigated by the corresponding masochism of black and indigenous women (e.g., 51).

The contradictory framing of the African male as both "impotent" and "rapist" belies the unspoken premise of Freyre's justification of the colonial sexual order: the fact that the exclusion of the black male from that normative heterosexual matrix must be actively maintained; or better, the schizoid reduction of the male slave to that dangerous supplement that must be contained, if not through the taming effects of scientific fact, then through the occasional resurrection of the timeworn threat of the raping savage. Either way, the black man is understood as a deviation within the colonial procreative ideal. In short, the eugenic force of hybridity—indeed, the relationships most appropriate to the laws of natural selection (442)—is realized not just between masters and slaves, but between masterful men and enslaved women.

Internal to the logic of Freyre's rhetoric, there is an implicit function to this containment of black masculinity. The exhaustive development of the racialized, gendered, and normative colonial relationship, to which Freyre dedicates much of his five-hundred-page tome, leaves a conspicuous silence hovering around the "other" reproductive possibility: romantic affairs between white women and black men. On this theme Freyre is almost entirely mute. He dedicates a total of one paragraph to its consideration, pausing briefly to dismiss Manuel Bomfim's thesis that sexual relations between "the young mistress" and the "sturdy slave lads" were "not infrequent" (339/353). This, Freyre argues (brushing aside documentary evidence supporting Bomfim), would have been a logistical impossibility, given the vigilant regulation of white women's sexuality during the colonial era. Although he later treats the theme of the repressed, slave-owning matron who takes lovers, there is no mention that these lovers may have been chosen from the ranks of the male slaves who populated the *casa-grande e senzala* circuit, the black men Elizabeth Agassiz had once described as the "fine-looking athletic negroes" of Brazil (1869, 82).[50] And in a passage where he analyzes newspaper want ads seeking good-looking house slaves of both sexes, he offers no further comment about "the aesthetic selection of housemen," yet qualifies the "housemaids" as the "Negro women who were in closest contact with the white men of the Big Houses, the mothers of the young mulattoes who were reared in the home" (314/321).

Is this silence on black masculine heterosexuality the unspeakable outside, the discursive limit of Freyre's voice? I would argue that there is nothing exterior about it. Rather, it is a strategic blindness within his project. Foucault speaks to the problem: "Silence itself . . . is less the absolute limit of discourse, the other side from which it is separated by a strict boundary, than an element that functions alongside the things said, with them and in relation to them within over-all strategies" (1978, 27).[51] To what "overall strategy" does Freyre's silence speak? Not merely tactical, it is the *strategy* that resides at the very heart of his hybridity: the production and reification of a normative discourse of national family that at once sublimates an eroticized brown woman (in this case, fundamentally the *mulata*) and authorizes her colonial subordination to a white master. What Freyre achieves through this silence is the ability to openly condemn colonial sexual mores—the virtual imprisonment of the white mistress, the sadism of the white master that Freyre claims led to a dissolution of the black woman's morality (379)—yet simultaneously naturalize and reify a relation of colonial power as deterministically inevitable; for this racialized and gendered hierarchy, in *Casa-grande e senzala*, is not the work of men, but of nature, or better, an evil genius that puts into motion a cruel tropical theater in which the actors simply play their prescribed part. That deity is the colonial system itself, a historical accident that allows for no alternatives, normalized through discourses of anthropology, religion, literature, and their hybridization: "What was given expression in those relations [between slave master and enslaved mistress] was the spirit of the economic system that, like a powerful god, divided us into enslaver and enslaved. And it was from that system that the exaggerated tendency toward sadism was derived that is so characteristic of the Brazilian born and reared in the *casa-grande*" (379/403). Like a powerful god, the discourse of slavery is an ontological given, leading to a generalized naturalization of sexual, economic, and racial roles.

Between *Iracema* and anthropology, Freyre's hybridity at once rests on and reinforces the coloniality of power, exhibiting all of the ambivalence of colonial discourse. While enabling a sharp and sustained critique of Eurocentric race science by confronting it with its own tools of analysis (e.g., 296), those same tools are appropriated in the naturalization of the racial contract—and neutralization of racialized protest—that governs Brazil's tolerance and cordiality. That contract tacitly solidifies the coloniality of power and its racial division of labor, perfectly reiterated in the 2000 made-for-TV docudrama on *Casa-grande e senzala* directed by Nelson Pereira dos Santos. In the film, a white, male narrator (Edson Nery da Fonseca, a scholar of Freyre's work and a personal friend of the writer) recites lessons from Freyre's text to a series of young women, each one an embodied metonym of Brazil's dominant "races." The structure could not have been more appropriate: the white man who speaks, the subaltern who listens, and the man of color who does not participate at all. Whether earnest or ironic, it is a precise rendition of the normative discourse of national family that recodifies and reifies the colonial relations between *casa-grande* and *senzala*. In the words of the normally sexually tolerant Freyre himself, any other configuration of race and gender would have been an "irregularity" (338), and, in the end, distinctly non-Brazilian.

The hybridity that emerges from the space-in-between—whether occupied by the Latin American writer or constructed as Brazil itself— is an ambivalent hybridity, an irresolution at the heart of the dialogue with the writable text: not an automatic transgression of that text, but, as Santiago concludes, *between* "prison and transgression." It is the work of critical (re)reading to (re)consider how the coloniality of power continues to operate on the site of the nation, which of its operations is transgressed, which maintained, which reinforced, and which might be stopped.

Notes

Introduction

1. The work often credited with launching colonial discourse studies is Edward Said's *Orientalism* (1978). Walter Mignolo (1993) has criticized colonial discourse theory for assuming an overly transparent relationship between colonial power and Eurocentric notions of alphabetic writing. He has proposed in its place a theory of "colonial semiosis." Although both Said and Mignolo are famously attentive to the realities of ongoing colonialism, it is Quijano's formulation, the "coloniality of power," that most succinctly captures the dynamic that I will attend to in this study. For Quijano, the "racial axis" that sustains "the model of power that is globally hegemonic today" while emerging from a "colonial origin . . . has proven to be more durable and stable than the colonialism in whose matrix it was established" (Quijano 2000, 533).

2. *Biopolitics* names the historical merging of the mere fact of organic living and political activity, whereby the regulation of life as such becomes the principal object of the political. I say more about this in chapter 1. See Foucault (2003) and Agamben (1995).

3. The context for this comment is Stuart Hall's article "When Was the 'Post-Colonial?'" which ends with a brief critique of Robert Young's *Colonial Desire* (1995). Young's book offers methodological leads that have been important for my own project. It is also an object of critical engagement, insofar as it largely elides the idea of "hybridity" as thought in the Latin American scene.

4. A number of scholars have analyzed examples of this politicization of hybridity, whereby a particular group's identity-based rights claims are attacked

on the basis of their racial, ethnic, cultural, or historical "mixedness," that is, their lack of "purity," "authenticity," and, ultimately, "legitimacy." Some studies that deal with this phenomenon include work by Bonfil Batalla (1987), Hanchard (1994), Warren (1998), and Wicomb (1998).

I. Theorizing Hybridity Today

1. Throughout this book I will occasionally indulge in tagging the suffix "-ist" onto "Latin American." I do so when I want to emphasize that I am not talking about cultural criticism that necessarily emerges from the geographical space known as "Latin America" or that is articulated by critics who might identify themselves as "Latin Americans." Rather, I refer to what Román de la Campa calls a "transnational discursive community" (1999, 1) that contextualizes its scholarly production through the object of study called "Latin America." Although most of the writers I write about here are indeed Latin Americans working (or who worked) in Latin America, *Latin Americanist* indicates a broader professional and interdisciplinary notion of thinking critically about Latin America. I realize that this conflation creates the danger of effacing important differences between "here" and "there." Although I will strive to be vigilant against such risks, a better consideration of the stakes can be found in de la Campa's *Latin Americanism* (1999, esp. 1–30).

2. I will dwell on this theme extensively over the coming pages, but for now I would point the reader to Ángel Rama's classic study of Latin American narrative fiction, *Transculturación narrativa en América Latina* (1982).

3. All translations from the Spanish and the Portuguese, unless otherwise noted in the bibliography, are mine.

4. The fiction of "four great races" has dominated the West at least since Immanuel Kant's inaugural attempt to endow the idea of race with scientific credibility (1777). Nearly a century later, Charles Darwin would note a number of competing models that counted the human races from as few as two to as many as sixty-three (1871).

5. Cornejo reports that "in the *Velázquez* English–Spanish dictionary, the word 'hybrid' raises a somewhat brutal meaning: '*mula*'" (1998, 7). While *mula* (mule) provides the root for *mulato*, the 1995 *Pequeño Larousse Ilustrado* makes the connection to race explicitly brutal by offering *mal definido* as a figurative definition of *híbrido*, and *mestizo* as a synonym; Corripio's *Gran Diccionario de Sinónimos* (1971) makes a similar move, linking *híbrido* to both *mestizo* and *bastardo*. The 1992 Real Academia Española defines "hybrid" as relating to "individuos cuyos padres son genéticamente distintos con respecto a un mismo carácter." In the English context, the *Oxford English Dictionary* notes that Webster (1828) defines it as "a mongrel or mule; an animal or plant produced from the mixture of two species." By the mid-nineteenth century, precisely with the

rise of race science, such adjectives as *grotesque* and *sickly* begin to be attached to the word (*OED*). More up-to-date, *Random House* (1983) calls a hybrid "anything derived from heterogeneous sources." However, note the suggestive "etc." with which it leaves hanging the racial implications of the hybrid: "a person or group of persons produced by the interaction or crossbreeding of two unlike cultures, traditions, etc." It mentions the synonymous *mongrel* as an outdated, "depreciatory" reference to dogs ("mixed, nondescript or degenerate breed or character"), but evades the long history of attributing the name "mongrel" to people.

6. Serge Gruzinski's comment (citing a typescript by Carmen Bernand) on the politico-religious origins of *metis* in medieval Spain, far from delinking *mestizaje* from race (as he seems to indicate), in fact points to the political origins of the naturalization of difference that would later come to be called *race* (1999, 211 n. 11).

7. Although *híbrido* does not yet appear in the 1732 *Diccionario de Autoridades*, it is noted that *mestizo* ("que se aplica al animal de padre y madre de diferentes castas") *"Viene del Latino Mixtus. Lat. Hybrid, idis. Hybridus."* However, Corominas, followed by García Yerba, points out that the Latin-Spanish route is not a dircet one. *Híbrido*, they argue, enters the Spanish not from the Latin, but rather as a gallicism, appearing in French as early as 1596, with no documented use in Spanish until 1817. This happens to be the late Enlightenment, not coincidentally the period that witnessed the beginnings of the modern current of evolutionism, whose first systematic expression is found in the early-nineteenth-century work of Lamarck, and that would sweep Western scientific thought in the following decades.

8. Although it is clear that the "fact of race"—as objective human difference—obeys no law of segregation, the idea of race necessarily does. Without discarding a constructivist idea of race—whereby race is understood not as a reflection of ethno-cultural difference, but as the production of the naturalization of that difference—we can find a number of antiessentialists who posit race's political force as essentially segregationist, for example, Foucault (2003, 255), Derrida (1985, esp. 331), and Quijano (2000). This claim should not imply a call to end race, as if that were possible. Neither is it a call for more race, as if discourses could be quantified, or their effects measured (what, exactly, is the material toll of the discourse "race"?). Rather, it should imply the need to think race "under erasure" (Spivak 1976, xiv–xx), asserting both its metaphysical contingency and its social-material immediacy. While always easily revealed as a convenient fiction, it is equally the case that a Western concept of race has founded a Eurocentric reason that scientifically organizes "man" at once into existential and ecological models of, on the one hand, self and other (e.g., Sepúlveda's famous dialogue with Las Casas; later polygenists such as Agassiz), and, on the other hand, standard and deviation (e.g., Kant and Hegel; later, this model would

underpin monogenetic theories and the paradoxical racism of, for example, Western abolitionists; for some striking examples in the U.S. case, see Talty [2000] and Menand [2001]; in the French case, see Trouillot [1995, 70–108]). A number of critics have theorized variations on these duplicitous vicissitudes of racism, such as Balibar's racism and differentialist or metaracism (17–29). Both models (binaristic self-other, or serial standard-and-deviation), however, consistently serve to regulate a segregationist, unequal distribution of social benefits ascribed to classes of people specifically constructed along racialized lines (as "races," "ethnicities," "nationalities," "tribes," etc.).

9. Some major instantiations of this debate include the *Latin American Research Review* 28(3) (1993) (with commentary by Adorno, Mignolo, Seed, and Vidal), *Revista Iberoamericana* 62(176–77) (1996) (e.g., Achugar, Cornejo, Larsen, and Moreiras), and *Cuadernos Americanos* 67(1) (1998) (e.g., Castro-Gómez, Mignolo, and Moraña). The short-lived journal *Nepantla* briefly became a kind of clearinghouse for this conversation, explicitly installing itself in between Latin Americanist and more Anglophone-oriented postcolonial or subalternist theory and criticism. See also the introduction to John Beverley's *Subalternity and Representation* (1999) and any of the essays that constitute the first part of Neil Larsen's *Determinations* (2001).

10. Both Larsen and Beverley produce admirable contributions to a more generalized critique of hybridity (articulated most forcefully against Bhabha and García Canclini). While it will take me too far afield to engage their arguments directly at this point, what I am attempting to suggest is that by *reducing* hybridity to questions of *national* politics, and thus placing it *against* "the nation," Larsen and Beverley can only reassert the very binary structures that hybridity theory tends to work between, and thus depends on. They thus leave standing, largely undisturbed, hybridity's strongest foundations. See especially their readings of Bhabha, in Beverley (via Dimitrov) (1999, 85–114) and in Larsen (via Mariátegui) (2001, 83–96).

11. My invocation of "biopolitics" is informed by Giorgio Agamben's revision of Michel Foucault's idea. In Foucault's 1976 lectures, biopolitics is limited to the new model of sovereignty, emerging decisively in the eighteenth century, in which the business of the sovereign (the state) becomes the maintenance, care, and purification of populations (public health, welfare, insurance, rehabilitation). He sums up this historical transition in sovereign power as the move from the right to "take life or let live" to the right to "make live or let die" (2003, 241). Agamben radicalizes Foucault insofar as he invokes biopolitics as the name for the "decisive event of modernity" whereby the politicization of life as such—what he calls "bare life" *(la nuda vita)*—reveals the true calling of the Western metaphysical tradition. Biopolitics, then, is the "politicization of bare life" (1995, 4) whereby "the humanity of living man is decided" (8). The incremental merging of the "realms" of bare life and political life becomes the

defining problematic of modern Western politics, and enables the conversion of classical politics (with its distinction between bare life and political life) into biopolitics (with its totalizing emphasis on the discriminatory maintenence of *all life* through typification, standardization, segregation, etc.). Without using the term, Arendt (1958, 22–78) traces a provocative history of this process. Both Foucault (e.g., 252–58) and Agamben (e.g., 130–32) understand the science of race, its articulation to nation, and its management by the state as central to the work of biopolitics. Moreover, Foucault, lending weight to Agamben's expansion of the historical parameters of biopolitics, notes something like a prehistory of biopolitics when he links it to racism, and then says that "Racism first develops with colonization, or in other words, with colonizing genocide" (257). If Foucault is serious about this statement, then we would have to take the genocide of indigenous Americans—first through war and disease in the Caribbean, later through forced work in the Andean mines—as a paradigmatic moment in the articulation of race and sovereignty.

12. On the supplementary relations between race and nation that I am following here, see Balibar and Wallerstein (1988).

13. For a good example of the complexity of the institutional transformation of Latin American cultural production (especially in terms of writing), see Ramos's (1989, 7–81) revisions of Rama (1984).

14. This claim finds support in Quijano, who notes that basic elements of the genealogy of race in Latin America are "still an open question" (2000, 575 n. 5). A number of scholars are contributing to rethinking the nexes of race and power in Latin America that Quijano is getting at here. Some good (among many) examples include Andrews (2004), Appelbaum, Macpherson, and Rosemblatt (2003), Branche (2002), Fiol-Matta (2002), Chor Maio and Ventura Santos (1996), and the contemporary classic book on eugenics by Stepan (1991), all of whom at once complicate and build on the important mid-century analyses of Latin American race relations carried out by Gonzalo Aguirre Beltrán, José María Arguedas, Florestan Fernandes, and Magnus Mörner. I take the concept of "racial exceptionalism" from Michael Hanchard (1994b).

1. Genres Are Not to Be Mixed

1. Although he never uses the term, a significant object of engagement for García Canclini is what in Bourdiean critique is often generalized as *doxa*, but what Bourdieu himself once more precisely called "class-centrism" (1968, 217), that is, the naturalization of the "way of perceiving" of a particular social class as the "real" way of perceiving art and society. García Canclini explicitly notes his debt to and displaces Bourdieu in *Culturas híbridas* (37).

2. Santiago is exemplary, but by no means exceptional, when he conflates religious syncretism, biological miscegenation, and literary discourse as all governed,

in Latin America, by the same principle of mixing that "destroys" the "unicity and purity" of Europe and becomes the "greatest contribution of Latin America to Western culture" (1971, 18).

3. The preface in question extracts sections from the original preface of the first Brazilian edition of *Casa-grande e senzala*, where the same anecdote appears, with the wording as follows: "E dos problemas brasileiros, nenhum que me inquietasse tanto como o da miscegenação" (1933, xlvii). I have been unable to verify to what extent Freyre collaborated with Samuel Putnam in translating the prefaces to the English edition, which differ from the prefaces in Portuguese.

4. For example, Gruzinski speaks to the desire to categorize the uncategorizable when he notes his efforts to produce an "inventory" of "mestizo phenomena" (1999, 20).

5. The etymology linking words such as *casta*, *castizo*, and the adjectival *casto* (chaste) to questions of both purity and mixing is fascinating, and far too complex to pursue here. Tellingly, to call something *castizo* in Spanish is not only to designate one of the many human products of race mixing (alongside *mestizo*, *mulato*, etc.), but also to speak of the authenticity of a thing's origins. Thus *lo castizo* is *lo puro*, but also *lo típico*, by which context and inflection can link *lo castizo* to *lo popular* and *lo tradicional*.

6. Konetzke (1953) offers a set of primary documents regarding colonial Spanish America, a number of which are juridical edicts regulating social privileges and restrictions along the lines of social-racial categories. Mörner's classic studies give an overview of the relations between the system of *castas*, race, and law in colonial Ibero-America (1967, 35–74; 1970).

7. The concepts of metropole and political-economic center that I employ here do not stem from a traditional, relatively static model of colonial center (e.g., Spain) and colonized periphery (e.g., New Spain), which would be inapplicable in most of Latin America since at least the late eighteenth century. Rather, I am working (at the level of both theory and practice) through the context of Enrique Dussel's more flexible revision of world-systems theory (see Dussel 1998), which understands Latin America as a peripheral participant (vis-à-vis Europe and North America) in the North Atlantic circuit of both commerce and ideas. Quijano's influential theorization of the "coloniality of power" draws upon the same model.

8. This idea is all over Bhabha's work, but see as two examples 1994, 86, 112; cf. Larsen (2001, 81–82).

9. Or again: how does "[t]he poverty of historical interpretation from the center [become] precisely the structural condition of possibility of the unequal exchange" (Gómez 2002, 367) of products and ideas? The ultimate futility of the binary strategy of insisting on the nondeficiency of knowledge generated from the so-called periphery is here suggested by rendering Fernando Gómez's insightful comment as a question. See Oliveira (2003).

10. Cf. Moreiras (1996), who also compares Borges and Candido, but takes that comparison in something like the opposite direction from which I take it here, that is, toward a positive genealogy of the basic questions that both found and complicate the effectivity of a Latin Americanist subalternism. Moreiras has both refined and expanded upon this important essay in his book *The Exhaustion of Difference* (2001, 162–83).

11. Both Borges and Derrida are participating in a long-standing critique of genre here. See Michael Beaujour's "Genus Universum" (1980).

12. Candido is here speaking through the old language of "underdevelopment" and "dependency," whose critical insight is summed up nicely, in the African context but with worldwide implications, by Paulin Hountondji when he notes that "if the economic activity of the colony was characterized by a kind of industrial vacuum, scientific activity, too, was characterized by a crying theoretical vacuum" (1992, 240). See also, for example, the way in which a theorist of the stature of Bronislaw Malinowski attempts to reconvert Fernando Ortiz's theory from the periphery into a kind of raw material for metropolitan appropriation and consumption in Ortiz's *Contrapunteo cubano del azúcar y el tobaco* (1940) (Coronil 1995, xxx–xlvi; Lund 2001, 64–68). That this center–periphery model has been fully decentered is made patently obvious less by "postcolonial theory" than by the bare fact of the cultural and intellectual industries of nation-states such as Brazil, Cuba, Mexico, and many others; that it is still a concern is made equally obvious by the financial evisceration of Latin American universities since the 1970s and the subsequent crises and dislocations of Latin Americanist humanism.

13. For a similar argument in the case of Mexico, see Reyes. Other prominent scholars have made the case for the scientific efficacy of the essay as, in the words of Clifford Geertz, "the natural genre in which to present cultural interpretation and the theories sustaining them," because, reiterating what I take to be Candido's point, "[t]heoretical formulations hover so low over the interpretations they govern that they don't make much sense . . . apart from them" (1973, 25). Citing Geertz, García Canclini says that he prefers the "scientific essay" over the "literary" because of the way that it "bases itself . . . on empirical investigations, and to the extent possible subject[s] its interpretations to a controlled handling of the data" (1989, 23–24). I think that Candido, at least within the context of Brazilian writing that he engages here, would read García Canclini's distinction as a red herring: the scientific essay *is* a literary genre. What García Canclini calls a "controlled handling of the data" Candido might call "rhetoric."

14. De Certeau radicalizes Geertz's and García Canclini's case for the essay (see note 13) granting to "fiction" (specifically, the novel) the theoretical function "which allows [history] to be thought" (1986, 20). De Certeau's reading of Freud, by which rhetoric, literature, and fiction are "the deployment of formal operations which organize historical effectiveness" and hence rise to challenge

the "logic . . . of accepted scientificity" (23), is homologous with Candido's reading of Brazilian literature. This dynamic is crucial to both the scientificity and the historicity that Freyre attempted to communicate in *Casa-grande e senzala*, as we will see in Part III.

15. Cf. Fernández Retamar (1971, 60) for the latter reading.

16. On the articulation of disciplinary and regulatory power, see Foucault's lecture of March 17, 1976, translated in *"Society Must Be Defended"* (2003).

17. I owe a debt of gratitude to Adam Sitze for helping me pull these terms out of Agamben's extremely dense treatment of "the example." Agamben sketches out this necessary relationship between example and exception as follows: "The example [as representative of the set] is thus excluded from the normal case [within the set] not because it does not belong to it but, on the contrary, because it exhibits its own belonging to it. The example is truly a *paradigm* in the etymological sense: it is what is 'shown beside' [from the Greek, *para-deigma*], and a class can contain everything except its own paradigm" (1995, 22). Now paradigmatic, the example suddenly exhibits the qualities of the exception: "The exception is what cannot be included in the whole of which it is a member and cannot be a member of the whole in which it is always already included" (25).

18. When I speak of the "limits" of Eurocentric universalism, I am thinking specifically about the "comparative advantage" (Dussel 1998, 5) known as colonialism that enabled Europe to claim its own local epistemologies as universal vis-à-vis the rest of the world. This "rest of the world" is the place wherein universality finds no purchase, and exceptions become the norm. The classic example is Hegel's African exception: "The peculiarly African character is difficult to comprehend, for the very reason that in reference to it, we must quite give up the principle which naturally accompanies all *our* ideas—the category of Universality" (1837, 93). It is worth pointing out that these comments appear in his *Philosophy of History*, and have as their goal the *exemplification* of Africa as the *exception* from *universal* History, along with America, which "as a Land of the Future . . . has no interest for us here" (87).

19. The bibliography on the relations between the topos "America" and the category of savagery spans five hundred years. Some good contemporary (among many) studies of the topic include Jáuregui (2000), Jara (1996), Dussel (1995), Mignolo (1995), Greenblatt (1991), Mason (1990), Hulme (1986), and White (1978).

20. Outside of the universal and thereby outside History, non-Europe must constitute something like, as Hegel writes in the *Phenomenology of Spirit*, "organic nature [which] has no history; from its universal, namely life, it precipitates immediately into the singularity of the existing entity" (cited in Agamben 1994, 81). Participating without belonging, Africa and America become the inner (organic nature) exteriority (savagery) of Universal History.

21. This obnoxious cascade of metonyms is one of the conclusions drawn in

Professor and Mrs. Louis [Elizabeth] Agassiz's narrative of their celebrated expedition, *A Journey in Brazil* (1869), which they undertook for the express purpose of scientifically proving polygenesis, that is, the essential nature of racial difference (Menand 2001): "The natural result of an uninterrupted contact of half-breeds with one another [in Brazil] is a class of men in which pure type fades away as completely as do all the good qualities, physical and moral, of the primitive races, engendering a mongrel crowd as repulsive as the mongrel dogs, which are apt to be their companions, and among which it is impossible to pick out a single specimen retaining the intelligence, the nobility, or the affectionateness of nature which makes the dog of pure type the favorite companion of civilized man" (1869, 298–99). The long-standing systematization of this kind of race theory is specifically what many foundational Latin American hybridologists write against. But, as I noted earlier, even Gilberto Freyre, famous popularizer of Brazilian procreative "tolerance," confesses a certain "anxiety" over "miscegenation" when confronted (during his studies in New York) with the physical evidence of the "fearfully mongrel aspect" of the Brazilian working classes (1946, xxvi–xxvii). Analogously, Pierre Bourdieu and Loïc Wacquant, just after calling for a recuperation of Freyre for the study of race relations in Brazil (1999, 71), note a similar repulsion when confronted with the "mongrel discipline" of cultural studies (74).

22. In spite of Borges's optimistic cosmopolitanism, nothing that he does makes the social and discursive force of "the nation" irrelevant, for it is the ground on which his essay stands. Indeed, his move to empty the nation of its political content as *nation-state* and turn instead to a more old-fashioned aesthetics of *nationness* (Q: "What is an Argentine?" A: "He who disavows his Argentineanness") serves only to highlight the existential and juridical crisis in which the concept "nation" was explicitly entangled by the mid-twentieth century (Agamben 1995, 130). As Larsen shows through his reading of Schwarz's concept of "as ideias fora de lugar," even a false problem may "in its very falsity [obey] a social and historical *necessity*" (2001, 80); that is, Borges's "pseudo-problem" is likely symptomatic of the most pressing, interesting, and difficult cultural "problems."

23. Writing in the wake of the Third Reich's "final solution," Borges's arguments here, articulated with his studied parsimony, are really deceptively extreme, at once suggestive and risky, as a reading of the last part of Agamben's *Homo sacer* (1995) demonstrates. The strategies of revalorization and association with which Borges links "the Jew" and the "Argentine writer" are the same strategies—invoked with something like the opposite intention—that the architects of German National Socialism used to frame the "exemplary" Jew (of "superior" talents and intellect) as the exception at the national margins and that propelled their biopolitical discourse of genocide, tied precisely, as Agamben emphasizes (132), to "denationalization." Arendt's pioneering history of Jewish

identity formation as caught "between pariah and parvenu" demonstrates the political limitations of this kind of "exceptionalism" (1951, 56–68). The fearful difference of the Jew as perceived by Nazi anti-Semitism, like today's constant exaltation of a "shadowy enemy" whose duplicity is without peer (and who is immediately denationalized as an "enemy combatant" or "foreign fighter"), is not a radical difference, but rather a common difference, an inner exteriority, an exceptional example. See also Žižek (2002, 100–101).

24. Freud here is neither constructing a discourse on the mestizo nor making a historiographical claim about the mestizo, but rather uses that figure—as an example, no less—to illustrate specific psychic processes of the unconscious. Nonetheless, his formulation is telling in the association that it draws between race, exemplification, and exception, and remarkably germane to a long-standing Latin American discourse on mestizaje and hybridity.

25. Mignolo's (2000b) introduction to the first issue of *Nepantla* offers a programmatic example of the sublimation of hybridity, broadly construed as a generalized status of being in-between.

2. Erasing Race and the Persistence of Teleology

1. De Grandis concludes her comparison of García Canclini and Bakhtin by exhorting us to consider race (2000, 223); Yúdice comments on the underdevelopment of race and ethnicity in García Canclini's mid-1990s work (2001, xxxvi–viii).

2. All translations are mine and are from the 1989 Sudamericana edition of *Culturas híbridas.* For the published English translation, see *Hybrid Cultures: Strategies for Entering and Leaving Modernity,* trans. Christopher L. Chiappari and Silvia L. López (Minnepolis: University of Minnesota Press, 2005). García Canclini uses the terms "hybridity" *(la hibridez)* and "hybridization" *(la hibridación),* as well as the nominal and adjectival form of "hybrid" (e.g., "a hybrid," or "hybrid cultures"), more or less interchangeably. In recent work he has noted a preference for "hybridization" based on the way that it implies a process, as opposed to a state or condition (1999, 56; 2001b, x). For consistency throughout this book, I defer to "hybridity." It should also be noted that García Canclini's characterization of *mestizaje* here is somewhat anachronistic. Many critics have used the term in a way that simultaneously retains its racial implications while also referring to other cultural processes of mixture. See especially Rama's elaboration of the "gesta del mestizo" (1982), Martín-Barbero's pluralized *mestizajes* (1987), and Gruzinski's *pensée métisse* (1999).

3. Although the politics and value placed around the two terms are almost opposite, the distinction between hybridity and *mestizaje* here is already at work in Gamio's 1916 formulation.

4. His introduction to Grijalbo's 2001 reedition of *Culturas híbridas* reit-

erates the case for *hibridación* over *mestizaje*, sincretism, and so on, but even there the distinction breaks down on a number of occasions (e.g., 2001b, i, viii, ix, x, xiv).

5. On the question of definition, García Canclini will find support from Friedrich Nietzsche, by way of Fredric Jameson's comments on globalization: "Nietzsche famously warned about the inevitable recursiveness of definitions. In much the same way, one often has the feeling that the call for a definition of globalization [or, in this case, hybridity], preliminary to any discussion of the thing itself, betrays a certain bad faith; and that those who insist on it already know what it is in the first place, at the same time seeking to prove its nonexistence by way of the confusion of the hapless definer" (1998, xi).

6. Even *proto*-Latin American identity. Compare, for example, the seventeenth-century thesis of religious syncretism promulgated by the Society of Jesus and later appropriated into a discourse of creole consciousness by intellectuals such as Sor Juana Inés de la Cruz and Carlos de Sigüenza y Góngora (see Jáuregui 2003), or Fray Servando Teresa de Mier (see Jara 1989, 356–57, 364). Although the stakes and motivations of these colonial writers are vastly divorced from García Canclini's, he repeats their strategic hybridization of Hispanic and indigenous cultural traditions.

7. Although this point is sometimes interpreted as a kind of revelation, it has also been widely noted that Latin American thinkers have been elaborating versions of this turn toward mixed temporalities for some time. In Part II we will see how this preoccupation is resolved by the nineteenth-century Mexican positivists; Kraniauskus (2000) has shown similar concerns in the writings of Sarmiento; and a comparable problematic runs through the anthropologically oriented work in the Andean context by Antonio Cornejo Polar (1978), Ángel Rama (1982) and José María Arguedas (see Rama 1982, 173–93). Beyond the Latin American context, Raymond Williams's notion of the "residual" (1977, 121–28), Ernst Bloch's 1930s-era concept of "noncontemporaneity" (1962, 97–148), and Bhabha's "time lag" (1994) obviously resonate here as well. García Canclini's more important contribution is to bring the notion of multitemporal heterogeneity to bear upon the nonliterary culture industries, both popular and mass.

8. For a more recent articulation of this project, see García Canclini (2001a, 12–13; 2001b). García Canclini's contribution to this reconsideration of the popular in modernity is a specific intervention within a long trajectory in Latin American cultural theory. In the genealogy of this project we would include pioneering work such as Freyre's *Casa-grande e senzala* (1933), and contemporaries such as Jesús Martín-Barbero, whose *De los medios a las mediaciones* (1987) offers an excellent, metahistorical analysis of this project in the Americas and Europe.

9. For a review of the incredibly detailed and voluminous material on racial

hybridity in the English, Anglo-American, French, and German contexts, see Young (1995, esp. 6–19). Although Young does not engage the similarly vast bibliography and participation in debates on hybridity produced in the Spanish-speaking and Lusophone world (which will be drawn upon in the following chapters), he does highlight the northern European tendency to look toward Latin America as a hotbed of hybridity (175–77).

10. A clear example of the notion of Latin American hybridity as a "harmonious" resolution of cultural antagonism can be found in Rama's uncharacteristically one-dimensional review of Arguedas called "La gesta del mestizo" (Rama 1982, 173–93).

11. See also Cornejo Polar (1996, 841) and Moraña (1998, 215). Cf. García Canclini's response (1999) to Cornejo.

12. Silvia López provides the most insightful of these critiques, reading García Canclini via the institutional perspective of critical theory: "In effect what is announced as a liberation from the social and cultural hierarchies of modernity and as a democratizing process, in reality reveals a new domination: that of the market" (2000, 258; see also 266–68). Misha Kokotovic (2000) offers a critical review of both García Canclini and his detractors (i.e., Yúdice, Beverley) in an article that incorporates a wide spectrum of García Canclini's works (*Culturas híbridas, Las culturas populares en el capitalismo* [1982], and *Consumidores y ciudadanos* [1995]). Alan O'Connor (2003) traces García Canclini's move from Marxist-oriented sociology of art to a "consumerist" (neoliberal?) theory of culture.

13. Beverley is more explicit about this choice in his critique of Bhabha and Spivak, where he asks up front, "Hybrid or binary?" (1999, 98–113). Whereas I am interested in the racialized logic of hybridity as such, Beverley's largely insightful discussion focuses on the problematic of culture within the state–civil society relation. Nevertheless, his text represents one of the most sophisticated and trenchant critiques of hybridity theory, which is why I drag it into this.

14. The insistent tone of García Canclini's frequent references to exploitation, underdevelopment, and the fact that he is not about a depoliticized postmodernism, suggest that he saw this critique coming, and that he self-consciously wants to outflank any neoconservative or neoliberal implications in his work. For example: "The accumulation of earlier examples [of how *some* marginalized groups have managed to strike a profitable balance between their worldview and customs and the onslaught of capitalist modernity] refutes nothing regarding what is known about worker exploitation and educational inequality" (221; see also 25, 149–58, 347–48). This is not to say that his treatment of power is unproblematic, or that its critique is unwarranted (see Kraniauskus 2000, 131). It is to say that his recurrent entry into the postmodernism debate is more agile than his critics tend to suggest (see 13–25, 263–347).

15. Besides Beverley (1999), this position is also staked out by Rosaldo (1995, xv–xvi).

16. This thesis is most convincingly developed in chapter 5, "La puesta en escena de lo popular" (191–235), especially in the first and fifth of his six "refutations of the classic view of the folklorists" (200): "Modern development does not suppress traditional popular cultures" (200–203) and "The popular is not lived by popular subjects as a melancholic complacency with traditions" (205–18).

17. Some of the many examples that García Canclini offers include artisans that combine modernized industrial technique with communal needs, collaborate with the state, and transform their modes of production and aesthetic expression in accordance with tourist market demands. Conversely, he mentions the persistence of caudillismo (strongman politics) within structures of modern democracy and the hybridization of popular taste and mass production with high art.

18. I would argue that the return of coevalness was anthropology's dominant project of the twentieth century, despite stereotypes that present the field as only interested in the purity of primitives. This genealogy runs from Boas, to Malinowski, to Geertz. Current examples of this long-standing critique of the denial of coevality include Lévi-Strauss's comments on "false evolutionism" (1952, 13–15), Fabian (1983), and Mignolo (1995), who does some exciting things in the Spanish colonial context with Fabian's work. García Canclini challenges the implications, though not the spirit, of Lévi-Strauss's position (1982, 3–9).

19. García Canclini takes pains to present "peasant" and "indigenous" as problematic—which is not to say empty— signifiers, and asserts that "Las culturas campesinas y tradicionales ya no representan la parte mayoritaria de la cultura popular" (203). I associate the two at great empirical risk, and only in the sense that both can be imperfectly generalized as members of the subaltern sectors of society whose cultural production is at issue in the aspect of García Canclini's work under analysis here. Still, old schemata die hard: even though urbanized, pluralized, and de-essentialized "recent migrants" to the city are framed as more closely associated with a "peasant origin" in process of "acquir[ing] the character of 'urbanoid groups'" (ibid.), precisely tracing the old anthropological teleology of acculturation.

20. As George Yúdice incisively puts it, cultural reconversion is, in the last instance, nothing more radical than "making cultural production marketable" (1993, 552).

21. In note 5 to chapter 1, I mentioned the synonymity, in Spanish, between *lo puro* and *lo tradicional*. Balibar notes that "cultural tradition" is an important element in segregationist discourses of culturalism (Balibar and Wallerstein 1988, 56).

22. We saw this same gesture in a different cultural register through his discussion of "impure genres" (see chapter 1). When García Canclini endorses Rosalba Campra's thesis that Fontanarrosa's comic-strip caricature "Inodoro

Pereyra es un gaucho que no nace de la pampa sino de la literatura gauchesca" (cited in García Canclini, 317), he obscures the fact that gaucho literature itself was a hybrid of belles lettres, a romantic, urban construction of the pampa, and nationalist-folklorist desire (Borges 1964). Thus García Canclini's conclusive "conclusion that today all cultures are border cultures" (261) may leave us wondering when it was that they weren't. Cf. Anzaldúa (1987, preface).

23. See Herlinghaus (2000, 2004) for book-length studies on the challenge of a model of competing or heterogeneous modernities for critical thought.

24. See Žižek (1993, 223) for a brief, though very suggestive, analysis of the Sendero Luminoso along the lines that I am thinking of here.

25. García Canclini has described the Zapatistas as "constru[ing the problem of hybridity and unequal material distribution] as a matter for debate concerning the nation and how it might be relocated within the framework of international conflicts. It is ultimately a critique of modernity" (2001a, 11). Unfortunately, the Sendero Luminoso would also fit into this definition. Other than the fact that the Sendero Luminoso is far less lovable than the new Zapatistas, what else differentiates their critique? García Canclini gives us no guidance here.

26. Cf. Spivak's "strategic essentialism" (1987), Gilroy's "anti-antiessentialism" (1993), and Fischer's "cultural logic" (1999; along with commentary and debate by Castañeda, Fabian, Friedman, Hale, Handler, Kapferer, and Kearney) for attempts to marry the epistemological force of (de)constructivist theory with the political necessity of essentialist ontology.

27. See Trigo (2000, 1–16).

28. It is a telling moment in the introduction to the 2001 version of *Culturas híbridas* when García Canclini presents a long list of the ways in which Mexico's large population of "indígenas mestizados" continue to hybridize, that is, modernize (travel to the United States, consumption of mass culture, education, maquiladora labor) (vii). No account of the "Indianization" of Mexico is presented.

29. William Finnegan traces the Bush administration's tendency to rhetorically link militant Islamic fundamentalism and "opponents of corporate-led globalization" (2003, 41).

30. See, for example, de Certeau (1981, 225–33).

3. The Ambivalence of Theorizing Hybridity

1. García Canclini specifically distances himself from the problem of representation, characterizing his task as "understanding and naming of the places [of conflict]" as opposed to "the representation of the voice of the silent" (2001a, 13). I am skeptical of the efficacy of this dichotomy.

2. Bhabha's texts that I find most suggestive for my intervention into Latin

Americanist theories of hybridity are his earlier work on colonial discourse and ambivalence. Thus the Bhabha with whom I dialogue in this section is primarily the mid-1980s Bhabha.

3. That Bakhtin's hybridity pointed to social relations beyond "mere" aesthetics can be seen in its suggestive affinity with Jacques Lacan's influential theory of mimetic desire, whereby a triangular structure of convergence-desire-contest sparks the role of aggressivity within the psychical production of subjection: "This form [that mediates the relations of the ego and its objects] will crystallize in the subject's internal conflictual tension, which determines the awakening of his desire for the object of the other's desire: here the primordial coming together *(concours)* is precipitated into aggressive competitiveness *(concurrence)*, from which develops the triad of others, the ego and the object" (1948, 19).

4. My reading of Bakhtin here attempts to put a finer point on Young's accurate observation of a distinguishing border between Bakhtin's natural and intentional hybridities, corresponding, respectively, to movements of fusion and of diffusion (1995, 21–22). I am arguing that this same dialectic of fusion and diffusion appears *within* that which Bakhtin alternatively refers to as intentional, conscious, or artistic hybridization. Conversely, his organic or natural hybridization is not exclusively reducible to a process of fusion, free of contest: "[L]anguage is something that is historically real, a process of heteroglot development, a process teeming with future and former languages, with prim but moribund aristocrat-languages, with parvenu-languages and with countless pretenders to the status of language—which are all more or less successful, depending on their degree of social scope and on the ideological area in which they are employed" (Bakhtin 1935, 357).

5. Cf. Spivak's discussion of two kinds of representing—*darstellen* and *vertreten*, portrait and proxy—in the context of Marx, Foucault, and Deleuze (1988, 70–74).

6. We could amass citations. Two good ones are Marx, who notes that "[t]he profound hypocrisy and inherent barbarism of bourgeois civilization lies unveiled before our eyes, turning from its home where it assumes respectable forms, to the colonies, where it goes naked" (1852, 335); and Fanon, who speaks of a "Europe where they are never done talking of Man, yet murder men everywhere they find them" (1961, 311).

7. I am going to have to leave underdeveloped, for now, the vexed question of "which colonialism?" (or, for that matter, "which hybridity?"). With Bhabha, I am using colonialism in the broadest sense, as what Quijano calls the "coloniality of power": in its literal form, as an extension of sovereignty effected by an institutionalization of primitive accumulation. I am not, then, at present, explicitly concerned with the spatiotemporal differences and historical specificities of various colonialisms: sixteenth-century Spain in the Americas; nineteenth-century British imperialism; nineteenth-century Argentine or

North American internal-colonial genocide; and so on. See Klor de Alva (1995) for an insightful consideration of this problem. Many critics have attacked the macro-theorizing that I am engaged in here. Bourdieu and Wacquant (1999) caution against the rise of imperial multiculturalists; Achugar (1997, 384) and Moraña (1998, 216) criticize the alleged universalization of the civil rights-oriented discourse of "las minorías [norteamericanas]"; and postcolonial theorists such as Said, Spivak, and Prakash are regularly chastised for generalizing. These dynamics of academic colonialism and exceptionalism are complex, and the discussions they have opened certainly are not unproductive. Nonetheless, I maintain that the loud demand for specificity (as opposed to accuracy) is a limited, and ultimately reductive, critique that replicates the divide-and-conquer strategy that defines (neo)colonial projects of all stripes. Many have made the case in favor of a (post)colonial studies that compares without effacing difference, such as Patricia Seed (1993, 150–51), Robert Young (1995, 165), and Ella Shohat and Robert Stam (1994). I also appreciate John Beverley's comment that "the issues that divide subaltern [and, I would add, postcolonial] studies from its Latin American critics may be less important in the long run than the concerns we share" (1999, 18).

8. From the 1987 article "Of Mimicry and Man: The Ambivalence of Colonial Discourse."

9. As one missionary, on the verge of hysteria, puts it: "there is no *unfeigned*, *undisguised* Christian among these Indians" (J. A. Dubois 1816; cited in Bhabha 1994, 121). This scene is also generic in the representation of Latin America's "Indians," not only within the colonial archive, but in modern critical fiction. For two striking examples, see Garro (1963, 258–59) and Castellanos (1962, 106–16).

10. The argument here is an updated version of the question of Manichaeanism (e.g., JanMohammed) and its complicators (e.g., Bhabha) that parallels the rise of postcolonial criticism. Henry Louis Gates Jr. (1991) offers a good summary of these earlier debates via a critique of the various appropriations of Fanon.

11. This is not, of course, a universal rule, as some Latin Americanists have drawn productively on aspects of Bhabha's work. A notable example would be Julio Ramos's delightful "El don de la lengua" (1993).

12. If we pretend, for a moment, that García Canclini and Bhabha represent Latin Americanist and postcolonial hybridity today, then clearly they are different. But, as a class, theories of hybridity are heterogeneous and overlap in numerous ways.

13. Besides the numerous classical myths that revolve around questions of hybridity (as genre/genus mixing), see also the book of Ezra in the Old Testament.

14. However, the *structure* of ambivalence, if not the word itself, is central to

the Freudian system of subjectification in general, namely, the Oedipal conflict. See Laplanche and Pontalis (1973, 282–86).

15. Young's reading of Gobineau is an informative review of this racially gendered dynamic (1995, 90–115).

16. The gendered structure of Freud's ambivalence is enacted in the memorable performance by Gwenyth Paltrow in Merchant and Ivory's otherwise ghastly *Jefferson in Paris*. As Thomas Jefferson's daughter, her ambivalence toward the family slaves exhibits itself symptomatically through her visibly neurotic state; Jefferson (Nick Nolte), meanwhile, remains the transparently "good slave owner" throughout. For a more complex filmic treatment of this dynamic in the masculine scene, see Tomás Gutiérrez Alea's *La última cena* (1976).

17. Malinowski's *Diary in the Strict Sense of the Term* (1967) is the key text here.

18. Far from paradoxical, as Balibar points out, this inclusive exclusion on the part of the colonizer is one of racism's founding moves, and underpins the expansion of sovereignty known as colonialism: "The heritage of colonialism is, in reality, a fluctuating combination of continued exteriorization [vis-à-vis colonial and/or national competitors] and 'internal exclusion' [vis-à-vis 'natives']" (Balibar and Wallerstein 1988, 43). Agamben calls "exclusive inclusion" the key to the "very codes of political power" in Western thought (1995, 8). Klor de Alva (1995) is very helpful in fleshing out the nuances of this abstract inclusion with concrete exclusion in the context of Latin American nation-state consolidation.

19. A good example would be the anti-pan-Mayanist writings analyzed in Warren (1998, 176–77) and Fischer (1999).

20. My argument is not an absolutist one; I am not negating *all possibility* of enlisting theories of hybridity as part of a discourse of emancipation in the service of ethnopolitical struggles. Cf. de la Cadena (2001, 22–23) for such a perspective on hybridity (as *mestizaje*).

21. I have relied on the work of others to help track down the explicit or implicit critiques of hybridity signaled in this paragraph. Especially helpful have been the already-cited Hewitt de Alcántara (on anthropology in Mexico), Gould (on *mestizaje* in Nicaragua), and Fischer (on Maya cultural activism), as well as the extraordinary volume on contemporary Latin American social movements edited by Alvarez, Dagnino, and Escobar (1998), and the articles contained therein by Warren (on Maya cultural activism), Gomes da Cunha (on black movements in Brazil) and Yúdice (on the cultural politics of *zapatismo*).

22. Although some would argue that postcolonialism is, in fact, a kind of postnationalism. See Qadri Ismail (1999).

23. The ambiguity between agency and its absence here is deliberate, and mirrors the long-standing Latin American tension around what García Canclini

calls "entering modernity" versus whether Latin America should "modernize" at all, if by modernization is meant succumbing to one of the dominant, sanctioned models of development.

24. See Lund (2001) for further consideration of this point.

25. For a convincing critique of the dominant readings of illness in Latin American writing, see Benigno Trigo's *Subjects of Crisis* (2000).

26. The copy, however, should not in and of itself be negated as a critical tool, despite forceful critiques that suggest as much (e.g., Schwarz 1992). Artists and theorists from Andrade (1928) to Richard (1993) have asserted and exemplified the critical, dialogic power harbored within the copy. For reasons of sociohistorical specificity, however, this Latin Americanist discourse of "copy as critique" (i.e., parody) should not be conflated with Bhabha's notion of "mimicry" (1994, 85–92).

27. Roberto González Echevarría (1990) has called anthropological discourse a master code of Latin American narrative fiction in the twentieth century.

28. By anthropological discourse, I refer to a loose matrix of representational strategies that bases its legitimacy on the Western scientific study, description, and interpretation of the social practices of groups of people, with a deliberate privileging of empirical questions of cultural difference. This is a wide view of the discourse. In other words, following Michel Foucault's (1971a) and Edward Said's (1978) pathbreaking theorizations of "discourse," I am not limiting these representational strategies, or this "discursive formation," to accounts that call themselves "anthropology" (e.g., the ethnography) or that explicitly engage in a critical dialogue with the academic discipline that goes by that name (e.g., *testimonio*). Rather, I am speaking of a way of knowing and representing the world that can show up in an array of narratological guises, or genres.

29. Ángel Rama's theory of the *transculturador* (1982) recognized the importance of anthropological discourse for the possibility of a critical Latin American literary production, perhaps with insufficient attention to its pitfalls and too much awe vis-à-vis the "inevitability" of modernity, whose denial he equated with "suicide."

30. The historical moment that I have in mind here is the rapid urbanization—and accompanying regional and national dislocations and crises—often summarized as "modernization," whose first wave of intensity runs from the last third of the nineteenth century to the mid-twentieth century. It is a process, of course, that (especially in the form of urbanization and dislocation) has not abated through today. Because the texts that I will be treating represent distinct areas of Latin America (Mexico and Brazil), I will not attempt to summarize a pan–Latin American historical context here. For a good review of the stakes of these social transformations, and their impact on popular culture, see Martín-Barbero (1987, esp. 149–87).

31. This theme of blurred genres is as old as anthropology itself, and has

been in vogue in North American and European anthropology for a few decades now. See, among others, Geertz (1973, 1983) and Clifford and Marcus (1986).

II. Mexico

1. See Nancy Leys Stepan's characterization of *mestizaje* as a kind of "constructive miscegenation" (1991, 138). In its most basic and common usage, *mestizaje* refers to the biological reproduction between humans of "different races," making it synonymous with terms such as race mixing, racial amalgamation, and hybridization. However, a trajectory of thinkers running from Manuel Gamio (1916) to Jesús Martín-Barbero (1987) has theorized notions of "cultural *mestizaje*" that give more or less weight to the concept's origins in biological race mixing.

2. The distinction between "discourse" and "ideology" in literary and cultural studies is full of confusion, and still an open topic. This confusion may stem from the overlapping and complementary critique of humanism developed by way of the evolving notions of ideology and discourse in the work of Louis Althusser and Michel Foucault, respectively. Each is ambiguous on the precise point of articulation between ideology and discourse (see Althusser and Balibar [1968, 64–69] and Foucault [1969, 184–86]). I will state for the record that more useful for my project is Foucault's near conflation of the two concepts, and prescription to "tackle the ideological functioning of a science [in this case, "hybridology"] . . . [by] question[ing] it as a discursive formation . . . [and hence] tackle . . . the system of formation of its objects, its types of enunciation, its concepts, its theoretical choices" (1969, 186). The point, in short, is to treat "ideological functioning" not as the enabler of illusions or false consciousness, but as a system of material representations, or a discourse. Alan Knight is one of many authoritative Mexicanists who refers transparently to *mestizaje*, especially in concert with *indigenismo*, as an essentially "ideological" aspect of the postrevolutionary state (1990, 86).

4. New Cultural History and the Rise of Mediation

1. See Kraniauskus (1998), Klor de Alva (1995, 244), Marcos (1994). This is not to say that *all* Indians live in a condition of colonialism. Nor is it to say that *only* Indians live in a condition of colonialism. Nor is it to say that *all* exploitation constitutes colonialism. As Klor de Alva has put it, a bit too glibly, but succinctly: "One does not have to be colonized to suffer" (1995, 270).

2. See Villoro (1950, 183) for a less political, and more existential, formulation of this same idea.

3. The question "Who is an Indian?" speaks to the great "paradox" of race,

whereby identifying marks are the key to informal and formal social discrimination, and yet their negation can constitute what Bonfil Batalla calls "etnocidio estadístico" (1981, 21), or the systematic negation of minority, or even majority, nationally internal ethnicities. This lack of official recognition can complicate claims to official redress on issues of race-based social inequalities. I happened to be in one of the major Afro-Brazilian centers (Salvador da Bahia) during a census year, and there was a massive campaign (called *Negro, Sim!*) on the part of activists in *o movimento negro* to mobilize blacks in favor of marking "negro" as their official ethnic identity, heretofore a centuries-old social stigma. In recent years, attempts to erase ethnoracial specificity, and hence debilitate claims to land rights or special constitutional protection, have proliferated in Guatemala, Colombia, and the United States.

4. See also Bonfil Batalla (1987, 19–40; 1981, 19–22). Joanna O'Connell offers a particularly efficient review of the historical conditions of indigenousness (1995, 47–51). More recent considerations of the problem include Montemayor (2001, 157–67), Valdés (2003), and Warman (2003, 15–40).

5. Here he is following up on the pioneering work of Villoro (1950).

6. Given the nature of ambivalence, it is striking that Villoro identifies "el mismo amor al indígnea" (1950, 184) as the generic mark of divergent, contemporary *indigenismos*. Hewitt de Alcántara links the "contradiction" to the drive to modernize that governed first-generation *indigenismo* (1984, 10–11). O'Connell, noting that "*indigenismo* has often colluded in the modernization of colonial relations rather than their elimination" (1995, 53), emphasizes—instead of contradiction—two general veins ("hegemonic" and "counterhegemonic") of *indigenismo* (57), the latter of which contains a kind of "radical potential" (53). *Indigenismo* as a term casts a wide net, but is useful in generalizing various intellectual movements, government policies, and aesthetic projects that take as their primary subject matter the social and cultural condition of the Indian or indigenous communities. It is important to point out, though, its emanation from state actors or hegemonic social sectors, and its articulation through the dominant trends and debates of what Hewitt calls "a world philosophical subculture" (1984, 181). In short, although the history and continuing threat of local or widespread rebellion makes Knight's assessment that *indigenismo* "cannot be attributed to any direct Indian pressure or lobbying" (1990, 82) somewhat misleading, O'Connell is correct in concluding that "one thing *indigenismo* is not is indigenous" (1995, 57).

7. Corrigan and Sayer note an alternative formulation of this gesture when they say that "in a materially unequal society [i.e., in any society] assertion of formal equality can be violently oppressive" (cited in Joseph and Nugent 1994, 14).

8. Michel de Certeau's turn to the agency of popular cultures in the mid-1970s (see 1981, 225–33), Bonfil Batalla's various projects on indigenous resistance (1981, 1987), the boom in *testimonio*, Subcomandante Marcos's spokesmanship in

Chiapas, and Patrick Tierney's exposure of genocidal anthropological projects carried out against the Yanomami (2000) are all exemplary in this regard.

9. Like almost all academic endeavors, the new cultural history is an internally divisive field. The lively 1999 special issue of the *Hispanic American Historical Review*, titled "Mexico's New Cultural History: ¿*Una Lucha Libre?*" provides a good overview of the contemporary insider positions on the field, along with some of its polemical opponents. In it, Mary Kay Vaughn provides a lucid summary of what kind of historiographical practice the new cultural history might be, noting four general characteristics: a decentered notion of subjectivity; the assumption of "culture" as an object of struggle; an understanding of "power" as dispersed, multiple, and cultural; and a methodological bias toward ethnography (1999, 275). In a strong critique of the new cultural history, Knight (2002) finds seven generic markers: an interest in subalterns; an emphasis on the agency of those subalterns; explicit political commitment on the part of the historian; an emphasis on the inseparability of politics and culture; attention to "mentalities" and representation; a tendency toward textual criticism; and interdisciplinarity. The main thrust of Knight's critique, however, centers on what he perceives as a reckless deployment of "jargon" within the genre, a "problem" to which he dedicates several didactic pages (148–53). Demystifying the Mexican Revolution, or rescuing the role of popular culture from the romanticizations of "revisionists" and "neopopulists," has been a major aim of what has become known as the new cultural history (Joseph and Nugent 1994, 11). Without anywhere declaring itself a work of the new cultural history, I think it is fair to consider both the collection and opening essay of Joseph and Nugent's *Everyday Forms of State Formation* (1994) as a kind of mission statement in this regard (see esp. 10–15). Florencia Mallon's *Peasant and Nation* (1995) is also foundational. An unfortunate tendency in the new cultural history is to frame it as a North American movement (Vaughn discusses this briefly [1999, 304–5]; see also Knight [2002, 148]), which it is only in name, not in practice. Not only do a number of Latin Americanists working in Latin America both anticipate (e.g., Luis González y González, José Luis Romero, Carlos Monsiváis) and theoretically inform (e.g., García Canclini, Martín-Barbero) the field, but excellent, contemporary work from Latin America that fits within the new cultural history paradigm is prevalent. See, as one example, Leticia Reina's edited volume *La reindianización de América, Siglo XIX* (1997).

10. This alliance has not always been a happy one, with Roger Chartier recently worrying that American cultural history "may be getting out of hand" in its emphasis on the cultural (cited in Deans-Smith and Joseph 1999, 204).

11. The rather orthodox notion of historical interpretation that underlies these comments is highlighted by the absence of any mention of the "novela de la Revolución" as a historical comment on the revolution. The critical tone of the best artistic representations of the revolution (e.g., Azuela, Guzmán,

Campobello, Usigli, even Orozco's murals) stands in distinct contrast to the enthusiasm of the pro-revolutionary "orthodoxy" (e.g., Tannenbaum) that Joseph and Nugent are writing against at this point.

12. Both Vaughn (1999) and Joseph and Nugent (1994, 16–17) cite Martín-Barbero as an important influence for new cultural historians. It is not a detraction from Martín-Barbero's work to note that the tone of epistemic shift that he implies here is something of an exaggeration. Indeed, the emphasis on *mestizajes* and the urban mediations between elite, popular, and mass updates, but does not go beyond, Freyre's 1933 project, which took as its object the spaces-in-between big house and slave barracks. And Martín-Barbero's formulation of indigenous culture as always already implicated in a process of *mestizaje* that links it to mass culture, though certainly a productive demystification of folklorist discourse, echoes Manuel Gamio's 1916 formulation of indigenous culture as always already implicated in a process of *mestizaje* that links it to the national culture.

13. One of the contributions of the new cultural history has been its inquiry into various emergent nationalisms, and hence it offers an important complication of the sociological determinism that haunts the work of both Gellner (see esp. 1983, 3–7) and Anderson (1983). See Chatterjeee (1986, 21). Joseph and Nugent note that an aim of the historiography represented in their volume is to "deepen our appreciation of the state's unremitting effort to contain and depict [political participation across the social-class spectrum]" (1994, 23). Deans-Smith and Joseph indicate a general underattention to the processes of containment in the new cultural history (1999). Knight skeptically quips: "Is elite ('high') cultural history not really cultural history? Or should we conclude that 100 percent new cultural history involves culture plus subalterns, while culture plus elites is a kind of watered-down version, like the 'small beer' given to callow novices in medieval monasteries?" (2002, 141).

5. Back toward a Positive *Mestizaje*

1. In thinking the relations between race, nation, and time, I am most closely following the conclusions drawn by Étienne Balibar in his work on "fictive ethnicity and ideal nation" (Balibar and Wallerstein 1988, 96–100). For further elaboration on the relations between nation and time, see Anderson (1983) and Bhabha (1994, 139–70).

2. Gamio explicitly poses the question as follows: "¿Pueden considerarse como patrias y naciones, países en los que los dos grandes elementos que constituyen a la población difieren fudamentalmente en todos sus aspectos y se ignoran entre sí?" (Can we consider as *patrias* and nations countries in which the two largest elements [Indian and criollo] that constitute the population fundamentally differ in all their aspects and are ignorant of each other?") (1916, 7).

3. Gamio actually rejects the threat of active indigenous resistance, replac-

ing the colonialist "pacification" with "incorporation" (12 ff.). Hale notes that this pacification of indigenous communities, which explicitly meant the privatization of communal lands, was an important objective for nineteenth-century Mexican liberalism: "If property, including the property of traditional Indian communities, could be freed from corporate, monopolistic, or governmental restrictions, then individual initiative, a natural division of labor, and free exchange between individuals and nations would flourish, leading ultimately to the general enhancement of wealth" (1989, 4).

4. I associate "hegemony" with the process of interclass and intercultural negotiation that leads to the formation of a body politic, a coherent, imagined community of "Mexicanness." I associate "sovereignty" with the right to "rule over," in other words, a state's exclusive legitimacy in demanding recognition and tribute from its subjects, and its capacity to regulate behavior through punishment and forgiveness. Hegemony marks the process of negotiating a national identity out of a multiplicity of "nationals"; sovereignty is the recognition of that identity in an institution, or a set of institutions such as the state, hence delegating to that institution the power to govern. Schematically, hegemony operates horizontally while sovereignty operates vertically along axes of power. For Balibar, the nation form is one of "several forms of hegemony" (Balibar and Wallerstein 1988, 90). For Deleuze and Guattari, the "State is sovereignty" (1980, 360).

5. I invoke "literate" not as a compliment, but as a generic classification. On what could be called "alphabetic racism," see Mignolo (1989).

6. I want to stress that I am attempting to think through the articulation of race and nation, and do not want to reduce race *entirely* to nation. A chain of signifiers is at work here that articulates not just race and nation, but each of them to gender, social class, sexuality, deviance, and so on. However, the race–nation articulation is fundamental. Even "imperial racism" (Hardt and Negri 2000, 190–95), from Sepúlveda to Hegel to Ashcroft and Rumsfeld, has an explicitly nationalist component. Cf. Anderson, who I think is in error in proposing that nationally internal racism can be peeled away from nationalism: "racism and anti-Semitism manifest themselves not across national boundaries, but within them. In other words, they justify not so much foreign wars as domestic repression and domination" (1983, 136). The current millenarian and militaristic discourse on "Islam," "Muslims," and "Arabs" emanating from the United States, and its explicit link to a foreign war—a "permanent" war against a "shadowy" enemy—is only one example that seems highly problematic for Anderson's assertion.

7. The basis of Barreda's educational program, and the basis of his notion of science in and of itself, is the notion of a universal positivism; in other words, positivism as not simply a method or practice, but as an ideology that names an entire way of life. Its commitment to "science" underscores the ascension of

the political appropriation of many of its precepts by the group that would both depend on and often challenge the Díaz dictatorship, and who, beginning in 1893, would be called the *Científicos* (see Hale 1989, 11, 21–22).

8. I will resist the temptation to repeat Hale's majesterial untangling of the differences between Comtian and Spencerian positivism within the positivist movement in Mexico (1989, 205). Suffice it to say that Barreda was a Comtian who understood progress as ending in a "collective and hierarchical whole" (ibid., 213) and rejected Spencer's social and Darwin's biological notion of constant transformation undergirded by a struggle for survival (ibid., 208–9, 215–17). Eventually, however, with the ascent of Justo Sierra, Comte and Spencer were reconciled under the banner of the *Científicos* (ibid., 217).

9. See Zea (1943, 55–56). The commission was called the Junta Directiva de la Instrucción Pública del Distrito Federal, and represented, in the words of Agustín Aragón, "una progresiva y completa relación entre el poder público y la educación popular" (a progressive and complete relation between public power and popular education; cited in Mares's preface to Barreda 1867, xi). Mares's preface to Barreda's *Estudios* (1941) offers an efficient account of Barreda's professional life. Barreda's contributions to the national preparatory educational system were influential for several decades, and formed most of Vasconcelos's generation of the Ateneo de la Juventud that would later undertake a fierce rebuke of its positivist principles. See, for example, Vasconcelos's 1910 speech "Don Gabino Barreda y las ideas contemporáneas" (Vasconcelos 1957–61, vol. 1), in which Barreda is applauded for dethroning the church and Hispanism, and then promptly displaced in favor of an extended critique of positivism and defense of idealism.

10. I am, of course, guilty here of a gross flattening of the dynamic and diverse intellectual movement known as "positivism." As Zea (1943) repetitively points out in his classic study, and as Hale (1989) corroborates, Mexican positivism develops within the context of vigorous debates, and it has legacies on both left and right in terms of today's political spectrum. Zea proposes a positivism that emerges out of Mexican liberalism from its combative phase (Mora, Melchor; anticlerical), to its dynamic phase (Juárez, Barreda, Sierra; anticlerical and anti-Jacobin), to its static, militant phase (the *Científicos*, Díaz, replacement of *liberty*, order, and progress with *peace*, order, and progress). Hale's study of late-nineteenth-century liberalism is widely regarded as the most sophisticated treatment of the tensions and contradictions that mediate positivism, liberalism, conservative liberalism, and "scientific politics." However, despite his critique of what he perceives as Zea's reductionism, he concurs that liberalism and positivism are interdependent and often name each other (23; see also 17, 18, 22), and ultimately reaffirms the same historical trajectory of ideas that Zea traces (3). According to Zea's interpretation, positivists see their competitors (clericalism and Jacobinism) as dangerous because they attempt to "impose"

their ideas on others. This imposition of ideas is the ultimate sin for positivists, and also their blind spot, in that they exempt scientific "demonstration" from the taint of "imposition" because it allegedly operates in a set of terms (logical exposition and material demonstration) that anybody can understand. Militant positivists, however, will reserve this right of demonstration only to those who can speak and understand the language of science, belying the exclusivity of their universality. In the end, I find that Zea's conclusion is unassailable: positivism, despite vigorous internal debates within the liberal state, is the name of the ideology of the Mexican bourgeoisie (or, for Hale, the "liberal establishment"), and privileges social order (i.e., static hegemony) over all else. But cf. Hale (23), who ascribes this ideological function to "liberalism."

11. The key texts here include Riva Palacio's contributions to the mammoth *México a través de los siglos* (1884), Sierra's *Evolución política del pueblo mexicano* (1900–1902), and Molina Enríquez's *Los grandes problemas nacionales* (1909).

12. The study in question was published in 1922 under the title *La población del Valle de Teotihuacán*.

13. See Paz (1950, and throughout later work); Anzaldúa (1987, 5). Contemporary indigenous activists are well aware of the power of this trope, and appropriate it into their own strategies of resistance and revolt in multiple ways. Thus it is common to find activists performing antiquity by invoking a transhistorical narrative of cultural and territorial heritage. In turn, statements on the vigor, and even youth, of indigenous movements are not contradictory to this stance, but rather complementary insofar as they operate within the same discursive formation. Subcomandante Omar, of the Ejército Zapatista de Liberación Nacional, is emblematic in declaring: "Nos persiguen por ser diferentes. Ya quisieran que fuéramos viejitos o viejitas para que ya no se preocupen. Se equivocan, porque nunca seremos viejitos. Unos vamos muriendo y otros retoñando, así que aquí la lucha va a estar todo el tiempo joven" (in Bellinghausen 2003). This could be read against Anzaldúa, for whom the appropriation of the Indian is consistently an appropriation of an old Indian, overcome by a new culture: "By 1650, only one-and-a-half-million pure-blooded Indians remained. The *mestizos* who were genetically equipped to survive [Old World diseases] founded a new hybrid race and inherited Central and South America" (1987, 5). Perhaps Anzaldúa is speaking in pure metaphors here, but it is worth pointing out the well-known fact that many living, even flourishing, communities that configure themselves as some version of "pure-blooded Indian" have actively questioned this inheritance.

14. The notion of an America-yet-to-be is still strong in representations of Latin America, and can be seen in the common references to the "potential" or "opportunity" of Latin American economies in the business press. On a June 2003 trip to Sweden, Mexican president Vicente Fox urged European investors to "take advantage" of the "potential" of Mexico's emerging markets (members

of his entourage were subsequently conned and mugged in downtown Stockholm). Two good artistic representations include Carlos Fuentes's *Una familia lejana* (1980), which ends with a vision of Euro-American twins in utero, and Jorge Bodansky's film *Iracema: Uma Transa Amazónica* (1975), which juxtaposes exploitative poverty (indigenous women who prostitute themselves to survive) with constant references to road construction (and exclamations of Brazil as a "pais grande"), and then these development projects with the biopolitics of colonization (*transa* refers at once to the trans-Amazon highway project and to an "Amazonian fuck"). Thanks to Malcolm McNee (personal communication) for pointing out this wordplay to me.

15. In a reading of Hegel in the context of anticolonial resistance, Susan Buck-Morss concludes that "[w]hat *is* clear is that in an effort to become more erudite in African studies during the 1820s, Hegel was in fact becoming dumber . . . It is sadly ironic that the more faithfully his lectures reflected Europe's conventional scholarly wisdom on African society, the less enlightened and more bigoted they became" (2000, 863–64).

16. On nineteenth-century indigenous and peasant resistance to the state, see Reina (1980, 2002).

17. The nineteenth-century race scientists would invert these "dangers" and worry about the excessive assimilation of racial endogamy and the infertility of racial exogamy.

18. By way of clarification, I should note that I am not attempting to determine any kind of direct "influence" between Kant and Hegel and, say, Barreda and his Mexican contemporaries. Neither, however, are they invoked at random. I am simply harnessing them as prominent examples of late Enlightenment thought, which is to a large extent reproduced as it is transformed through the specific historical needs of later nineteenth-century Western philosophers and scientists. The state intellectuals of the Reforma and the Porfiriato are active participants in these trends.

19. The texts where they most explicitly work through this paradox are Gobineau's *Essay on the Inequality of the Human Races* (1853–55) and Gumplowicz's *Rassenkampf* (1883).

20. Basave Benítez (1992) has an excellent book-length study that informs my reading of Molina Enríquez.

21. Many had already made this case, but none developed it with the sophistication of Molina Enríquez. See Ibid.

22. For Molina Enríquez, *amificación* is Díaz's mode of political action: "ofrece todos los matices de la mutua consideración y del mutuo sacrificio, [y así] todas las unidades sociales han podido pedir al señor general Díaz, según sus necesidades y tendencias propias, y el señor general Díaz les ha podido ir concediendo lo que han pedido; pero, en cambio, les ha podido pedir a su vez, sacrificios proporcionales" (it offers all the nuances of mutual consideraton and mu-

tual sacrifice, [and thus] all of the social units have been able to make requests of the señor general Díaz, according to their own necessities and tendencies, and the señor general Díaz has been able to concede to them that which they have requested; but, in exchange, he has been able at the same time to ask of them proportional sacrifices") (136). For Molina Enríquez, these various "social units" were reducible to race, as his work shows with numerous charts and tables coordinating profession, social status, real estate, and so on with racial designators. Hale notes that "[o]nce in power Díaz pardoned and then openly recruited the partisans of his three former opponents . . . Díaz could thus be portrayed as the indispensable perpetuator of national unity within the Liberal party, and the way was cleared for revisions in the constitution to legalize his successive reelections" (1989, 9).

6. They Were Not a Barbarous Tribe

1. The fatalistic quality of Knight's critique of race intensifies throughout the essay. He concludes that racism in Mexico will continue until "Indian ethnic identity is rendered socially neutral, that is, until ethnically patterned forms of subordination are completely replaced by class relations, a process that is well advanced, but still far from complete. If radical change does not solve the 'Indian problem,' continued 'development' will eventually remove it altogether" (1990, 102).

2. Benítez-Rojo asserts that the protagonist's various features "make him an Indian in the eyes of the Mexican reader of the period" (1996, 464). The book, however, is never explicit. But here is the physical description of Fernando, the protagonist, which does seem to meet certain indigenous stereotypes and social conventions of the time: "Tenía ojos pardos y regulares, nariz un poco aguileña, bigote pequeño y negro, cabellos lacios, oscuros y cortos... Taciturno, siempre sumido en profundas cavilaciones, distraído, metódico, sumiso con superiores... severo y rigoroso con sus inferiores, económico, laborioso, reservado, este joven tenía aspecto repugnante, y en efecto era antipático para todo el mundo" (Altamirano 1869, 22–23).

3. See Reina (1980) and García Cantú (1969, 55–92).

4. Myriad examples could be brought forth that run counter to Krauze's claims of the non-*mestizaje* of Mexico's historical regions of unrest. Limiting the scope to the bibliography that I am handling here, see Hu-DeHart (1988) and Reina (1980, 45–57). For examples of the varied *mestizaje* at play in regions whose unrest was neither short-lived nor "politically" resolved, see Reina (1980, 64–82) and the reports of the Centro Regional de Derechos Humanos Bartolomé Carrasco Briseño, cited in *La Jornada* (June 3, 2002).

5. Gamio's "culturally representative census" wanted to measure levels of indigenousness by taking as its standard the everyday use of a range of cultural

artifacts denominated "indigenous," "European," or "mixed." Thus a subject's or community's use of huaraches would increase indigenousness, while use of marijuana would decrease it. Ultimately, if it so happens that "la cifra de objetos de cultura indígena presente un alto porcentaje respecto al total de objetos," then "pueden considerarse como indígenas a las familias clasificadas" (187), regardless of genealogical "race." The recognized opacity of race is thus confronted with the transparent purity of "culture" in the form of racially designated "cultural objects."

6. Gamio speaks of the "pristina pureza" of the "tipo mestizo" that serves as his historical protagonist of Mexican national identity formation (1916, 66). Perhaps it is predictable to find Krauze, a writer in the same liberal tradition as Gamio, similarly repeating an uncritical exaltation of the mestizo, at the expense of indigenous communities (on Krauze's commitment to monumentalist historiography, see Lomnitz 1998). And yet even Gloria Anzaldúa, although her critical motives lie elsewhere, makes the same move with all of the biopolitical implications intact (1987, 5).

7. See, among others, Barreda (1867), Altamirano (1869), Sierra (1885, 7; 1900–1902, 291), Riva Palacio (1889, viii, 471, 478, 481), Molina Enríquez (1909). The postrevolutionary intelligentsia will only strengthen this cultural link between metaphors of (racial, cultural, and philosophical) *mestizaje* and Mexico. Some notable examples include Reyes ([1915] 1936, 16–17), Gamio ([1916] 1942), Caso (1923, 70–71, 86), Vasconcelos (1925, 1926), Brenner (1929) (whose perspective was from the North), and Lombardo Toledano (1930, 45–47). Ramos, Paz, Villoro, Zea, and a host of others carry on the tradition, sometimes articulated melancholically, but largely unproblematized.

8. The classic study of this history is Villoro (1950). Villoro's existentialist problematic is already thematized in a more historico-materialist register in López y Fuentes's *El indio* (1935; see esp. the chapters "Sumisión," "La tradición perdida," and "El líder"). See also Stabb (1959), Hale (1989, 9), Knight (1990, 79) and, for an eloquent and visual rendering of the Porfirian inauguration of *indigenismo*, Krauze (1997, 25–32). For more extensive treatment, see Bonfil Batalla (1987) and O'Connell (1995, 47–57). I invoke *indigenismo* here as a long historical trajectory of the Occidentalist appropriation of indigenous cultural practices, and do not, for the purposes of this book, abide by the traditional distinction between *indigenismo* and Romantic "Indianism."

9. These included the large-scale invasion of indigenous territories with modernized federal forces, bombardment with heavy artillery, and mass race- or ethnicity-based imprisonment and deportation. Although these were not always Díaz's first resort, they were rigorously applied as the last.

10. The nineteenth-century policy of "colonización" referred to the occupation of "terrenos baldíos" (barren lands) by small landholders, preferably immigrants from Europe. Although its goals differ from traditional "colonialism,"

it shares the structural similarity of expanding sovereignty through primitive accumulation—in this case, the alienation of communally held (often indigenous) lands by appropriating them as private property and fomenting the "liberal ideal of creating a rural bourgeoisie through colonization" (Hale 1989, 237). The history of its emergence as state policy, with ample references to the need to "improve the blood" of the Mexican citizenry, exemplifies the tightly woven discourses of race and space in Porfirian Mexico. See Hale (1989, 234–38) for a brief review, and González Navarro (1960) for a book-length study of this history.

11. The publication of *Tomochic* is a story unto itself. For the best account, see James Brown's 1968 introduction to the Porrúa edition (1989). The 1893 edition was printed anonymously in the opposition newspaper *El Demócrata*. It was soon revealed that Frías was the author. His activity in the army exposed him to charges of sedition (specifically, "revealing military secrets" and "causing false alarm") and gave the Díaz regime a reason to shut down the periodical. Frías was scheduled to be shot, but friends destroyed the hard evidence that would link him to the serial (manuscripts, notes, etc.). In one very biblical episode, a lady friend hid a publisher's letter of acceptance in "un canasto de ropa sucia" and was able to thwart the federal police by feigning "la dignidad femenina herida con tal éxito que no continuaron la búsqueda" (Brown 1968, xi–xii). Frías's death sentence was rescinded, but he was expelled from the army. Despite his fame among the opposition, his reputation for bohemianism made it hard to find work. He soon developed a morphine habit (ibid., xiii). The periodical's director, Joaquín Clausell, had diligently protected Frías during his incarceration by arguing that *he* was the serial's true author. This episode has led Antonio Saborit to write a fascinating monograph, *Los doblados de Tomóchic* (1994), in which he argues that Clausell *was*, in fact, the true author of the book. Whatever the case, there seems to be little doubt that the narrative is based on Frías's lived experience, and Brown indicates a stylistic commonality throughout his other novels.

12. The centrality of biopolitics as the conflation of citizenship with the state's selective preservation and elimination of bare life is what distinguishes the national narrative of Frías from the neoclassical narrative of, for example, Altamirano, where citizenship hinges on the voluntaristic patriotism of the individual.

13. This is precisely the structure of Renan's famous "What Is a Nation?" (1882) speech, where the polemical role that "forgetting" plays at the beginning of the speech is slyly replaced by terms such as "consent" and "sacrifice" at the end (1882, 11, 19–20).

14. In the 1906 edition (Porrúa 1989) that I am handling, chapter 8 reviews the historical conditions of the uprising at Tomochic. These include abandonment of services, but not of tax collection, by the federal government and the

church (23); the influence of a messianic movement centered on the mystic Teresa Urrea, the Santa de Cabora (ibid.); an attempt by the governor of Chihuahua to transfer the religious paintings of Tomochic's church to the state capital (24); the rape and impregnation of a village girl by a judicial authority from Guerrero (ibid.); the chastisement by a priest for the town's recognition of the villager José Carranza's status as the reincarnation of San José (ibid.); the rise of Cruz Chávez to rebuke the priest, and lead the crowd to evict him from the town (ibid.); the attempt by the mayor to fine Cruz for his actions, which Cruz refuses to pay (ibid.); and the arrival of a military battalion, which is promptly routed by the Tomoches under Cruz's leadership (25); things escalate from there. In his introduction to the Porrúa edition, Brown implies that these are a reasonably accurate summary of the historical facts surrounding the uprising (Brown 1968, xx). Most are confirmed in Vanderwood's (1998) study of the uprising.

15. See Azuela (1947, 666–67), Brown (1968, xvi–xvii), and Benítez-Rojo (1996, 478–79).

16. Thanks to Pat McNamara (personal communication) for historical verification in this regard.

17. The love story is a clear point of distinction from Sommer's foundational fictions, in which "the romances are invariably about desire in young chaste heroes for equally young and chaste heroines, the nations' hope for productive unions" (1991, 24). Frías's allegory of national (dis)articulation precisely reverses this model. The young heroes, the embodiment of a fragmented nation, are not chaste ("pure"), but soiled. At every turn, Julia is at once a "niña santa" (29) and a victim of "la monstruosa violación" (28) of a "despotismo de pirata musulmán" (21), "violada ya, pero sana y firme todavía" (21). Miguel is an alcoholic, a slave to his "vicios" (6). Moreover, there is nothing chaste in the consummation of their affections. The love scene is graphic (41–42), yet ambiguous in its reciprocity, and Miguel spends much of the remaining narrative convincing himself that it was not, in fact, a rape (43–44, 83). Julia's death at the hands of the federal siege symbolizes the effective impossibility of nonviolent, productive national union. It is significant, too, that Bernardo is alone among the Tomoches in his ignobility, and even his death is a study in treason, as he guns down a national hero who is about to grant him mercy (98–101).

18. "Quasi-colonial attitudes and methods became hallmarks of the Porfiriato: the army resembled a colonial force (pale officers, dark troops) and resorted to the usual counterinsurgency excesses" (Knight 1990, 80).

19. Although it is certainly likely that some of the rebel combatants at Tomochic were ethnically Indians, the important point is that Frías never suggests this in his work. In fact, the construction of a "criollo" and/or "mestizo"—that is, "non-Indian"—Tomochic by Frías is much more than a passing reference, indeed, is quite methodical. Later in the narrative, Frías contrasts the Sonoran

Indians ("aquellos recios indios [los pimas]") with the Tomoches, whom he describes as "criollos serranos chihuahenses" (124). This differentiation is made increasingly explicit in the later editions, with the 1906 version considered definitive (Brown 1968, xix). For example, neither reference just cited (26 or 124), nor the mention of the "white faces" of the officers (70), appears in the 1899 version. However, even there a clear distinction is made between the Tomoches and their Indian enemies, such as the Apaches, the Pimas, the Tarahumaras, and the Navajoas, of whom the latter three fight as mercenaries on the side of the federal army (1899, 13, 41, 133, 157, 165, 221). In one passage of the 1899 version, the heroic fight against the cattle-rustling, "ferocious Indians" (41) is noted as the source of the famous Tomoche valor. Finally, in the two illustrations of Tomoches (Bernardo and Julia, see ibid., 1, 51), both are depicted with stereotypically mestizo or criollo features (full beard, modern dress, etc.). In short, nothing in the 1899 version suggests that the Tomoches should be understood as "Indians." It is unlikely that any of the critics I mentioned would have been handling an edition earlier than the 1906 edition (where the mestizo and criollo identification of the Tomoches becomes explicit), which has served as the basis of subsequent publications. Brown notes that Azuela's citations pertain to the 1906 edition (1968, xix).

20. Hale cites one influential metropolitan newspaper (Justo Sierra's *La Libertad*), commenting on a rural uprising a decade prior to Tomochic, as "warning that although the Indians were fighting today for 'a few hundred square yards *(varas)* of ground,' tomorrow they would want 'the destruction of the white race'" (1989, 224). He goes on to argue that this was the long-standing "response of an intellectual and governing elite to attacks upon property and the established social order" (ibid.).

21. Frías notes the federal rationale for the crackdown on Tomochic: "En efecto, el histerismo bélico religioso de los tomochitecos podía ser un foco de contagio para los demás pueblos de la sierra que sufrían un malestar sombrío pronto a resolverse en rebelión" (26; see also 143). Moreover, the material interests of the elite classes are slyly suggested by Frías as the ulterior motive for the military action at various moments in the text. At the very outset, a functionary at a London-based mining company threatens the Tomoches with "meterlos de soldados" (24) and a railway engineer with the same company decides to avoid the region and inform the government of "la actitud belicosa del pueblo." By the time the Tomoches can assure him that they are not "bandidos vulgares," it is too late: "Mas el grito de alarma se propagaba, se multiplicaba" (26).

22. The durable Yaqui resistance, like the uprising at Tomochic, took place in northwestern Mexico, although centered one state to the west, in Sonora. Díaz's attempted "resolution" of that resistance, however, did not begin in earnest until 1897 (five years after the siege of Tomochic), with the massacre and deportation of the Yaqui at the hands of eight thousand federal troops in 1902

(see Hu-DeHart 1988, 162–65). I have heard the thesis that Yaqui fighters could have been present at Tomochic, but I have not been able to find verification. Historically, Tomochic was a center of Tarahumara culture, peripheral to the Jesuit Yaqui missions to the west (see Vanderwood 1988, 51–53), and Frías's Tomoches are constantly beset by Apaches (1906, 5, 23; 1899, 13, 41), who were not traditional rivals of the Yaqui (Hu-DeHart 1988, 155). The one reference in *Tomochic* to the Yaqui precisely opposes that resistance movement to the rebellion at Tomochic (1906, 137).

23. In a prelude to his famous works on the evolution of Mexican society and politics, Sierra refers to the "familia mestiza," thus conflating national singularity with *mestizaje* ("la mestiza constituye la familia mexicana") (1885, 7). Krauze secures the trope for future generations in his discussion of Mexican origins under the heading "The Mestizo Family" (1997, 51–59).

24. Cannibalism emerges in a passage in which Frías implies that the troops have been eating the meat of "cerdos voraces que se cebaban en la humana carnaza" and hence have been "nourished with human flesh" (139). The historic weight of this accusation could not be heavier, especially as it is launched against an army under a tyrant's command. Beyond the local references to Aztec blood sacrifice, Agamben notes that it is precisely cannibalism that mediates the transition from leader to tyrant, at least since Plato: "[W]hoever tastes one bit of human entrails minced up with those of other victims is inevitably transformed into a wolf . . . Thus, when a leader of the mob . . . , seeing the multitude devoted to his orders, does not know how to abstain from the blood of his tribe . . . will it not then be necessary that he either be killed by his enemies or become a tyrant and be transformed from a man into a wolf?" (cited in Agamben 1995, 108).

25. More precisely, the government's strategy relied on constructing the Tomoche rebels as outside the nation on three counts: Indianness, banditry, and fanaticism (Vanderwood 1998, 137). A similar process can be seen in a peasant uprising in Reformist Mexico documented by Reina, wherein the military communiqués report "una gavilla" (gang of thugs), "ladrones" (thieves), "bandidos" (bandits), "rebeldes" (rebels), "sublevados" (insurrectionists), and "indios" (Indians) (67–70). Today, this discourse has come full circle, in Chiapas, where attempts to delegitimize the neo-Zapatistas (the EZLN) often rest on "exposing" them as inauthentic Indians, that is, as urban mestizos. Whereas the statist logic in Tomochic was that the Indians were always already antinational in their non-*mestizaje*, the logic in contemporary Chiapas is that the rebels, as urban mestizos, have never been the victims of colonialism and hence must be national traitors.

26. See Azuela (1947, 663–64) and Magaña Esquível (1964, 60). Katz goes as far as to suggest that the historical uprising at Tomochic became an enabling memory for the outbreak of the revolution itself (1986, 20).

27. Vanderwood reports that the Díaz version of the massacre was so effective that even in the immediate, local aftermath, "imagination ran amok as anxious settlers in the Sierra spotted here, there, and everywhere dangerous and vengeful Tomochic 'Indians'" as opposed to "hard-working mestizos like themselves" (1998, 318).

28. Thus it is not surprising that, as the anti-Yaqui propaganda of the government increases, so do the increasingly sophisticated versions of *Tomochic* construct an increasingly explicit mestizo and criollo Tomochic.

29. See Brown's note in Frías (1906, 137). For more elaborate treatment of *teresismo*, which reached international proportions, finding receptive audiences in New York and California, see Vanderwood (1998). Gill (1957) offers a thorough, if excessively anti-Porfirian, account of the life of Teresa.

30. On the concept of "conservative liberalism," see Hale (1989, 34).

31. Frías: "Cruz convocaba a los principales vecinos a rezar el rosario, un rosario fantástico, donde aquella gente intercalaba oraciones extrañas, letanías estupendas, gritos de odio y bélicas proclamas, imprecando 'al gran poder de Dios'" (1906, 27). Mexican intellectuals have long distinguished between a good and a bad hybridity, with the former falling under terms such as *mestizaje* and *integral* (associated with the organicism of autochthonous national development), and the latter historically (at least until García Canclini salvaged the term) denominated as some derivation of *hibridismo* (associated with the imposition of colonialism and cultural imperialism).

7. *Mestizaje* and Postrevolutionary Malaise

1. The so-called Sovereign Revolutionary Convention was an alliance of generals and factions of the revolution that rejected the legitimacy of the new Carranza presidency. Among others, it included Francisco "Pancho" Villa and some supporters of Emiliano Zapata. José Vasconcelos wrote the argument that defended the Convention's legitimacy as national sovereign. Frías participated in the Convention as a "member and journalist," and wrote a "ferocious critique" of the Carranza regime. Upon the consolidation of Carranza's power, Frías was captured and, for the second time in his life, sentenced to death. This time the sentence was commuted to an eight-month prison term. See Brown (1968, xv).

2. In the opening pages of *Indología*, Vasconcelos himself notes the surprisingly strong reception of *La raza cósmica* in greater Latin America. Marentes points out that *La raza cósmica* was not actually published in Mexico until 1948 (Marentes 2000, 196).

3. See Knight (1990, 80–83) for a brief summary, with bibliography, of indigenous participation in the revolution: "The Indian contribution to the Revolution had not been premised on any Indianist project, but it had revealed

the 'Indian problem' and brought non-Indians into contact with Indians on a grand scale" (83).

4. Cited in Zea (1943, 29) from a 1922 speech by Vasconcelos, published in *La Revista del Maestro*.

5. *Zapatismo* is complex, and is more properly characterized as a kind of popular anarchism than as any kind of Indian movement. However, although Zapata himself was ethnically and culturally mestizo, much of his political platform was premised on questions central to indigenous rights, such as the partial restoration of indigenous communal lands. See Womack (1969), Krauze (1997, 274–304).

6. In 1928 Calles inaugurated the Partido Nacional Revolucionario, which he formally led until 1931, and which would transform into the Partido Revolucionario Institucional in 1946. See Krauze (1997, 404–37).

7. See, for example, Marentes (2000, 32–74), Fiol-Matta (2000, 500), Paredes (2000), Castillo (1995), Stepan (1991, 147–53), Monsiváis (1968). As early as 1927, Mariátegui offers a critique of *La raza cósmica* in his famous *Siete ensayos de interpretación de la realidad peruana*.

8. After a mobile childhood that included an influential period on the Mexican–U.S. border, Vasconcelos became part of the Mexico City cultural elite, and was a founding member of the first major postpositivist cultural center, the Ateneo de la Juventud. He was an active participant in the first phase of the revolution, and held an important cultural post under Madero. In the early 1920s, he served as secretary of education during the Álvaro Obregón presidency. During that time, he was a driving force in the postrevolutionary cultural renaissance: he commissioned the muralist movement that would make Diego Rivera famous, and he began an ambitious campaign of public education and hygiene that would be emulated in many of the early-twentieth-century populist governments of Latin America. He traveled and lectured extensively, drawing huge crowds after the publication of *La raza cósmica*. He was defrauded of the presidency in 1929, and his supporters were harrassed and sometimes killed. His thinking turned toward a kind of Hispano-fascism, and intense anti-Marxism, in the 1930s, and in 1940 he briefly directed a journal, *Timón*, run by German Nazis, in which he wrote of Hitler's "inteligencia penetrante" (Krauze 1997, 502). Shortly before he died in 1959, he applauded the success of the Cuban Revolution. There are several major studies on Vasconcelos and his life. Besides his four-volume, somewhat hyperbolic autobiography, panoramic treatments of his life's work include de Beer (1966) and Marentes (2000). On his role as secretary of education, see Fell (1989). On his ill-fated presidential campaign, see Skirius (1982). There are also a number of biographical treatments of Vasconcelos written by his friends and disciples.

9. Vasconcelos was prolific, and wrote in a number of genres, including the essay, the journalistic editorial, the travelogue, the philosophical treatise, the

historical inquiry, the autobiography, theater, short story, poetry, and a number of speeches *(discursos)* that were then published. The dominant genre that overarches all others for Vasconcelos, however, is the manifesto: there is an urgency to his writing that almost always leads him to the first-person plural mandate ("Let's") in which he articulates precisely what is to be done.

10. Indeed, his law thesis, *Teoría dinámica del derecho* (1907), contains the basic concerns that will stay with him forever: synthesis and heterogeneity, race and civilization, art and science, aesthetics and mechanics, and an obsession with totality that will later be articulated via terms such as "cosmic," "universe," "unity *[unidad]*," and "monism." See Vasconcelos (1957–61, 1:13–56).

11. Although Vasconcelos tends to refer back to Bolívar on this point, he is also in dialogue with other key pan–Latin Americanists, such as Rodó and Martí (see Gabilondo 1997), as well as nationalists such as Gamio.

12. He condemns the positivist appropriation of Spencerian natural selection with great regularity, but a particularly succinct statement comes in *Indología*: "La selección natural, según la interpretaron los darwinistas políticos a lo Herbert Spencer [es] uno de esos argumentos implícitos en todo imperialismo, con el cual de una manera inconsciente la filosofía de los dominadores de una época justifica el vandalismo de los portadores de la conquista" (1926, 70–71).

13. Cf. Paz, who, throughout his writing career, will propose precisely the opposite: that Mexico has *too much past* (e.g., 1979, 370).

14. Again, as a sign of a discourse that has turned 180 degrees, we can compare Vasconcelos to another contemporary critic, this time Silviano Santiago (1971), who—taking up a point elaborated by Lévi-Strauss (1955)—also comments on a New World temporal paradox whereby the "New" World is always slightly "behind" modernity.

15. This thesis can be found in virtually any work by Vasconcelos prior to 1930, but see *La raza cósmica* (1925, 60) for one clear example. The equivocation that Latin America *should* have much to look forward to stems from his model of a cosmic battle for the future of humanity, to be waged between Anglo and Latin America, whose outcome is still in doubt. See, for example, the last lines of *Indología* (1926, 230). In this, without citing him, he echoes Hegel (cf. 1837, 86).

16. It is interesting to note that even Vasconcelos, a radical universalist, cannot seem to proceed without identifying a constitutive outside. His special case is the Asian, who "multiply like mice" and hence risk overwhelming the new race (1925, 59–60). The Asian here functions as the American version of the European Jew, in other words, as the "stateless other" that a multiplicity of nationalisms can be defined against. It is important to remember that Vasconcelos is operating within a competition between colonizing projects (i.e., Anglo versus Iberian), and that both (the United States and Mexico) had at the time recently banned Asians from their ports, a point to which Vasconcelos

makes reference in the same passage (59). Hence the Asian serves as a kind of mediating other that can help construct an equivalence between the two. On anti-Chinese racism in Mexico, see Knight (1990, 96–97). Later, in Vasconcelos's autobiographical *Ulises Criollo* (1935), the Apache will serve this same function as a mediating other, the barbarian in between the warring camaraderie of civilizing missions. See Marentes (2000, 40).

17. He notes the "abismos contenidos en la pupila del hombre rojo, que supo tanto, hace tantos miles de años, y ahora parece que se ha olvidado de todo" (1925, 61).

18. The works that I have in mind are Guzmán, *El águila y la serpiente* (1926), Orozco's dark murals, and Usigli, *El gesticulador* (1938).

19. Azuela was once accused of plagiarizing *Tomochic*. See Azuela (1947).

20. There is a passing description of Demetrio in which it mentions "sus mejillas cobrizas de indígena de pura raza" (122), which could identify him as Indian, or as having Indian ancestry. Either way, he is constructed culturally as "Mexican," and his social sector is a generally mestizo sector. His *compañeros*, described from the perspective of the urban, *letrado*, and white Cervantes, would definitely fall on the wrong side of Vasconcelos's plan of aesthetic eugenics: "Uno, Pancracio, agüerado [light meztizo], pecoso, su cara lampiña, su barba saltona, la frente roma y oblicua, untadas las orejas al cráneo y todo de un aspecto bestial" (97). Another is described as "piltrafa humana" (ibid.).

21. Or, better, they articulate a revolution that is what Deleuze and Guattari characterize as a "war machine" (1980, 358), completely detached from any realizable project of nation or state, a force of nature. A while after Demetrio has announced his intention to support Carranza at the Aguascalientes Convention (the Convention was convened for the express purpose of deposing Carranza), his ally, the "romantic poet" Valderrama declares: "¿Villa?... ¿Obregón?... ¿Carranza?... ¡X... Y... Z...! ¿Qué se me da a mí?... ¡Amo la Revolución como amo al volcán que irrumpe! ¡Al volcán porque es volcán; a la Revolución porque es Revolución!... Pero las piedras que quedan arriba o abajo, después del cataclismo, ¿qué me importa a mí?" (Azuela [1915] 1992, 198).

22. See Paz (1985, 338–45), Fuentes (1992, 306), Krauze (1997, 296–99).

23. I am unaware of any rigorous analysis of Vasconcelos's turn to fascist anti-Semitism. Most critics express some kind of bafflement at it (e.g., Krauze 1997, 502), attempt to explain it through psychohistorical factors, or apologize for it. Marentes offers an extended analysis (2000, 48), and rightly points out a number of consistencies with Vasconcelos's larger oeuvre (ibid., 53). But he also seems to downplay the anti-Semitism by emphasizing Vasconcelos's "pragmatism" and his defense of Catholicism (54), and misses Vasconcelos's support for Nazism (52).

24. The slogan that Vasconcelos would bestow upon the ministry of educa-

tion was "Por mi raza hablará el espíritu" (Through my race the spirit will speak). Vasconcelos's embrace of *mestizaje* as a vehicle toward a new purity speaks to his pragmatism noted in both Marentes (2000) and Basave Benítez (1992, 134).

25. Vasconcelos inaugurated the spectacular ministry of education in 1922 (see 1957–61, 2:796–803). The principal patio (the Patio del Trabajo) contains allegorical frescoes that place Mexico alongside Spanish, Greek, and Indian (South Asian) civilizations. The statues of the races and the central monument, however, were never realized. Vasconcelos's spirit still resonates in the palace: a new contribution is a mural titled *El mestizaje* by Raúl Anguiano, which includes an image of Vasconcelos alongside Cortés.

26. The defense of idealism is central for Vasconcelos (1926, 202–30).

27. Monsiváis (1968) has spoken to Vasconcelos's essentially conservative nature. I think this is a fair assessment, and is seen even in Vasconcelos's most literally revolutionary text, the argument that he produced in favor of the Revolutionary Convention's sovereignty, in which he argues that the fundamental aim of revolution is to restore order, in this case the order of the Constitution of 1857 (1914, 13).

III. Brazil

1. The *Requerimiento* was the declaration of sovereignty that Spanish conquistadors were legally obligated to read aloud before entering into any kind of relations (including war) with newly encountered civilizations in the New World.

2. In a famous article titled "The Brazilian Family" (1951), Antonio Candido calls Freyre "our great authority on the sociology of the family" and reproduces a number of the basic theses of *Casa-grande e senzala*. See Christopher Dunn's article "A Retomada Freyreana" (2006) for a detailed review of the lasting influence of Freyre's thought in contemporary Brazilian cultural politics.

8. The Brazilian Family

1. Translated by Malcolm McNee, who also reproduces the section of Caminha's 1500 letter that Oswald here poeticizes (2001, 207).

2. Space, Alice Jardine has argued, is "coded as *feminine*, as *woman*" (1985, 25) in Western discourse, from classical Greek philosophy to French poststructuralism (24–25).

3. Although JanMohamed's articulation of racialized sexuality suffers from a geocentrism (in his case, Anglo/North American) similar to the Eurocentrism that he criticizes in Michel Foucault, his thesis that the "force relations" that govern the exchanges that take place across the "racial border, which is in fact always a sexual border [or discourse of gender differentiation]" (1992, 109), is

germane to the discussion that will unfold here. Foucault has demonstrated how the "dynamic racism" of the modern bourgeoisie that would later coalesce as race science emerges within the eighteenth-century rise of a discourse of sexual hygiene that marked off a eugenic elite from the unwashed masses (1978, 125). Robert Young has argued that sexuality is the "third term" that mediates the articulation of race and culture in colonial race theory (1995, 97). Balibar posits that "it is not in practice simply the case that an 'ethnic racism' and a 'sexual racism' exist in parallel; racism and sexism function together and in particular, *racism always presupposes sexism*" (Balibar and Wallerstein 1988, 49; see also 56).

4. There are, of course, exceptions to this Latin American "rule," as the scandal in Argentina around the "mixed" lineage of the hero of independence, San Martín, suggests. And colonial Latin America was not the interracial free-for-all that many of the hybridologists would have us believe. Alongside the official (national) discourses of mixing there has also existed a complementary (colonial) discourse of segregation. The *régimen de castas* of late-colonial Mexico, or the Portuguese restrictions against official recognition of mixed-race marriages beginning in 1755 (Marx 1998, 34), are only two well-known examples.

5. These nomenclatures of the *castas* abound in studies of Latin American colonial race relations. Rosenblat lists a series of them in his study on *mestizaje* (1954, 168–79). See also Katzew (1996) for many reproductions of the ethnological picto-ideographic genre known as *las castas*.

6. But cf. Metcalf (1996) and Rabell Romero (1996). Metcalf offers statistical analysis of eighteenth- and nineteenth-century Brazil that shows the scarcity of officially recognized marriages between blacks and whites, with white men married to black women at a significantly higher rate than free blacks and *pardos* (mulattos) married to white women (1996, 68). She concludes that the main barriers to interracial marriage were social-class attitudes, with the white-dominated elite almost exclusively marrying intraracially (72). Rabell Romero shows that in eighteenth-century Oaxaca, Spaniards (criollos) and Indians rarely cohabitated (within or outside of marriage), but in the cases verified, there was no significant gender bias, with Indian men paired with creole women at a slightly higher rate. It should be pointed out that the conclusions of these kinds of survey analyses, though suggestive, are made tenuous when the historically transformative nature of racial identification and the political vicissitudes of state- or church-sponsored population counting are taken into account.

7. In his memoirs, *Tempo morto e outros tempos* (1975), Freyre speaks of his "oblique" introduction to sexual relations with a "morena pálida em plena adolescência" (18, 14) and alludes to his homosexual experiences in Europe (80–122). However, Ventura (2000) reports that he is much more explicit on both subjects

in a March 1980 interview that he gave to *Playboy*, where he speaks openly about his "aventuras homossexuais na Europa" and his "apetite sexual pelas mulatas ternas e dengosas, sempre de posição social inferior."

8. It is by way of this logic that Gobineau himself could unproblematically marry a "creole whose unadulterated whiteness would always remain open to doubt" (Young 1995, 115).

9. Examples of studies of the "mediating woman" applicable to colonial discourse that inform my thinking here include Jean Franco's (1989, 1992) pathbreaking work in the Latin American context, and Eve Sedgwick's brief review of erotic triangulation in homosocial desire (1985, 21–27).

10. The Law of the Free Womb, initiated in 1871, held that children born to slaves should be free, provided that the slave owner was willing to accept governmental compensation. It was not an effective mode of abolition. See Skidmore (1974, 16).

9. On the Myth of Racial Democracy

1. See Vianna (1995, 53–54) for a brief review of the impact of Freyre's work on Brazilian social and humanistic sciences.

2. One symptomatic example would be the otherwise comprehensive collection of essays on ideas of race in Brazil, *Raça, Ciência e Sociedade* (1996), organized by Marcos Chor Maio and Ricardo Ventura Santos. Although two of the essays make brief forays into *Casa-grande e senzala* (Martínez-Echazábal and Sansone), there is no sustained reading of the text, nor a single essay dedicated to Freyre's work on race in its historical context.

3. One could amass citations, but a paradigmatic example is Michael Hanchard's *Orpheus and Power* (1994), which traces and appropriates the trajectory of the critique of "the myth of racial democracy" that runs from the 1960s (e.g., Florestan Fernandes) to the late 1980s (e.g., Hasenbalg and Valle Silva).

4. Htun (2004) provides an efficient review of the current relations between state policy and racial politics in Brazil, including an ample bibliography and statistics on race-based inequality in Brazil.

5. Htun (ibid., 61–62, 79–81) argues that the drastic and exciting shift in the national conversation around race that emerged in 2000 had as a primary condition of possibility the "conviction" among a number of (white) elites that racism was a problem worth addressing, in other words, that the "racial democracy thesis" was worth abandoning.

6. I was able to witness this reaction firsthand in 2000 when I had the opportunity to observe the filming of Nelson Pereira dos Santos's television docudrama on Freyre's *Casa-grande e senzala*. A number of the crew and cast were reading Freyre's text, and the universal response to it was amazement at how reflective it was of real, contemporary Brazilian social life and attitudes.

7. My invocation of the "logic of the example" stems from the work of Derrida and Agamben discussed in chapter 1.

8. On the ultimate weakness of this approach vis-à-vis discourse, see White (1978, 3).

9. Editions of *Casa-grande e senzala* continue to be produced, and 2000—the simultaneous one hundredth anniversary of Freyre's birth and five hundredth anniversary of the Portuguese invasion of Brazil—witnessed a surge of almost universally favorable interest in Freyre's work. Major projects included a four-part, made-for-television docudrama directed by Cinema novo legend Nelson Pereira dos Santos and starring Freyrian scholar Edson Nery da Fonseca; and extensive newspaper supplements in the *Folha de São Paulo* and the *Jornal do Brasil*.

10. Hanchard (1994b, 48–49) cites a number of revisionist historians who have documented the economic dynamics of the Portuguese slave trade that set the conditions for a kind of disposable slavery in Brazil whereby slave owners, contrary to the U.S. South, found it most efficient to simply replace exhausted (dead) labor with new imports. See also Viotti da Costa (1985) for further elaboration of comparisons between Brazilian and U.S. slavery.

11. Owing to the extensive and sometimes quite technical translations of *Casa-grande e senzala* in what follows, I have relied on the definitive and eloquent translation of Samuel Putnam for all citations of *Casa-grande e senzala* longer than a couple of words. In the case of references with a slash (as here), the page number before the slash refers to the Portuguese, which is the primary text that I am handling, and the reference following the slash refers to the Putnam translation. I will indicate any modifications of my own. A single parenthetical reference is to the Portuguese.

12. A refreshing exception to this tendency is Benzaquen de Araújo's study (1994) of Freyre's 1930s work.

13. It is thus unsurprising to find within the text several turns that equate sex and food (e.g., 250–51).

14. Freyre attributes to the Portuguese in Brazil the invention of the plantation system: "a new type of colonization . . . based upon agriculture and with the colonist remaining permanently upon the land, in place of a mere chance contact on his part with the environment and the native folk. It was in Brazil that the Portuguese began a large-scale colonization of the tropics by means of an economic technique and a social policy that were entirely new" (17/24).

15. I treated this aspect of Bhabha's work in chapter 3, but to reiterate: the ambivalence that Bhabha teases out of colonial discourse ushers forth from authoritative attempts to construct rhetorical "transparency" through a "discursive closure" that always ultimately reveals the rules of "ethnocentric, nationalist intelligibility," or the discursive and material violence that underwrites

the reason, right, and objectivity of colonial or national order and progress (1994, 110).

16. On these topics, see especially chapters 1 and 3 of *Casa-grande e senzala*.

17. The contemporary (or immediate predecessor) who receives the most of Freyre's scorn on this point is the sociologist Francisco Oliveira Vianna, and his classic studies *Populações meridionais do Brasil* (1920) and *Evolução do povo brasileiro* (1922), whose often sharp insights are overshadowed by his famous dedication to Aryanism. Aryanism was a prominent thesis of late-nineteenth- and early-twentieth-century Brazil that subscribed to the idea that race mixing would eventually "wash out" all black and indigenous traces, and yield a Europeanized race. This process was called "Aryanization" and its proponents "Aryanists" *(aryanistas)*. This notion, in fact, was long promoted as Brazil's solution to racial tension, even capturing the imagination of U.S. president Theodore Roosevelt, who commended Brazilians for their ingenious strategy (i.e., sexual reproduction) for diluting African blood, and hence, it was supposed, racial conflict. He lamented that this technique had purportedly escaped his own country. See Skidmore (1974, 75–76).

18. But cf. Skidmore, who argues that precisely this point had the "practical effect" of serving "to enforce the whitening ideal" by displaying the Portuguese ability to absorb its others (ibid., 192). This is a hoary debate in Brazil, and has more recently been reinvoked in Heloísa Buarque de Hollanda's critique of *antropofagia* (2000).

19. For Freyre, the African slave was "the white man's greatest, and most plastic collaborator in the task of agrarian colonization . . . [and] came to perform a civilizing mission" not only among the Indians (289/285), but among newly arrived slaves—who became Brazilians not in the *casa-grande* but in the *senzala* (357)—and among the Portuguese themselves, who would undergo a process of "Africanization" (290).

20. Contrary to standard interpretation, Freyre considered the *casa-grande* "as a part and not as the dominating center of the system of colonization and the patriarchal society in process of formation in Brazil" (357/375).

21. In this regard, Freyre is especially enthusiastic about the slaves from Muslim cultures. Against the stereotype of the barbarous slave, he asserts: "The fact of the matter is that the Mohammedan Negroes brought to Brazil . . . were culturally superior not only to the natives, but to the great majority of white colonists—Portuguese and the sons of Portuguese, with almost no education, some of them illiterate, most of them semi-literate . . . Almost none [of the colonists] were able to do more than sign their own names, and when they did so, it was in a broken script, like that of a child learning to write" (299/298; translation altered). He goes on to surmise that the rate of literacy in many *senzalas* exceeded that of the *casa-grande*. Against the stereotype of the dirty

slave, he notes the Portuguese tradition of growing "an enormous [finger]nail" for the "purpose of [complacently] scratching lice, and . . . their sores as well" (479/471), concluding that "the African slave . . . very often experienced a genuine repugnance at the unclean habits of his master" (462/471), and pointing to the contemporary dominance of blacks in the hygienic arts—barbers, dentists, launderers, soap merchants—as further proof against the stereotype of "spreading filth" (ibid.).

22. This thesis of a hybrid, semiperipheral (vis-à-vis Europe) Portugal finds itself in vogue again today. See José Saramago's *The Stone Raft* (1995) and Sousa Santos (1996, esp. chapter 3).

23. "The scholarly figure of Franz Boas is the one that to this day makes the deepest impression upon me" (xlvii/xxvi).

24. For example: "In the South of the United States, there evolved, from the seventeenth to the eighteenth century, an aristocratic type of rural family that bore a greater resemblance to the type of family in northern Brazil before abolition than it did to the Puritan bourgeoisie from the other half of North America, which was similarly of Anglo-Saxon origin, but which had been influenced by a different kind of economic regime" (377/401; translation altered).

25. In the same set of entries, the young Freyre also noted the terrible conditions of the "black neighborhood" and the hypocrisy of "this philistine civilization" that sends missionaries to the "pagans" around the globe: "Tais misionários antes de atravessar os mares, deveriam cuidar destes horrores domésticos. São violentamente anticristãos" (32).

26. Although Freyre does not cite the source of his "American traveler," it is likely Agassiz. Compare this obnoxious cascade of metonyms from the Professor Louis and Mrs. [Elizabeth] Agassiz's narrative of their celebrated expedition, *A Journey in Brazil* (1869), which they undertook for the express purpose of scientifically proving the polygenesis thesis, that is, the essential nature of race (Menand 2001): "The natural result of an uninterrupted contact of half-breeds with one another [in Brazil] is a class of men in which pure type fades away as completely as do all the good qualities, physical and moral, of the primitive races, engendering a mongrel crowd as repulsive as the mongrel dogs, which are apt to be their companions, and among which it is impossible to pick out a single specimen retaining the intelligence, the nobility, or the affectionateness of nature which makes the dog of pure type the favorite companion of civilized man" (1869, 298–99).

27. An interesting and telling implication of this scene is the way that social class goes uninterrogated within the shift of emphasis from race as biological essence to culture as environmental contingency. Freyre goes on to resolve the scene by "wishing" that he had known then what he knows now: that these were not just any *mestiços*, but rather "*sickly*" ones (1946, xxvii). Thus, in Freyre's self-reflection, the problem is not the confluence, in and of itself, of racial, cul-

tural, and social class markers that enable his perception and produce his judgment on the sailors' "sickliness." Rather, he assumes that the problem is that his perception—ultimately correct in its diagnosis of incompleteness, as the sailors move from "caricatures of men" to "sickly men"—was displaced into a faulty arrangement of those generic markers. Once this arrangement is "corrected," recognizing race (as biology) as an effect of culture (as environment), he feels better, less anxious.

28. Although some have argued that Nazism as such never really caught on in Brazil, this is a difficult claim to sustain in the face of the far right and openly anti-Semitic Ação Integralista Brasileira that became a fast-growing political party after its inauguration in 1932, especially in the European immigrant communities of southern Brazil. In response to the rise of the racist right at home and abroad, Freyre (who had also been accused of anti-Semitism, a not implausible assessment of some aspects of *Casa-grande e senzala*) and others issued a "Manifesto against Racial Prejudice" in 1935 (Skidmore 1974, 205–6).

29. My understanding of Kant's "affirmative criticism" is guided by John Mowitt's discussion of the same (1992, 42–43).

30. Hanchard makes a similar point (1994b, 55). On the concept of scientificity, and its relationship to literature, see de Certeau (1981, 19–21, 26). An avid reader of Freud, Freyre was among an entire generation of intellectuals who were interested in problematizing the border between science and literature, in effect returning to literary discourse the explanatory power of "positivist scientificity" (ibid., 25–26; see Freyre 1946, xxi). Euclides da Cunha's *Os sertões* (1901) is typically read as a hybrid of literary discourse and scientific observation, leading Antonio Candido to propose a particularly Brazilian genre that lists da Cunha and Freyre as its ultimate exemplars (1950, 153), an assessment later echoed by Darcy Ribeiro (1977). For more extended discussion of this point, see chapter 1 of this volume and Lund (2001, 64–72); cf. Costa Lima's (1984, 152–68) problematization of this reading of Cunha, and, by implication, of Freyre.

31. It is generally acknowledged that *Casa-grande e senzala* can be variously approached as a novel, an essay, a sociological treatise, or a historiographical study. With Candido, I would argue that it belongs to none, yet participates in all, of these generic categories. In the preface to the second English edition of *Casa-grande e senzala*, Freyre himself discusses at length his attempt to bring to Brazilian historiography the "psychological time" that would be necessary to write a domestic and intimate history of national character, and that was missing in the arid scientism that dominated the preceding generation. In this he classifies his method as "Proustian" (1946, lviii), and, calling his work a "heresy" (xviii), notes the resistance that his style often received from academics, especially in the United States. Many commentators, no less weighty than Braudel (1965) and Barthes (1953), considered him an innovator in these

questions of bringing literary sensibilities to scientific research, and of taking the subtleties of "everyday life" as a legitimate subject matter of historical inquiry. And although he desires to be taken seriously as a scholar, he cleverly ends up apologizing to "literature" for being "too scientific" rather than accept the opposite charges leveled by his critics: "this essay pretends to be not so much a conventional literary work as a piece of research and an attempt at a fresh interpretation of a determined group of facts having to do with the formation of Brazilian society" (lviii). There are many studies on the "literary aspects" of Freyre's work. See the 1962 collection of essays *Gilberto Freyre: Sua ciência, sua arte, sua filosofia* (1962), Leal et al. (1981), and Lund and McNee (2006). On the "sociological aspects" of Freyre's work, see Vila Nova (1995). Peter Burke reads Freyre as a foundational practitioner of what is today called "cultural history" (2006). Freyre also wrote works explicitly proposed as novels; see Arroyo (2003) for a reading of these works.

32. Candido provides an early modification—though not rejection—of Freyre's model in "The Brazilian Family" (1951), showing the very narrow social stratum from which Freyre drew his theory of the patriarchal, slave-owning family as a metonym for greater Brazil. For the best sustained rejection of Freyre's model, derived from demographic analysis, see Mesquita Samara (1989, esp. 15–45). See also Metcalf (1996, 59–61) and Borges (1992, 4–9).

33. Freyre mentions the regular burning of slave archives that took place in the late nineteenth century, effectively making impossible the thorough study of Brazil's slavocratic past (300–301).

34. In these quotations Freyre is largely citing, favorably, the *Ensaios brasileiros* (1930) of Azevedo Amaral.

10. The Iracema Effect in *Casa-grande e Senzala*

1. The "foundational national romance" could serve as a narrative structure that operates in the service of normalizing a discourse of national family. On the concept of the foundational national romance in nineteenth-century Latin America, see Sommer (1991).

2. Freyre wrote two short works on Alencar: *José de Alencar* (1952) and *Reinterpretando José de Alencar* (1955). The latter essay (which is also reproduced in the collection *Vida, forma e cor* [1962]), is a lyrical homage to the Brazilian language, whose "softness" Freyre attributes in part to the influence of Alencar's writing. He also notes that in his own work "creio ter, inconscientemente, seguido sugestões de um Alencar lido com entusiasmo e até fervor na meninice" (1955, 30).

3. As discussed in chapters 1–3, the construction of this positionality of the Latin American cultural producer has a long trajectory, and marks a place of convergence between Latin Americanism and postcolonialism.

4. Barthes most clearly complements Bhabha's hybridity in his discussion

of "connotation": "Functionally, connotation, releasing the double meaning on principle, corrupts the purity of communication: it is a deliberate 'static,' painstakingly elaborated, introduced into the fictive dialogue between author and reader, in short, a countercommunication (Literature is an intentional cacography)" (1970, 9).

5. "Yet reading is not a parasitical act, the reactive complement of a writing which we endow with all the glamour of creation and anteriority" (ibid., 10).

6. "[T]he writerly text is *ourselves writing*" (ibid., 5). Thus the bulk of *S/Z* is a thorough rewriting of Honoré de Balzac's readerly *Sarrazine.*

7. Mowitt is here working from the later "De l'œuvre au texte" (1971), but the implications of his reading of Barthes are apparent in *S/Z* as well. For a fuller discussion of this politicized reading of Barthes, see chapter 1 of Mowitt's *Text* (1992).

8. Roberto Schwarz's widely cited 1986 critique of Santiago (1992, translated as "National by Elimination") seems to miss this key aspect of Santiago's essay. Thus, Schwarz's baiting question, "Would the innovations of the advanced world suddenly become dispensable once they had lost the distinction of originality?" (6), seems irrelevant in the face of Santiago's recognition of the productive centrality of the economic center; that is, Santiago would likely respond in the negative.

9. From the perspective of the critique of Barthes that sees textuality as ultimately an abandonment of the historical, contextual, and political (e.g., Jameson, McNee), Santiago's appropriation would be understood as a radical reading of Barthes. From the perspective of the critique of that critique (e.g., Mowitt), I think Santiago's appropriation would be understood as an appropriate reading of Barthes.

10. Barthes explicitly rejects the priority of any model text (1970, 6, 10, 16), which I understand Santiago to be framing as an impossibility for the Latin American writer.

11. For commentary on the social exceptionalism that corresponds to Brazil's production of an "amphibious" literature, see the comments by Roberto Schwarz (2003) on Francisco de Oliveira's theory of Brazil as the "platypus country." Santiago continues to develop nuances of his theory of the "in-between," such as his lecture titled "Literatura Anfíbea" (2002).

12. Despite his rejection of appealing to force, Barthes seems to concur, concluding that "the work of the commentary [i.e., the "secondary" text, which for Santiago *is* the condition of Latin American textuality], once it is separated from an ideology of totality, consists precisely in *manhandling* the text, *interrupting* it" (1970, 15).

13. It is interesting to read Santiago's assessment alongside Borges's own conflation of European and Indian in his famous story "Historia del guerrero y de la cautiva" (1949).

14. See McNee (2001) for an analysis of Brazilian *modernismo* and its relationship to Santiago's theory of the writable text.

15. This phrasing is much more wonderful in the original: "Esses códigos perdem o seu estatuto de pureza e pouco a pouco se deixam enriquecer por novas aquisições, que transformam a integridade do Livro Santo e do Dicionário e da Gramática europeus. O elemento híbrido reina" (Santiago 1971, 18).

16. I prefer to categorize literary narratives on the Indian as *indigenismo*, rather than make the standard distinction between it and *indianismo*, which is usually the generic term applied to the Romantic treatments of the Indian. In short, I think that the idea of an "Indianism" opposed to "indigenism" creates an arbitrary and misleading division within the Latin American discourse on the Indian or Indianness. (See chapter 4 for further discussion of this point.)

Romero attacked the artificiality of the Romantic construction of the Indian in *Literatura brasileira e a crítica moderna* (1880). He was ambivalent concerning the effects of *mestiçagem*, at times heralding it as the only route of return to "the white type . . . pure and beautiful as in the old world," other times blaming it for producing "a shapeless nation with no original or creative qualities" (cited in Skidmore 1974, 36, 37).

17. Even Santiago's "contraction" is, of course, a kind of expansion, a filling up of space, of *national* territory, à la James Fenimore Cooper. See Van Doren (1921, 350).

18. *Paremos* ("let us stop") is the word he chooses to end his brief treatment of the nationalization of the Indian. Incidentally, Borges also attempts to produce a naturally critical space of Latin American writing in "El escritor argentino y la tradición" (1955). See chapter 1.

19. Schwarz frames the model–copy debate that governs Santiago's deconstructive critique as fundamentally about soothing the collective inferiority complex of an elite class of cultural producers and consumers who obsess over the misdiagnosed problem of cultural copying. He seems to take great pleasure in pointing out the irony of First World high theory rescuing the Third World from "the humiliation of having to imitate" (1992, 6). Here is a summary of his position: The problem of imitation, *even as* a false problem, is one that has historically been misdiagnosed—from Sílvio Romero to the *tropicalistas*—and is only resolvable through close attention paid to the class dynamics of social realities. The copying class, or the class for whom imitation has always been a problem, is the elite class. In fact, their dedication to the foreign follows the logic of global capital, by falsely posing the problem as one between local elite classes and a Eurocentric model, when the real problem is the separation of the poor from the structural means of (cultural) production (16). Poststructuralism, deconstruction, and spaces-in-between do nothing for us, argues Schwarz, when faced with this "specific set of historical imperatives" (7) (wrought by colonialism and slavery) and the reemergence of "relations of actual subordination"

(6) between First and Third Worlds. Although I am generally sympathetic to Schwarz's diagnosis, I would argue that he underreads the critical impulse of his target. He understands Santiago to be performing simple inversions, and engaging in an easy deconstruction of the aura and anxiety of influence. Thus Santiago's project becomes abstract, elitist, and completely divorced from concrete national problems and their corresponding social realities. What Schwarz misses, however, is what I have been trying to problematize and push forward from another direction: Santiago's discovery of the radical possibilities and politicized applicability of poststructuralism in Brazil, not incompatible with Schwarz's own keen use of dialectical materialism.

20. If it hasn't become apparent yet, I am also in oblique dialogue with the legacies of the critical project brought forth by a much wider set of thinkers than Santiago, such as Homi Bhabha (see chapter 3), Judith Butler (see esp. the last chapter of *Gender Trouble* [1990]), and Nelly Richard (1993). All have put forth important arguments around the question of repetition and differentiation, through themes of hybridity, mimicry, parody, travesty, and so on.

21. This theoretical apparatus imports from the crisis of modernity to the construction of Brazilian national essence what Jardine has identified as "gynesis," defined as "the putting into discourse of 'woman' or the 'feminine' as problematic" (1985, 236). The "writable text," which Barthes's commentator "manhandles"; the space-in-between, which becomes a lack, between this and that but neither one nor the other; and hybridity itself, whose enabling vehicle is the uterine function of the womb, all connote territory that registers in a feminine code, with real women neutralized, sublated into the conceptual.

22. Frías's *Tomochic* can be read as a narrative of civilization and barbarism, but the classic articulations of the Latin American discourse are Domingo Sarmiento's *Facundo: Civilización y barbarie* (1845) and Euclides da Cunha's *Os sertões* (1901). Beyond these and other nineteenth-century debates, which took up everything from purging of the South American plains (the pampa) of its indigenous inhabitants to perceived crises of linguistic purity (e.g., Bello versus Sarmiento), the grammar of civilization and barbarism can be traced back to the originary moments of the conquest (e.g., Columbus declaring that he will bring back to Castile a half-dozen Taino captives "so that they may learn to speak") and forward to contemporary debates surrounding indigenous rights and land reform.

23. I am, of course, only sketching, in broad strokes, the general parameters of a discursive formation. Theoretical relations of center–periphery—like all theoretical schemata—always leave something to be desired as real-life reflections of a global or national reality. Thus the discourse of civilization and barbarism has a multiplicity of nuances that far transcend a simple urban/rural dichotomy. Issues of race, gender, social class, poverty, citizenship, human rights, language, literacy, and so on, have all, at various moments, been plugged into the discourse.

24. On the notion of the racialized, allegorical economy of colonial discourse, see JanMohamed (1985). Although I think that Freyre's text would problematize the somewhat mechanistic nature of JanMohamed's famous Manichaeanism, his insistence that the European subject eventually be fixed in a position of superiority within "a field of diverse yet interchangeable oppositions" (63) is an important insight for my analysis.

25. Jara writes: "Para descubridores y conquistadores... [l]os indios eran incapaces de discriminar adecuadamente en sus hábitos culinarios, religiosos y sexuales... Sus desviaciones sexuales se producían por el favorecimiento de compañeros equivocados; ello aclaraba su inclinación al lesbianismo, la bestialidad, la sodomía y el incesto entre otras prácticas consideradas no-naturales... Además, se creía ["verified" in reports by witnesses like Vespucci and Léry], el amor socrático era una buena manera de culminar un festín de humano a la barbacoa" (1996, 23–24).

26. The bibliography on this topic is vast, but see Franco's sharp reading of the complexities surrounding the agency of La Malinche for an example in the specifically Latin American scene (1992, esp. 77). Cf. Young (1995, 108).

27. Skidmore's (1974) sources—besides Freyre, also Smith (1972) and Saunders (1958)—do not help his case. Neither speaks of the agency of "colored" women at all. Both specifically speak of the "extramarital proclivities" (Smith 1972, 74) for dark women on the part of white, upper-class men, with Saunders (citing Rene Ribeiro) also mentioning the "preferential choice by the man of a woman of lighter color" (1958, 59). Saunders also speaks of a "handicap in mating" that afflicts "black women" (62). Saunders's piece is the more scientific of the two, but its logic is highly dubious, and its findings incredible. Neither seems interested in fully acknowledging the fluid nature of racial classification, and both make judgments based on census data that cannot be tested against contemporary social reality. In today's Brazil, a *Folha de São Paulo* survey on racial prejudice implies that, at least in terms of sexual desire, black women prefer intraracial relationships at a significantly higher rate than either white or *mulata* women (Turra and Venturi 1995, 135).

28. See Sommer (1991, 140–41) on the cultural diffusion of *Iracema* and its precursor *O Guaraní* (1857). Although Sommer notes that *O Guaraní* would compete with *Iracema* as "Brazil's national novel" (140, 154), it is the latter that is generally recognized as having achieved the greater symbolic significance (Lindstrom 2000, xxii), and whose gendered configuration of the national family serves more obviously as Freyre's writable text. Several adaptations—for theater, cinema, and television—of *Iracema* have appeared, with the most irreverent rewrite attributable to Jorge Bodansky's 1975 Cinema novo classic *Iracema: Uma Transa Amazônica*. This reinterpretation explicitly points to the nexus between the coloniality of power and national development.

29. The love scene is interesting. When Iracema reports that she is now

Martim's wife, she implies that she seduced him. Iracema: "The daughter of Paje [Iracema] betrayed the secret of the *jurema* [the drug]" (69). But in the love scene itself, Martim, after praying for moral fortitude ("Christ! . . . Christ! . . .") in the presence of the beguiling virgin, is overcome by a seemingly divine "inspiration" to request the drug, and he orders Iracema to bring it to him (60). He does not seem to realize the implications of the aphrodisiac. In the same chapter, Araquém, Iracema's shaman father, has a "troubling vision of the [future] race of his children" (ibid.). It is as if all divine signs—Christian inspiration, shamanistic visions—foretell the inevitability of the birth of mestizo Brazil.

30. Klobucka (2003) has a suggestive essay on the relations between Camões and Freyre.

31. Sedgwick's model of triangulation (1985) is an important influence on my thinking here, but, as will become clear, this particular text deviates in important ways from the standardized operations of its gendered dynamics.

32. The latter is what happens, as the warrior brothers go off to battle, leaving Iracema bereft and pregnant. Martim, speaking to Poti: "'Your brother leaves with you. Nothing separates two warrior comrades when the battle trumpet sounds' . . . They embraced and departed" (102).

33. Chapter 13: Iracema: "the foreigner loves [Poti]"; Martim: "Martim does not fear the warriors of Irapuã; he fears the eyes of the maiden of Tupã [Iracema]." Chapter 14: Martim: "The words of Poti enter his brother's [Martim's] soul"; Narrator: "Martim pulled the maiden close; but then pushed her away. The sweet touch of her body . . . pained his heart as he remembered the terrible words of [her father]," who requires death of any man who possesses Iracema, owing to her sacred functions.

34. One of these speeches reads like a defense of Poti's presence: "The happiness of a young man is his wife and his friend; the first gives joy, the second, strength. The warrior without a wife is like a tree without leaves or flowers: it never bears fruit; the warrior without a friend is like a solitary tree that the wind lashes in the middle of the field: its fruit never matures" (94).

35. In this sense, Fiedler's (1979) reading of Cooper's *Leatherstocking* sagas as narratives of the relations between male bonding, sublimated erotic desire, and nation formation is suggestive.

36. An allegorical reading of *Iracema* (Iracema = America) is not extravagant, indeed, quite conventional. The important point for my particular reading is that Alencar's national allegory, whose referential equivalences transform over time (via Freyre, Santiago, Bodansky, etc.), functions discursively in that it is a rhetorical tool that operates within a discourse whose institutional underpinning is the coloniality of power packed into a national aesthetic of eugenics. Although I (like everybody) do not subscribe to Fredric Jameson's (self-acknowledged) hyperbole that *all* Third World texts should be read as "national

allegories," his complication of allegory from metaphorical parallelism to an "allegorical spirit [that] is profoundly discontinuous, a matter of breaks and heterogeneities . . . [that may lead us] to entertain the more alarming notion that such equivalences are themselves in constant change and transformation" (1986, 73) works well for my purposes here. This despite the fact that the historical situation of the "Third World literature" that he takes as his object is incommensurable with nineteenth-century Latin American fiction. For important critiques of Jameson's relevance for "reading the Third World," see Ahmad (1986) and Colás (1992); and for the specific case of Brazil, see McNee (2002). In her own critique, Sommer seems to want to reject Jameson, but then confirms the force of his attempt to reconcile allegory and dialectic by adopting the same approach (1991, 41). This ambivalence notwithstanding, I think that her unorthodox deployment of allegory (which, like Jameson, she traces to Benjamin) is a good one, and one that I am indebted to.

37. Later, the child becomes "O primeiro cearense" (The first [child] of Ceara), the Brazilian state that is the setting of *Iracema*.

38. *O Guaraní* (1857), Alencar's other major novel, places an Indian character (Peré) as the romantic lead, sparking the desire of the white Ceci. However, there is no explicit coupling as in *Iracema*, with the interracial national family merely an allusion, a utopia, at the end of the story. Only in the 1865 *Iracema* is the foundation of national family rendered literally.

39. Freyre is here citing Adlez via Alfred Crawley's influential *Studies of Savages and Sex* (1929), which he draws on extensively. The citation of Thomas refers to William Isaac Thomas, *Sex and Society* (1907).

40. Freyre immediately contradicts this argument for "sexual hunger" by noting that "among the more primitive tribes there was even a fixed period for the union of male with female" (102/98), suggesting that performance on demand was not only possible for the primitive, but necessary.

41. The wording in this phrase must have been altered in later editions of *Casa-grande e senzala*. The thirty-second edition that I am handling here weakens the "It is indeed a known fact" with "Segundo alguns observadores, entre certos grupos de gente de cor os órgãos genitais apresentam-se em geral menos desenvolvidos que entre os brancos" (102). However, both the Putnam translation (1946) and Benjamín de Garay's 1942 Spanish translation (which renders the phrase with the more definitive "Sábese, en efecto, que..." [It is in fact known that . . .]) would have been working off much earlier editions. Again, Freyre here cites the authorities in making his claims. On the underdevelopment of genitalia, he cites Ploss-Bartels, *Das Weib* (1927); on civilized versus savage libido, he cites Edward Westermarck, *The History of Human Marriage* (1891).

42. In her discussion of La Malinche in colonial Mexico, Jean Franco con-

cludes that "For the integration of the indigenous [in Latin America] into a system that was both pluralistic and hierarchical, they had to become like women or children" (1992, 74). Robert Young notes that the Western notion of "Race [has been] defined through the criterion of civilization . . . on an evolutionary scale of development from a feminized state of childhood (savagery) up to full (European) manly adulthood" (1995, 94). JanMohamed theorizes a "hysterization of the . . . oversexualized body of the black male" (1992, 107) and "the 'feminization' or 'infantilization' of the black man" (ibid.) within phallocratic and slavocratic societies.

43. "Genocide" here is used in the literal sense. Entire indigenous cultures were wiped out in Brazil's early colonial period. The total population of Indians diminished by more than half from 1570 to 1825 (Marx 1998, 49). Although the total population of Brazil has since more than doubled, the 1825 estimate of the indigenous population has not increased appreciably in the subsequent years (*Jornal do Brasil*, online, April 19, 2002). However, focusing on the preceding 40 years, Jonathan Warren (2001) argues for a resurgence in posttraditional Indian identity, as well as real indigenous peoples, in Brazil.

44. He cites Pitt-Rivers's classification of "cultural degradation" in colonial situations to draw up a "balance-sheet of European responsibilities for the racial and cultural degradation of the aborigines in Brazil, . . . find[ing] that at least nine [of fifteen] are applicable to the Jesuit padres and their civilizing methods" (110/109).

45. For example, although signature works of the era, like Mário de Andrade's *Macunaíma* (1929) or Oswald de Andrade's *Manifesto antropófago* (1928) both playfully reinvented colonial Brazil by appropriating indigenous cultures as positive signs of *brasilidade*, neither work is explicitly critical of the colonial project as such. I should also make clear that Freyre's position is by no means the first critique of the Portuguese and Jesuit conquest of the Brazilian Indians. For example, he gains support from an 1869 text by Gonçalves Dias (169).

46. Freyre is not the first to attempt this reinscription of the African as a positive element in the unfolding of Brazilian civilization. He was, however, the first to make it stick. Notable precursors whom he cites with regularity include Roquette-Pinto, and the much more ambivalent Afrânio Peixoto, Sílvio Romero, Joaquim Nabuco, and João Ribeiro. He also consistently credits Franz Boas's pathbreaking critiques of race science.

47. Sommer: "Where blacks are protagonists for Alencar . . . they figure as future, and desired, absences . . . [Iracema dies], but not before she produced a mestizo baby, nor before Martim realized that her absence was a loss. By contrast, the loss of blacks in Alencar's plays is felt like a relief" (1991, 155–56).

48. This is not a passing reference in *Casa-grande e senzala*, but rather a central point. Freyre transfers the same arguments on the "weak sexuality" of the indigenous male to the African male, including a reminder that "in the case of

civilized man the sexual appetite is ordinarily excited without great provocation. Without effort" (316/323).

49. "[U]nder a regime such as that of a slave-holding monoculture, where a majority labors and a minority does nothing but command, there will of necessity develop in the latter, by reason of its comparative leisure, a greater preoccupation with sexual matters, a greater degree of erotic mania" (320/329).

50. I arrived at this citation via Robert Young (1995, 150).

51. JanMohamed supplements the importance of this silence by racializing it, simultaneously displaying the limits of both Foucault's theory (the Eurocentric bourgeoisie) and the purview (which certainly does not include Brazil) that enables his own critique of that theory: "the most important characteristic that distinguishes racialized from white bourgeois sexuality is its strategic, rather than merely tactical, deployment of a peculiar 'silence.' Racialized sexuality has never been subjected to dense discursive articulation, which was the basis of bourgeois sexuality" (1992, 103; see also 104).

Bibliography

Achugar, Hugo. 1997. "Leones, cazadores e historiadores: A propósito de las políticas de la memoria y del conocimiento." *Revista Iberoamericana* 180: 379–87.

Agamben, Giorgio. 1993. *The Coming Community.* Trans. Michael Hardt. Minneapolis: University of Minnesota Press.

———. 1994 [1999]. *The Man without Content.* Trans. Georgia Albert. Palo Alto, Calif.: Stanford University Press.

———. 1995 [1998]. *Homo sacer: Sovereign Power and Bare Life.* Trans. Daniel Heller-Roazen. Palo Alto, Calif.: Stanford University Press.

———. 2002 [2004]. *The Open: Man and Animal.* Trans. Kevin Attell. Palo Alto, Calif.: Stanford University Press.

Agassiz, Professor Louis and Mrs. 1869. *A Journey in Brazil.* Boston: Fields, Osgood and Co.

Ahmad, Aijaz. 1986. "Jameson's Rhetoric of Otherness and the 'National Allegory.'" *Social Text* 17: 3–25.

Alencar, José de. 1865 [1948]. *Iracema.* Rio de Janeiro: Imprensa Nacional.

Altamirano, Ignacio. 1869 [1944]. *Clemencia.* Mexico City: Porrúa.

———. 1901 [1959]. *El Zarco.* In *Obras literarias completas.* Mexico City: Oasis.

Althusser, Louis, and Étienne Balibar. 1970. *Reading Capital.* Trans. Ben Brewster. London: New Left Books.

Alvarez, Sonia, Evelino Dagnino, and Arturo Escobar, eds. 1998. *Cultures of Politics, Politics of Cultures: Re-visioning Latin American Social Movements.* New York: Westview Press.

Anderson, Benedict. 1983. *Imagined Communities: Reflections on the Origin and Spread of Nationalism*. London: Verso.

Andrade, Oswald de. 1922. "As meninas da garé." In *Obras completas de Oswald de Andrade: Pau-Brasil*, ed. Haroldo de Campos. São Paulo: Globo.

———. 1928 [1970]. "Manifesto antropófago." In *Obras completas*. Vol. 6. Rio de Janeiro: Civilização Brasileira. 11–19.

Andrews, George Reid. 2004. *Afro-Latin America, 1800–2000*. New York: Oxford University Press.

Anzaldúa, Gloria. 1987. *Borderlands/La frontera: The New Mestiza*. San Francisco: Aunt Lute.

Appelbaum, Nancy, Anne Macpherson, and Karin Rosemblatt, eds. 2003. *Race and Nation in Modern Latin America*. Chapel Hill: University of North Carolina Press.

Arendt, Hannah. 1951. *The Origins of Totalitarianism*. New York: Harcourt.

———. 1958 [1998]. *The Human Condition*. Chicago: University of Chicago Press.

Arroyo, Jossianna. 2003. *Travestismos culturales: literatura y etnografía en Cuba y Brasil*. Pittsburgh: Instituto Internacional de Literatura Iberoamericana.

Ashcroft, Bill, Gareth Griffiths, and Helen Tiffin. 1998. *Key Concepts in Post-Colonial Studies*. London: Routledge.

Augé, Marc. 1994. *An Anthropology for Contemporaneous Worlds*. Trans. Amy Jacobs. Stanford, Calif.: Stanford University Press.

Azuela, Mariano. 1915 [1992]. *Los de abajo*. Madrid: Cátedra.

———. 1947 [1960]. "Cien años de novela mexicana." In *Obras completas*, vol. 3. Mexico City: Fondo de Cultura Económica. 569–668.

Bakhtin, Mikhail. 1935 [1981]. "Discourse in the Novel." In *The Dialogic Imagination: Four Essays*, trans. Caryl Emerson and Michael Holquist. Austin: University of Texas Press. 259–422.

Balibar, Étienne, and Immanuel Wallerstein. 1988 [1991]. *Race, Nation, Class: Ambiguous Identities*. London: Verso.

Barreda, Gabino. 1867 [1941]. *Estudios*. Mexico City: UNAM.

Barthes, Roland. 1953. "Maîtres et Esclaves." *Les Lettres Nouvelles* 1: 107–8.

———. 1957 [1972]. *Mythologies*. Trans. Annette Lavers. New York: Hill & Wang.

———. 1970 [1974]. *S/Z: An Essay*. Trans. Richard Miller. New York: Noonday.

Basave Benítez, Agustín. 1992. *México mestizo*. Mexico City: Fondo de Cultura Económica.

Beaujour, Michael. 1980. "Genus Universum." *Glyph: Textual Studies* 7: 15–31.

Bellinghausen, Hermann. 2003. "La Fiesta de *Los Caracoles*." *La Jornada*, August 11. http://www.jornada.unam.mx/2003/ago03/030811/003n1pol.php?origen=politica.php&fly=1

Benítez-Rojo, Antonio. 1996. "The Nineteenth-Century Spanish American Novel." In *The Cambridge History of Latin American Literature*, vol. 1, *Dis-*

covery to Modernism, ed. Roberto González Echevarría and Enrique Pupo-Walker. Cambridge: Cambridge University Press. 417–89.

Benzaquen de Araújo, Ricardo. 1994. *Guerra e Paz:* Casa-grande e senzala *e a obra de Gilberto Freyre nos anos 30.* Rio de Janeiro: Editora 34.

Bernd, Zilá. 1994. *Racismo e anti-racismo.* São Paulo: Moderna.

Beverley, John. 1999. *Subalternity and Representation: Arguments in Cultural Theory.* Durham, NC: Duke University Press.

Bhabha, Homi. 1994. *The Location of Culture.* London: Routledge.

Bloch, Ernst. 1962 [1990]. *Heritage of Our Times.* Trans. Neville Plaice and Stephen Plaice. Berkeley: University of California Press.

Bolívar, Simón. 1819 [1984]. "Discurso pronunciado por el Libertador ante el Congreso de Angostura el 15 de febrero de 1819, día de su instalación." In *Obras Completas*, vol. 6. 148–71.

Bonfil Batalla, Guillermo. 1981. "Utopía y revolución: El pensamiento político contemporáneo de los indios en América Latina." In *Utopía y revolución*, ed. Guillermo Bonfil Batalla. Mexico City: Nueva Imagen. 11–59.

———. 1987 [1996]. *México Profundo: Reclaiming a Civilization.* Trans. Philip Denis. Austin: University of Texas Press.

Borges, Dain. 1992. *The Family in Bahia, Brazil, 1870–1945.* Stanford, Calif.: Stanford University Press.

Borges, Jorge Luis. 1949a [1971]. "Historia del guerrero y de la cautiva." In *El Aleph.* Madrid: Alianza. 49–54.

———. 1949b [1971]. "El muerto." In *El Aleph.* Madrid: Alianza. 29–36.

———. 1964. *Discusión.* Madrid: Alianza.

Bourdieu, Pierre. 1968 [1993]. "Outline of a Sociological Theory of Art Perception." In *The Field of Cultural Production.* New York: Columbia University Press. 215–37.

———. 1998 [2001]. *Masculine Domination.* Trans. Richard Nice. Stanford, Calif.: Stanford University Press.

Bourdieu, Pierre, and Loïc Wacquant. 1999. "The New Global Vulgate." *The Baffler* 12: 69–78.

Brading, David. 1984. *Prophecy and Myth in Mexican History.* Cambridge: Center of Latin American Studies.

Branche, Jerome, ed. 2002. *Lo que teníamos que tener: Raza y revolución en Nicolás Guillén.* Pittsburgh: Instituto Internacional de Literatura Iberoamericana.

Braudel, Fernand. 1965. Introduction to Gilberto Freyre, *Padroni e Schiavi: La Formazione della Famiglia Brasiliana in Regime di Economia Patriarcale.* Turin: Einaudi.

Brenner, Anita. 1929. *Idols behind Altars: The Story of the Mexican Spirit.* Boston: Beacon Press.

Brown, James. 1968 [1989]. "Prólogo y notas." In *Tomochic* by Heriberto Frías. Mexico City: Porrúa. ix–xxv.

Buarque de Hollanda, Heloísa. 2000. "The Law of the Cannibal, or How to Deal with the Idea of 'Difference' in Brazil." *Revista Z.* http://acd.ufrj.br/pacc/z/quemsomos.html.

Buck-Morss, Susan. 2000. "Hegel and Haiti." *Critical Inquiry* 26: 821–65.

Burke, Peter. 2006. "Gilberto Freyre e a História Cultural." In *Gilberto Freyre e os estudos latinoamericanos*, ed. Joshua Lund and Malcolm McNee. Pittsburgh: Instituto Internacional de Literatura Iberoamericana.

Butler, Judith. 1990. *Gender Trouble: Feminism and the Subversion of Identity.* New York: Routledge.

Cadena, Marisol de la. 2001. "Reconstructing Race: Racism, Culture and Mestizaje in Latin America." *NACLA: Report on the Americas* 34(6): 16–23.

Candido, Antonio. 1950 [1967]. "Literatura e cultura de 1900 a 1945." In *Literatura e sociedade.* São Paulo: Nacional. 129–60.

———. 1951. "The Brazilian Family." In *Brazil: Portrait of Half a Continent*, ed. T. Lynn Smith and Alexander Marchant. New York: Dryden. 291–312.

———. 1970 [1995]. "Literature and Underdevelopment." In *Antonio Candido: On Literature and Society*, ed. and trans. Howard Becker. Princeton, N.J.: Princeton University Press.

Canessa, Andrew. 2000. "Contesting Hybridity: *Evangelistas* and *Kataristas* in Highland Bolivia." *Journal of Latin American Studies* 32: 115–44.

Caso, Antonio. 1923. *Obras completas.* Vol. 9. Mexico City: UNAM.

Castellanos, Rosario. 1962 [1998]. *The Book of Lamentations.* Trans. Esther Allen. New York: Penguin.

Castillo, Debra. 1995. "Postmodern Indigenism: 'Quetzacoatl and All That.'" *Modern Fiction Studies* 41(1): 35–73.

Castro-Gómez, Santiago. 1996. *Crítica de la razón latinoamericana.* Barcelona: Puvill.

Chatterjee, Partha. 1986. *Nationalist Thought and the Colonial World: A Derivative Discourse.* London: Zed.

Chiappari, Christopher. 2000. "Hybrid Religions in Highland Guatemala: Modernity, Tradition and Culture." In *Unforeseeable Americas: Questioning Cultural Hybridity in the Americas*, ed. Rita de Grandis and Zila Bernd. Amsterdam: Rodopi. 226–53.

Chor Maio, Marcos, and Ricardo Ventura Santos, eds. 1996. *Raça, Ciência e Sociedade.* Rio de Janeiro: Fiocruz.

Clifford, James, and George Marcus, eds. 1986. *Writing Culture: The Poetics and Politics of Ethnography.* Berkeley: University of California Press.

Cojtí Cuxil, Demetrio. 1996. "The Politics of Mayan Revindication." In *Maya Cultural Activism in Guatemala*, ed. Edward Fischer and MacKenna Brown. Austin: University of Texas Press. 19–50.

Colás, Santiago. 1992. "The Third World in Jameson's *Postmodernism or the Cultural Logic of Late Capitalism.*" *Social Text* 10(2–3): 258–70.

Con Davis-Undiano, Robert. 2000. "Mestizos Critique the New World: Vasconcelos, Anzaldúa and Anaya." *LIT*, vol. 11. 117–42.

Cornejo Polar, Antonio. 1978. "El indigenismo y las literaturas heterogéneas: su doble estatuto socio-cultural." *Revista de Crítica Literaria Latinoamericana* 4(7–8): 7–21.

———. 1996. "Una heterogeneidad no dialéctica: Sujeto y discurso migrantes en el Perú moderno." *Revista iberoamericana* 62: 176–77, 837–44.

———. 1998. "Mestizaje e hibridez: Los riesgos de las metáforas. Apuntes." *Revista de Crítica Literaria Latinoamericana* 47: 7–11.

Coronil, Fernando. 1995. "Transculturation and the Politics of Theory: Countering the Center, Cuban Counterpoint." In Fernando Ortiz, *Cuban Counterpoint: Tobacco and Sugar*, trans. Harriet de Onís. Durham, N.C.: Duke University Press. ix–lvi.

———. 1999. "Más allá del occidentalismo: hacia categorías geohistóricas no imperiales." *Casa de las Américas* 21(214): 21–49.

Corrigan, Philip. 1990 [1994]. "State Formation." In *Everyday Forms of State Formation: Revolution and the Negotiation of Rule in Modern Mexico*, ed. Gilbert Joseph and Daniel Nugent. Durham, N.C.: Duke University Press. xvii–xix.

Costa Lima, Luiz. 1984 [1988]. *Control of the Imaginary: Reason and Imagination in Modern Times*. Trans. Ronald W. Sousa. Minneapolis: University of Minnesota Press.

Darwin, Charles. 1871 [1997]. *The Descent of Man*. Amherst, Mass.: Prometheus Books.

Deans-Smith, Susan, and Gilbert Joseph. 1999. "The Arena of Dispute." *Hispanic American Historical Review* 79(2): 203–8.

de Beer, Gabriella. 1966. *José Vasconcelos and His World*. New York: Las Americas.

de Certeau, Michel. 1981 [1986]. *Heterologies: Discourse on the Other*. Trans. Brian Massumi. Minneapolis: University of Minnesota Press.

———. 1974 [1997]. *Culture in the Plural*. Trans. Tom Conley. Minneapolis: University of Minnesota Press.

de Grandis, Rita. 2000. "Pursuing Hybridity: From the Linguistic to the Symbolic." In *Unforeseeable Americas: Questioning Cultural Hybridity in the Americas*, ed. Rita de Grandis and Zila Bernd. Amsterdam: Rodopi. 208–25.

de la Campa, Román. 1999. *Latin Americanism*. Minneapolis: University of Minnesota Press.

Deleuze, Gilles, and Félix Guattari. 1980 [1987]. *A Thousand Plateaus: Capitalism and Schizophrenia*. Trans. Brian Massumi. Minneapolis: University of Minnesota Press.

Derrida, Jacques. 1980. "The Law of Genre." Trans. Avital Ronell. *Glyph: Textual Studies* 7: 202–32.

———. 1985. "Racism's Last Word." In *"Race," Writing and Difference*, ed. Henry Louis Gates Jr. Chicago: University of Chicago Press. 329–38.

————. 1990. "Force of Law: The 'Mystical Foundation of Authority.'" *Cardozo Law Review* 11: 920–1045.

Dirlik, Arif. 1994. "The Postcolonial Aura: Third World Criticism in the Age of Global Capitalism." *Critical Inquiry* 20: 331–50.

Dunn, Christopher. 2006. "A Retomada Freyreana." In *Gilberto Freyre e os estudos latinoamericanos*, ed. Joshua Lund and Malcolm McNee. Pittsburgh: Instituto Internacional de Literatura Iberoamericana.

Dussel, Enrique. 1995. *The Invention of Americas: Eclipse of the "Other" and the Myth of Modernity*. Trans. Michael Barber. New York: Continuum.

————. 1998. "Beyond Eurocentrism: The World-System and the Limits of Modernity." Trans. Eduardo Mendieta. In *The Cultures of Globalization*, ed. Fredric Jameson and Masao Miyoshi. Durham, N.C.: Duke University Press. 3–31.

Fabian, Johannes. 1983. *Time and the Other: How Anthropology Makes Its Object*. New York: Columbia University Press.

Fanon, Frantz. 1961. *The Wretched of the Earth*. New York: Grove.

Fell, Claude. 1989. *José Vasconcelos, los años del águila (1920–1925)*. Mexico City: UNAM.

Fernandes, Florestan. 1965. *A integração do negro na sociedade de classes*. São Paulo: Dominus.

Fernández Retamar, Roberto. 1971 [1973]. *Calibán*. Montevideo: Aquí Testimonio.

————. 1976. "Nuestra América y Occidente." *Casa de las Américas* 98: 36–57.

Fiedler, Leslie. 1979 [2001]. "James Fenimore Cooper: The Problem of the Good Bad Writer." In *The Last of the Mohicans* by James Fenimore Cooper. New York: Modern Library. xi–xxii.

Finnegan, William. 2003. "The Economics of Empire: Notes on the Washington Consensus." *Harper's Magazine* (May): 41–54.

Fiol-Matta, Licia. 2000. "'Race Woman': Reproducing the Nation in Gabriela Mistral." *Gay and Lesbian Quarterly* 6(4): 491–527.

————. 2002. *A Queer Mother for the Nation: The State and Gabriela Mistral*. Minneapolis: University of Minnesota Press.

Fischer, Edward. 1999. "Cultural Logic and Maya Identity: Rethinking Constructivism and Essentialism." *Current Anthropology* 40(4): 473–99.

Foucault, Michel. 1969 [1972]. *The Archaeology of Knowledge*. Trans. Alan Sheridan Smith. New York: Pantheon.

————. 1971a. "The Discourse on Language" (aka "The Order of Discourse"). Trans. Rupert Swyer. In *The Archaeology of Knowledge*, trans. Alan Sheridan Smith. New York: Pantheon. 215–38.

————. 1971b [1984]. "Nietzsche, Genealogy, History." In *The Foucault Reader*, ed. Paul Rabinow. New York: Pantheon. 76–100.

————. 1978. *The History of Sexuality*. Trans. Robert Hurley. New York: Pantheon.

————. 2003. *"Society Must Be Defended": Lectures at the Collège de France, 1975–1976.* Trans. David Macey. New York: Picador.

Franco, Jean. 1989. *Plotting Women: Gender and Representation in Mexico.* New York: Columbia University Press.

————. 1992. "La Malinche: From Gift to Sexual Contract." In *Critical Passions: Selected Essays*, eds. Mary Louise Pratt and Kathleen Newman. Durham, N.C.: Duke University Press. 66–82.

Freud, Sigmund. 1913 [1938]. "Totem and Taboo." In *The Basic Writings of Sigmund Freud*, ed. and trans. Dr. A. A. Brill. New York: Modern Library. 807–930.

————. 1916 [1989]. "Some Character-Types Met with in Psychoanalytic Work: [The Exceptions]." In *The Freud Reader*, ed. Peter Gay. New York: Norton. 589–93.

————. 1927 [1961]. "Fetishism." In *The Standard Edition of the Complete Psychological Works of Sigmund Freud*, trans. James Strachey and Anna Freud. London: Hogarth. 149–58.

Freyre, Gilberto. 1933 [1992]. *Casa-grande e senzala.* Rio de Janeiro: Editora Record.

————. 1942. *Casa-grande y senzala.* Trans. Benjamín de Garay. Buenos Aires: Mercatali.

————. 1946 [1966]. *The Masters and the Slaves: A Study in the Development of Brazilian Civilization.* Trans. Samuel Putnam. New York: Knopf.

————. 1955. *Reinterpretando José de Alencar.* Rio de Janeiro: Ministério da Educação e Cultura.

————. 1962 [1987]. *Vida, forma e cor.* Rio de Janeiro: Editora Record.

————. 1975. *Tempo morto e outros tempos.* Rio de Janeiro: José Olympio.

Frías, Heriberto. 1899. *Tomochic.* Barcelona: Maucci.

————. 1906 [1989]. *Tomochic.* Mexico City: Porrúa.

Friedlander, Judith. 1975. *Being Indian in Hueyapan: A Study of Forced Identity in Contemporary Mexico.* New York: St. Martin's Press.

Fuentes, Carlos. 1980. *Una familia lejana.* Mexico City: Era.

————. 1992. *The Buried Mirror: Reflections on Spain and the New World.* New York: Houghton Mifflin.

Gabilondo, Joseba. 1997. "Afterword to the 1997 Edition." In *La raza cósmica* by José Vasconelos. Baltimore: Johns Hopkins University Press. 99–117.

Gamio, Manuel. 1916 [1992]. *Forjando patria: Pro-nacionalismo.* Mexico City: Porrúa.

————. 1942 [1992]. "Las características culturales y los censos indígenas." In *Forjando patria: Pro-nacionalismo.* Mexico City: Porrúa, 1992. 185–92.

García Canclini, Néstor. 1982 [1993]. *Transforming Modernity: Popular Culture in Mexico.* Trans. Lidia Lozano. Austin: University of Texas Press.

————. 1989 [1992]. *Culturas híbridas: Estrategias para entrar y salir de la modernidad*. Buenos Aires: Sudamericana.

————. 1995a. *Consumidores y ciudadanos: Conflictos multiculturales de la globalización*. Mexico City: Grijalbo.

————. 1995b. "Narrar la multiculturalidad." *Revista de Crítica Literaria Latinoamericana* 21(42): 9–20.

————. 1999. "Entrar y salir de la hibridación." *Revista de Crítica Literaria Latinoamericana* 35(50): 53–57.

————. 2001a. *Consumers and Citizens*. Trans. George Yúdice. Minneapolis: University of Minnesota Press.

————. 2001b. "Las culutras híbridas en tiempos de globalización." In *Culturas híbridas: Estrategias para entrar y salir de la moderndidad*. Mexico City: Grijalbo. i–xxiii.

————. 2005. *Hybrid Cultures: Strategies for Entering and Leaving Modernity*. Trans. Christopher L. Chiappari and Silvia L. López. Minneapolis: University of Minnesota Press.

García Cantú, Gastón. *El socialismo en México, siglo XIX*. Mexico City: Era.

Garro, Elena. 1963 [2001]. *Los recuerdos del porvenir*. Mexico City: Joaquín Moritz.

Gates, Henry Louis, Jr. 1991. "Critical Fanonism." *Critical Inquiry* 17: 457–70.

Geertz, Clifford. 1973. *The Interpretation of Cultures*. New York: Basic Books.

————. 1983. "Blurred Genres: The Refiguration of Social Thought." In *Local Knowledge: Further Essays in Interpretive Anthropology*. New York: Basic Books.

Gellner, Ernest. 1983. *Nations and Nationalism*. Ithaca, N.Y.: Cornell University Press.

Gilberto Freyre: Sua ciência, sua filosofia, sua arte: Ensaios sôbre o autor de Casa-grande e senzala e sua influência na moderna cultura do Brasil. 1962. Rio de Janeiro: Olympio.

Gill, Mario. 1957. "Teresa Urrea, la Santa de Cabora." *Historia Mexicana* 6(4): 626–64.

Gilroy, Paul. 1992. "The End of Anti-Racism." In *"Race," Culture and Difference*, ed. Donald and Rattansi. London: Sage.

————. 1993. *The Black Atlantic: Modernity and Double Consciousness*. Cambridge: Harvard University Press.

Gobineau, Arthur de. 1853 [1970]. "Essay on the Inequality of the Human Races." In *Gobineau: Selected Political Writings*. London. Jonathan Cape. 37–176.

Gomes da Cunha, Olivia Maria. 1998. "Black Movements and the 'Politics of Identity' in Brazil." In *Cultures of Politics, Politics of Cultures: Re-visioning Latin American Social Movements*, ed. Sonia Alvarez, Evelina Dagnino, and Arturo Escobar. New York: Westview Press. 220–51.

Gómez, Fernando. 2002. "Francisco de Vitoria in 1934, Before and After." *MLN* 117(2): 365–405.

González Echevarría, Roberto. 1990. *Myth and Archive: A Theory of Latin American Narrative.* Cambridge: Cambridge University Press.

González Navarro, Moisés. 1960. *La colonización en México, 1877–1910.* Mexico City: Estampillas y Valores.

Gould, Jeffrey. 1998. *To Die in This Way: Nicaraguan Indians and the Myth of Mestizaje, 1880–1965.* Durham, N.C.: Duke University Press.

Greenblatt, Stephen. 1991. *Marvelous Possessions: The Wonder of the New World.* Chicago: University of Chicago Press.

Gruzinski, Serge. 1999 [2002]. *The Mestizo Mind.* Trans. Deke Dusinberre. London: Routledge.

Guha, Ranajit, ed. 1982. *Subaltern Studies: Writings on South Asian History and Society.* Vol. 1. Delhi: Oxford University Press.

Guillén, Nicolás. 1979. *Nueva antología mayor.* Ed. Ángel Augier. Havana: Letras Cubanas.

Hale, Charles. 1989. *The Transformation of Liberalism in Late Nineteenth-Century Mexico.* Princeton, N.J.: Princeton University Press.

Hall, Stuart. 1996a. *Race: The Floating Signifier.* Dir. Sut Jhally. Northampton, Mass.: Media Education Foundation.

———. 1996b. "When Was the 'Post-Colonial'? Thinking at the Limit." In *The Post-Colonial Question: Common Skies, Divided Horizons,* ed. Iain Chambers and Lidia Curti. London: Routledge. 242–60.

Hanchard, Michael. 1994a. "Black Cinderella?: Race and the Public Sphere in Brazil." *Public Culture* 7: 165–85.

———. 1994b. *Orpheus and Power: The* Movimento Negro *of Rio de Janeiro and São Paulo, Brazil, 1945–1988.* Princeton, N.J.: Princeton University Press.

Hardt, Michael, and Antonio Negri. 2000. *Empire.* Cambridge: Harvard University Press.

Hasenbalg, Carlos. 1996. "Entre o Mito e os Fatos: Racismo e Relações Raciais no Brasil." In *Raça, Ciência y Sociedade,* ed. Marcos Chor Maio and Ricardo Ventura Santos. Rio de Janeiro: Fiocruz.

Hegel, G. W. F. 1830 [1971]. *Hegel's Philosophy of Mind: Being Part Three of the "Encyclopaedia of the Philosophical Sciences."* Trans. W. Wallace and A. V. Miller. Oxford: Clarendon.

———. 1837 [1956]. *The Philosophy of History.* Trans. J. Sibree. New York: Dover.

Henríquez, Elio, and Rosa Rojas. 1996. "Queremos ser parte de la nación mexicana, como iguales." *La Jornada,* November 18.

Herlinghaus, Hermann. 2000. *Modernidad heterogénea: Descentramientos hermenéuticos desde la comunicación en América Latina.* Caracas: Centro de Investigaciones Post-Doctorales.

———. 2004. *Renarración y descentramiento: Mapas alternativos de la imaginación en América Latina.* Frankfurt: Vervuert.

Hewitt de Alcántara, Cynthia. 1984. *Anthropological Perspectives on Rural Mexico*. London: Routledge.

Hountondji, Paulin. 1992. "Recapturing." In *The Surreptitious Speech:* Présence Africaine *and the Politics of Otherness, 1947–1987*, ed. V. Y. Mudimbe. Chicago: University of Chicago Press. 238–48.

Htun, Mala. 2004. "From 'Racial Democracy' to Affirmative Action: Changing State Policy on Race in Brazil." *Latin American Research Review* 39(1): 60–89.

Hu-DeHart, Evelyn. 1988. "Peasant Rebellion in the Northwest: The Yaquí Indians of Sonora, 1740–1976." In *Riot, Rebellion and Revolution: Rural Social Conflict in Mexico*, ed. Friedrich Katz. Princeton, N.J.: Princeton University Press. 141–75.

Hulme, Peter. 1986. *Colonial Encounters: Europe and the Native Caribbean, 1492–1797*. London: Methuen.

Huntington, Samuel. 2004. "The Hispanic Challenge." *Foreign Policy* (March–April): 30–46.

"Índio brasileiro vive 502 anos de exclusão." 2002. *Jornal do Brasil*, online, April 19.

Ismail, Quadri. 1999. "Discipline and Colony: *The English Patient* and the Crow's Nest of Post Coloniality." *Postcolonial Studies* 2(3): 403–36.

Jameson, Fredric. 1986. "Third-World Literature in the Era of Mulitnational Capitalism." *Social Text* 15: 65–88.

———. 1998. "Notes on Globalization as a Philosophical Issue." In *The Cultures of Globalization*, ed. Fredric Jameson and Masao Miyoshi. Durham, N.C.: Duke University Press. 54–80.

JanMohamed, Abdul. 1985. "The Economy of Manichean Allegory: The Function of Racial Difference in Colonialist Literature." *Critical Inquiry* 12: 59–87.

———. 1992. "Sexuality on/of the Racial Border: Foucault, Wright and the Articulation of 'Racialized Sexuality.'" In *Discourses of Sexuality: From Aristotle to AIDS*, ed. Domna Stanton. Ann Arbor: University of Michigan Press. 94–117.

Jara, René. 1989. "The Inscription of Creole Consciousness: Fray Servando de Mier." In *1492–1992: Re/Discovering Colonial Writing*, ed. René Jara and Nicholas Spadaccini. Minneapolis: The Prisma Institute. 349–79.

———. 1996. *Los pliegues del silencio: Narrativa latinoamericana en el fin del milenio*. Valencia: Episteme.

Jardine, Alice. 1985. *Gynesis: Configurations of Woman and Modernity*. Ithaca, N.Y.: Cornell University Press.

Jáuregui, Carlos. 2000. "Saturno caníbal: fronteras, reflejos y paradojas en la narrativa sobre el antropófago." *Revista de Crítica Literaria Latinoamericana* 25(51): 9–40.

———. 2003. "'El plato más sabroso': Eucaristía, plagio diabólico y la traducción criolla del caníbal." *Colonial Latin American Review* 12(2): 199–231.

Joseph, Gilbert, and Daniel Nugent. 1994. *Everyday Forms of State Formation: Revolution and the Negotiation of Rule in Modern Mexico.* Durham, N.C.: Duke University Press.

Kant, Immanuel. 1777 [2000]. "Of the Different Human Races." In *The Idea of Race*, ed. Robert Bernasconi and Tommy Lott. Indianapolis: Hackett.

———. 1797 [1974]. *Anthropology from a Pragmatic Point of View.* Trans. Mary Gregor. The Hague: Martinus Nijhoff.

Katz, Friedrich. 1986. "Introducción." In *Porfirio Díaz frente al descontento popular regional (1891–1893)*, ed. Friedrich Katz and Jane-Dale Lloyd. Mexico City: Universidad Iberoamericana. 11–22.

Katzew, Ilona. 1996. *New World Orders: Casta Painting and Colonial Latin America.* New York: Americas Society.

Klobucka, Anna. 2003. "Lusotropical Romance: Camões, Gilberto Freyre, and the Isle of Love." *Portuguese Literary and Cultural Studies* 9: 121–38.

Klor de Alva, Jorge. 1995. "The Postcolonization of the (Latin) American Experience: A Reconsideration of 'Colonialism,' 'Postcolonialism,' and 'Mestizaje.'" In *After Colonialism: Imperial Histories and Postcolonial Displacements*, ed. Gyan Prakash. Princeton, N.J.: Princeton University Press. 241–78.

Knight, Alan. 1990. "Racism, Revolution and *Indigenismo*: Mexico, 1910–1940." *The Idea of Race in Latin America, 1870–1940.* Austin: University of Texas Press. 71–114.

———. 2002. "Subalterns, Signifiers and Statistics: Perspectives on Mexican Historiography." *Latin American Research Review* 37(2): 136–58.

Kokotovic, Misha. 2000. "Hibridez y desigualdad: García Canclini ante el neoliberalismo." *Revista de Crítica Literaria Latinoamericana* 36(52): 289–300.

Konetzke, Richard. 1953. *Colección de documentos para la historia de la formación social de Hispanoamérica, 1493–1810.* 3 vols. Madrid: Consejo Superior de Investigaciones Científicas.

Kraniauskus, John. 1998. "*Cronos* and the Political Economy of Vampirism: Notes on a Historical Constellation." In *Cannibalism and the Colonial World*, ed. Francis Barker, Peter Hulme, and Margaret Iversen. Cambridge: Cambridge University Press. 142–57.

———. 2000. "Hybridity in a Transnational Frame: Latin-Americanist and Postcolonial Perspectives on Cultural Studies." *Nepantla: Views from South* 1(1): 111–38.

Krauze, Enrique. 1997. *Mexico, Biography of Power: A History of Modern Mexico, 1810–1996.* New York: HarperCollins.

Kristeva, Julia. 1982. *Powers of Horror: An Essay on Abjection.* Trans. Leon Roudiez. New York: Columbia University Press.

Lacan, Jacques. 1948 [1977]. *Écrits: A Selection.* Trans. Alan Sheridan. New York: Norton.

Laplanche, Jean, and J.-B. Pontalis. 1973. *The Language of Psycho-analysis.* Trans. Donald Nicholson-Smith. New York: Norton.

Larsen, Neil. 1995. *Reading North by South: On Latin American Literature, Culture and Politics.* Minneapolis: University of Minnesota Press.

———. 2001. *Determinations: Essays on Theory, Narrative and Nation in the Americas.* London: Verso.

Leal, César, et al. 1981. *Expressão literária em Gilberto Freyre.* Recife: Conselho Estadual de Cultura.

Lévi-Strauss, Claude. 1952. *Race and History.* Paris: UNESCO.

———. 1955 [1997]. *Tristes Tropiques.* Trans. John Weightman and Doreen Weightman. New York: Modern Library.

Lindstrom, Naomi. 2000. "Foreword." In José de Alencar, *Iracema.* Oxford: Oxford University Press. xi–xxiv.

Lombardo Toledano, Vicente. 1930 [1988]. "El sentido humanista de la Revolución Mexicana." In *La Revolución Mexicana,* vol. 1, *1921–1967.* Mexico City: Instituto Nacional de Estudios Históricos de la Revolución Mexicana.

Lomnitz, Claudio. 1998. "An Intellectual's Stock in the Factory of Mexico's Ruins: Enrique Krauze's *Mexico: Biography of Power.*" *American Journal of Sociology* 103(4): 1052–65.

López, Silvia. 2000. "'Hybrid Cultures': Modern Experience and 'Institution Kunst.'" In *Unforeseeable Americas: Questioning Cultural Hybridity in the Americas,* ed. Rita de Grandis and Zila Bernd. Amsterdam: Rodopi. 254–70.

López y Fuentes, Gregorio. 1935 [1972]. *El indio.* Mexico City: Porrúa.

Lund, Joshua. 2001. "Barbarian Theorizing and the Limits of Latin American Exceptionalism." *Cultural Critique* 47: 54–90.

Lund, Joshua and Malcolm McNee, eds. 2006. *Gilberto Freyre e os estudos latinamericanos.* Pittsburgh: Instituto Internacional de Literatura Iberoamericana.

Magaña Esquível, Antonio. 1964. *La novela de la Revolución,* vol. 1. Mexico City: Instituto Nacional de Estudios Históricos de la Revolución Mexicana.

Malinowski, Bronislaw. 1967. *A Diary in the Strict Sense of the Term.* New York: Harcourt.

Mallon, Florencia. 1995. *Peasant and Nation.* Berkeley: University of California Press.

Marcos, Subcomandante. 1994. "Chiapas: El sureste en dos vientos, una tormenta y una profecía." http//www.ezln.org/documentos/1994/199208xx.es.htm.

Marentes, Luis. 2000. *José Vasconcelos and the Writing of the Mexican Revolution.* New York: Twayne.

Martí, José. 1891 [1973]. "Nuestra América." In *Cuba, Nuestra América, Estados Unidos.* Mexico City: Siglo Veintiuno. 109–20.

Martín-Barbero, Jesús. 1987 [1993]. *Communication, Culture and Hegemony: From the Media to Mediations.* Trans. Elizabeth Fox and Robert White. London: Sage.

Marx, Anthony. 1998. *Making Race and Nation.* Cambridge: Cambridge University Press.

Marx, Karl. 1852 [1977]. "The Future Results of British Rule in India." In *Selected Writings,* ed. David McLellan. Oxford: Oxford University Press. 332–37.

———. 1867 [1977]. *Capital: A Critique of Political Economy.* Vol. 1. Trans. Ben Fowkes. New York: Vintage Books.

Mason, Peter. 1990. *Deconstructing America: Representations of the Other.* London: Routledge.

McNee, Malcolm. 2001. "Chronicles, Ethnographies, and the Tension between Nostalgia and Destruction in Brazilian Modernism." *Romance Notes* 41(2): 199–208.

———. 2002. "Alegorizando as periferias: Pontos de articulação entre a crítica cultural de Fredric Jameson e Roberto Schwarz." *Veredas* 4.

Menand, Louis. 2001. *The Meta-physical Club: A History of Ideas in America.* New York: Farrar, Straus and Giroux.

Mesquita Samara, Eni de. 1989. *As mulheres, o poder e a família: São Paulo, Século XIX.* São Paulo: Marco Zero.

Metcalf, Alida. 1996. "El matrimonio en Brasil durante la colonia: ¿Estaba configurado por la clase o por el color?" Trans. Diana Murin. In *Familia y vida privada en la historia de Iberoamérica,* ed. Pilar Gonzalbo Aizpuru and Cecilia Rabell Romero. Mexico City: UNAM. 59–74.

Mignolo, Walter. 1989. "Literacy and Colonization: The New World Experience." In *1492–1992: Re/Discovering Colonial Writing,* ed. René Jara and Nicholas Spadaccini. Minneapolis: The Prisma Institute. 51–96.

———. 1993. "Colonial and Postcolonial Discourse: Cultural Critique or Academic Colonialism?" *Latin American Research Review* 28(3): 120–34.

———. 1995. *The Darker Side of the Renaissance: Literacy, Territoriality, and Colonization.* Ann Arbor: University of Michigan Press.

———. 1998a. "Globalization, Civilization Processes, and the Relocation of Languages and Cultures." In *The Cultures of Globalization,* ed. Fredric Jameson and Masao Miyoshi. Durham, N.C.: Duke University Press. 32–53.

———. 1998b. "Posoccidentalismo: El argumento desde América Latina." *Cuadernos Americanos* 67(1): 143–65.

———. 2000a. *Local Histories/Global Designs.* Princeton, N.J.: Princeton University Press.

———. 2000b. "The Many Faces of Cosmo-polis: Border Thinking and Critical Cosmopolitanism." *Public Culture* 12(3): 721–48.

Molina, Enríquez Andrés. 1909 [1978]. *Los grandes problemas nacionales.* Mexico City: Era.

Monsiváis, Carlos. 1968. "José Vasconcelos: La búsqueda del paraíso perdido." *Comunidad* 14: 347–55.

———. 1981. "Notas sobre el estado, la cultura nacional y las culturas populares en México." *Cuadernos Políticos* 30: 33–44.

———. 2000. "Notas sobre la cultura mexicana en el siglo XX." In *Historia general de México*, ed. Daniel Cosío Villegas† et al. Mexico City: El Colegio de México.

Montemayor, Carlos. 2001. *Los pueblos indios de México hoy*. Mexico City: Planeta.

Mora, José María Luis. 1830 [1994]. "De los medios de precaver las revoluciones." In *Obras completas*, Vol. 1, *Obra política 1*. Mexico City: Instituto Mora/ Conaculta.

———. 1849 [1994]. "Carta dirigida al Gobierno de México, Londres, julio 31 de 1849." In *Obras completas*, Vol. 7, *Obra diplomática*. Mexico City: Instituto Mora/Conaculta.

Moraña, Mabel. 1998. "El boom del subalterno." *Cuadernos Americanos* 67(1): 216–22.

Moreiras, Alberto. 1996. "Elementos de articulación teórica para el subalternismo latinoamericano: Candido y Borges." *Revista Iberoamericana* 62: 176–77, 875–91.

———. 2001. *The Exhaustion of Difference: The Politics of Latin American Cultural Studies*. Durham, N.C.: Duke University Press.

Mörner, Magnus. 1967. *Race Mixture in the History of Latin America*. Boston: Little, Brown.

———. 1970. *La corona española y los foráneos en los pueblos de indios en América*. Stockholm: Latinamerikanska-institutet, Almqvist & Wiksell.

Mowitt, John. 1992. *Text: The Genealogy of an Antidisciplinary Object*. Durham, N.C.: Duke University Press.

Narayan, Uma. 1997. *Dislocating Cultures: Identities, Traditions and Third World Feminism*. New York: Routledge.

O'Connell, Joanna. 1995. *Prospero's Daughter: The Prose of Rosario Castellanos*. Austin: University of Texas Press.

O'Connor, Alan. 2003. "Consumers and Citizens: On Néstor García Canclini." *Pretexts* 12(1): 103–20.

Oliveira, Francisco de. 2003. "The Duckbilled Platypus." *New Left Review* 24 (November–December): 40–57.

Oliveira e Oliveira, Eduardo de. 1974. "Mulato, um Obstáculo Epistemológico." *Argumento* 1(3): 65–73.

Ortiz, Fernando. 1940 [1995]. *Cuban Counterpoint: Tobacco and Sugar*. Trans. Harriet de Onís. Durham, N.C.: Duke University Press.

Paredes, Américo. 2000. "Interview with Américo Paredes." Interviewed by Héctor Calderón and José Rósbel López-Morín. *Nepantla* 1(1): 197–228.

Paz, Octavio. 1950 [1997]. *El laberinto de la soledad*. New York: Penguin.

———. 1970 [1985]. "Olympics and Tlatelolco." In *The Labyrinth of Solitude and Other Writings*, trans. Lysander Kemp, Yara Milos, and Rachel Phillips Belash. New York: Grove.

———. 1979 [1985]. "Mexico and the United States." In *The Labyrinth of Solitude and Other Writings*, trans. Lysander Kemp, Yara Milos, and Rachel Phillips Belash. New York: Grove. 355–76.

———. 1985. "Return to the Labyrinth of Solitude." In *The Labyrinth of Solitude and Other Writings*, trans. Lysander Kemp, Yara Milos, and Rachel Phillips Belash. New York: Grove. 327–53.

Quigley, Declan. 1993. *The Interpretation of Caste*. Oxford: Clarendon.

Quijano, Aníbal. 2000. "Coloniality of Power, Eurocentrism and Latin America." *Nepantla* 1(3): 533–79.

Rabell Romero, Cecilia. 1996. "Trayectoria de vida familiar, raza y género en Oaxaca colonial." In *Familia y vida privada en la historia de Iberoamérica*, ed. Pilar Gonzalbo Aizpuru and Cecilia Rabell Romero. Mexico City: UNAM. 75–118.

Rama, Ángel. 1982. *Transculturación narrativa en América Latina*. Mexico City: Siglo Veintiuno.

———. 1984. *La ciudad letrada*. Hanover, N.H.: Ediciones del norte.

Ramos, Julio. 1989. *Desencuentros de la modernidad en América Latina: Literatura y política en el siglo XIX*. Mexico City: Fondo de Cultura Económica.

———. 1993. "El don de la lengua." *Casa de las Américas* 34(193): 13–25.

Ramos, Samuel. 1938. *El perfil del hombre y la cultura en México*. Mexico City: Robredo.

Reina, Leticia. 1980 [1988]. *Las rebeliones campesinas en México (1819–1906)*. Mexico City: Siglo Veintiuno.

———, ed. 1997. *La reindianización de América, Siglo XIX*. Mexico City: Siglo Veintiuno.

———. 2002. "Reindianización: paradoja del liberalismo." *Nueva Época* 1(2).

Renan, Ernest. 1990. "What Is a Nation?" Trans. Martin Thom. In *Nation and Narration*, ed. Homi Bhabha. London: Routledge.

Reyes, Alfonso. 1915 [1992]. "Visión de Anáhuac." In *Última Tule y otros ensayos*. Caracas: Ayacucho. 3–17.

———. 1936 [1992]. "Notas sobre la inteligencia americana." In *Última Tule y otros ensayos*. Caracas: Ayacucho. 230–35.

Ribeiro, Darcy. 1977. "Prólogo." In Gilberto Freyre, *Casa-grande y senzala*. Caracas: Ayacucho.

Richard, Nelly. 1993. "The Latin American Problematic of Theoretical-Cultural Transference: Postmodern Appropriations and Counterappropriations." *South Atlantic Quarterly* 92(3): 453–60.

Riva Palacio, Vicente. 1889. *México a través de los siglos*. Vol. 2. Mexico City.

Rodrigues, Fernando. 1995. "Racismo cordial." In *Racismo cordial*, ed. Cleusa Turra and Gustavo Venturi. São Paulo: Ática. 11–56.

Rodriguez, Richard. 1991. "La Raza Cosmica" *[sic]*. *NPQ* (winter): 47–50.

Ronell, Avital. 1996. "The Uninterrogated Question of Stupidity." *differences: A Journal of Feminist Cultural Studies* 8(2): 1–19.

Rosaldo, Renato. 1995. Foreword to Néstor García Canclini, *Hybrid Cultures: Strategies for Entering and Leaving Modernity*, trans. Christopher L. Chiappari and Silvia L. López. Minneapolis: University of Minnesota Press. xi–xvii.

Rosenblat, Ángel. 1954. *La población indígena y el mestizaje en América*. Vol. 2. Buenos Aires: Nova.

Ruffinelli, Jorge. 1992. "From Unknown Work to Literary Classic." In *The Underdogs* by Mariano Azuela. Pittsburgh: University of Pittsburgh Press. 157–65.

Rugeley, Terry. 2002. "Indians Meet the State, Regions Meet the Center: Nineteenth-Century Mexico Revisited." *Latin American Research Review* 37(1): 245–59.

Saborit, Antonio. 1994. *Los doblados de Tomóchic: Un episodio de historia y literatura*. Mazatlán: Cal y Arena.

Sáenz, Moisés. 1936 [1966]. *Carapan: bosquejo de una experiencia*. Morelia (Mexico).

Said, Edward. 1978. *Orientalism*. New York: Pantheon.

———. 1989. "Representing the Colonized: Anthropology's Interlocutors." *Critical Inquiry* 15: 205–25.

Santiago, Silviano. 1971 [1978]. "O Entre-lugar do Discurso Latino-americano." In *Uma literatura nos trópicos*. São Paulo: Editora Perspectiva. 11–28.

———. 2002. "Literatura Anfíbea." *Revista Mais! (Folha de São Paulo)* 11–28. (June 30).

Saramago, José. 1995. *The Stone Raft*. Trans. Giovanni Pontiero. New York: Harcourt.

Sarmiento, Domingo. 1845 [1986]. *Facundo: Civilización y barbarie*. Barcelona: Planeta.

Saunders, J. V. D. 1958. *Differential Fertility in Brazil*. Gainesville: University of Florida Press.

Schwarz, Roberto. 1992. *Misplaced Ideas: Essays on Brazilian Culture*. London: Verso.

———. 2003. "Preface with Questions." *New Left Review* 24 (November–December): 31–39.

Sedgwick, Eve Kosofsky. 1985. *Between Men: English Literature and Male Homosocial Desire*. New York: Columbia University Press.

Seed, Patricia. 1993. "More Colonial and Postcolonial Discourses." *Latin American Research Review* 28(3): 146–52.

Shohat, Ella, and Robert Stam. 1994. *Unthinking Eurocentrism*. London: Routledge.

Sierra, Justo. 1885 [1960]. *Apuntes para un libro: México social y político*. Mexico City: Secretaría de Hacienda y Crédito Público.

———. 1900–1902 [1977]. *Evolución política del pueblo mexicano*. Caracas: Ayacucho.

Skidmore, Thomas. 1974 [1993]. *Black into White: Race and Nationality in Brazilian Thought*. Durham, N.C.: Duke University Press.

Skirius, John. 1982. *José Vasconcelos y la cruzada de 1929*. Mexico City: Siglo Veintiuno.

Smith, T. Lynn. 1972. *Brazil: People and Institutions*. 4th ed. Baton Rouge: Louisiana State University Press.

Sommer, Doris. 1991. *Foundational Fictions: The National Romances of Latin America*. Berkeley: University of California Press.

Sousa Santos, Boaventura de. 1996. *Pela mão de Alice: O social e o político na posmodernidade*. Porto: Edições Afrontamento.

Spivak, Gayatri. 1976. "Translator's Preface." In Jacques Derrida, *Of Grammatology*. Baltimore: Johns Hopkins University Press. ix–xc.

———. 1987. *In Other Worlds: Essays in Cultural Politics*. New York: Methuen.

———. 1988 [1994]. "Can the Subaltern Speak?" In *Colonial Discourse and Post-Colonial Theory: A Reader*, ed. Patrick Williams and Laura Chrisman. New York: Columbia University Press. 67–111.

———. 1999. *A Critique of Postcolonial Reason: Toward a History of the Vanishing Present*. Cambridge: Harvard University Press.

Stabb, Martin. 1959. "Indigenism and Racism in Mexican Thought, 1857–1911." *Journal of Inter-American Studies* 1: 405–24.

Stallybrass, Peter, and Allon White. 1986. *The Politics and Poetics of Transgression*. Ithaca, N.Y.: Cornell University Press.

Stam, Robert. 2000. "Tropical Detritus: *Terra em transe*, Tropicália and the Aesthetics of Garbage." *Studies in Latin American Popular Culture* 19: 83–92.

Stepan, Nancy Leys. 1991. *"The Hour of Eugenics": Race, Gender and Nation in Latin America*. Ithaca, N.Y.: Cornell University Press.

Talty, Stephan. 2000. "Spooked: The White Slave Narratives." *Transition* 85(10:1): 48–75.

Tierney, Patrick. 2000. *Darkness in El Dorado: How Scientists and Journalists Devastated the Amazon*. New York: Norton.

Trigo, Benigno. 2000. *Subjects of Crisis: Race and Gender as Disease in Latin America*. Hanover, NH: University Press of New England.

Trouillot, Michel-Rolph. 1995. *Silencing the Past: Power and the Production of History*. Boston: Beacon Press.

Turra, Cleusa, and Gustavo Venturi. 1995. *Racismo cordial*. São Paulo: Ática.

Valdés, Luz María. 2003. *Los indios mexicanos en los censos del año 2000*. Mexico City: UNAM.

Vanderwood, Paul. 1998. *The Power of God against the Guns of Government: Religious Upheaval in Mexico at the Turn of the Nineteenth Century.* Stanford, Calif.: Stanford University Press.

Van Doren, Robert. 1921 [2001]. "Commentary." In *The Last of the Mohicans,* by James Fenimore Cooper. New York: Modern Library. 349–50.

Vasconcelos, José. 1914 [1915]. *The Sovereign Revolutionary Convention of Mexico and the Attitude of General Francisco Villa.* Washington, DC: Confidential Agency of the Provisional Government of Mexico.

———. 1916 [1992]. "El movimiento intelectual contemporáneo de México." In *Obra selecta.* Caracas: Ayacucho.

———. 1925 [1979]. *The Cosmic Race/La raza cósmica.* Baltimore: Johns Hopkins University Press.

———. 1926. *Indología: Una interpretación de la cultura ibero-americana.* Barcelona: Agencia Mundial.

———. 1937. *¿Qué es la revolución?* Mexico City: Ediciones Botas.

———. 1957. *En el ocaso de mi vida.* Mexico City: Editora de Periódicos.

———. 1957–61. *Obras completas.* Vols. 1–4. Mexico City: Libreros Mexicanos Unidos.

Vaughn, Mary Kay. 1999. "Cultural Approaches to Peasant Politics in the Mexican Revolution." *Hispanic American Historical Review* 79(2): 269–305.

Ventura, Roberto. 2000. "Gilberto Freyre: Sexo no senzala." Paper delivered at the Sixth Congress of the Associação Brasileira da Literatura Comparada. Universidade Federal da Bahia, Salvador da Bahia, Brazil.

Vianna, Hermano. 1995 [1999]. *The Mystery of Samba: Popular Music and National Identity in Brazil.* Trans. John Charles Chasteen. Chapel Hill: University of North Carolina Press.

Vila Nova, Sebastião. 1995. *Sociologias e pós-sociologia em Gilberto Freyre.* Recife: Massangana.

Villoro, Luis. 1950. *Los grandes momentos del Indigenismo en México.* Mexico City: El Colegio de México.

Viotti da Costa, Emilia. 1985 [2000]. *The Brazilian Empire: Myths and Histories.* Chapel Hill: University of North Carolina Press.

Wagley, Charles. 1952. *Race and Class in Rural Brazil.* Paris: UNESCO.

Warman, Arturo. 2003. *Los indios mexicanos en el umbral del milenio.* Mexico City: Fondo de Cultura Económica.

Warren, Jonathan. 2001. *Racial Revolutions: Anti-Racism and Indian Resurgence in Brazil.* Durham, N.C.: Duke University Press.

Warren, Kay. 1998. "Indigenous Movements as a Challenge to the Unified Social Movement Paradigm for Guatemala." In *Cultures of Politics, Politics of Cultures: Re-visioning Latin American Social Movements,* ed. Sonia Alvarez, Evelina Dagnino, and Arturo Escobar. New York: Westview Press. 165–95.

White, Hayden. 1978. *Tropics of Discourse: Essays in Cultural Criticism*. Baltimore: Johns Hopkins University Press.

Wicomb, Zoë. 1998. "Shame and Identity: The Case of the Coloured in South Africa." In *Writing South Africa: Literature, Apartheid and Democracy, 1970–1995*, ed. Derek Attridge and Rosemary Jolly. Cambridge: Cambridge University Press. 91–107.

Williams, Raymond. 1977. *Marxism and Literature*. Oxford: Oxford University Press.

Womack, John. 1969. *Zapata and the Mexican Revolution*. New York: Knopf.

Young, Robert. 1990. *White Mythologies: Writing History and the West*. London: Routledge.

———. 1995. *Colonial Desire: Hybridity in Theory, Culture and Race*. London: Routledge.

Yúdice, George. 1993. "Postmodernism in the Periphery." *South Atlantic Quarterly* 92(3): 543–56.

———. 1998. "The Globalization of Culture and the New Civil Society." In *Cultures of Politics, Politics of Cultures: Re-visioning Latin American Social Movements*, ed. Sonia Alvarez, Evelina Dagnino, and Arturo Escobar. New York: Westview Press. 353–79.

———. 2001. "From Hybridity to Policy: For a Purposeful Cultural Studies." Translator's introduction to Néstor García Canclini, *Consumers and Citizens*, trans. George Yúdice. Minneapolis: University of Minnesota Press. ix–xxxvii.

Zea, Leopoldo. 1943. *El positivismo en México*. Mexico City: Fondo de Cultura Económica.

Žižek, Slavoj. 1993. *Tarrying with the Negative: Kant, Hegel and the Critique of Ideology*. Durham, N.C.: Duke University Press.

———. 2002. "*Homo Sacer* in Afghanistan." *Lacanian Ink* 20: 100–113.

Index

affirmative action: in Brazil, 142–43
Africa, 196n18
African: figure of, 152, 229n19. *See
    also negro, el*
Afro-Brazilian culture, 158, 184, 185
Agamben, Giorgio, xx, 19–20,
    192n11, 196n17, 197n23, 205n18,
    220n24
Agassiz, Elizabeth, 186, 196n21,
    230n26
Agassiz, Louis, 59, 86, 196n21,
    230n26
agency, 39, 40, 173–74, 205n23,
    236n27
Alencar, José de, xix, 129, 138, 161,
    167, 168, 174, 176–8, 181, 182, 184.
    See also Iracema
Altamirano, Ignacio, 90–91, 95,
    217n12. *See also Clemencia; Zarco, El*
ambivalence: of colonial discourse,
    xxi, 48–50, 51, 57, 61, 68, 94, 101,
    120, 125, 145, 148, 149, 150, 166,
    168, 182, 187, 204n14, 228n15.

See also Bhabha, Homi; Freud,
    Sigmund
amificacíon, 88, 214n23. *See also*
    Díaz, Porfirio; Molina Enríquez,
    Andrés
Anderson, Benedict, 126, 211n6
Andrade, Mário de, 52, 239n45
Andrade, Oswald de, 131, 133,
    239n45
anthropological discourse, 56–58,
    158, 170, 171, 181, 184, 185, 187,
    206n27, 206n28, 206n29
anthropology, 78, 150–51, 179,
    201n18
*Anthropology from a Pragmatic
    Point of View*, 87. *See also* Kant,
    Immanuel
anthropophagy. *See* cannibalism
anti-Semitism, 224n23, 231n28
antropofagia, 4, 5
Anzaldúa, Gloria, 107, 213n13,
    216n6
Aragón, Agustín, 212n9

51, 125, 148, 149, 168, 189n1. *See also* Bhabha, Homi; coloniality of power
colonialism, 149, 203n7, 205n18, 207n1, 216n10; "friendly," 146–47. *See also* coloniality of power
coloniality of power, ix, xi, xix, xx, xxi, 8, 43, 52, 55, 57, 61, 65, 72, 73, 94, 95, 120, 121, 125, 129, 135, 138, 139, 152, 168, 187, 188, 189n1, 194n7, 203n7, 237n36
Comte, Auguste: doctrine of, 81, 83, 212n8
Con Davis-Undiano, Robert, 107
Consumidores y cuidadanos, 38. *See also* García Canclini, Néstor
Cornejo Polar, Antonio, 4, 8, 14, 47, 190n5
Coronil, Fernando, 8, 52
Corrigan, Philip, 70
Cortázar, Julio, 165
Cortés, Hernan, 133
criollismo, 4
critique, xx. *See also* Derrida, Jacques
culturalism, 151, 201n21
Culturas Híbridas: Estrategias para entrar y salir de la modernidad. See García Canclini, Néstor; *Hybrid Cultures*
culturas híbridas, theory of, 4. *See also* García Canclini, Néstor; *Hybrid Cultures*
Cunha, Euclides da, 17, 231n30, 235n22

Darwin, Charles, 112, 190n4
de Certeau, Michel, 18, 20, 58, 195n14, 208n8
deconstruction, 23, 46. *See also* Bhabha, Homi; Derrida, Jacques
de la Campa, Román, 190n1
de Léry, Jean, 166

Deleuze, Gilles, 118, 132
De los medios a las mediaciones, 71. *See also* Martín-Barbero, Jesús
Derrida, Jacques, xiv, xx, 13, 14–15, 22–23, 150
developmentalism, 36, 37, 181, 183, 205n23
Díaz, Porfirio, 87–88, 94, 101, 103, 214n23. *See also* Porfiriato
discourse, 206n28, 207n2
Dussel, Enrique, 194n7

Ejército Zapatista de Liberacíon Nacional (EZLN), 213n13, 220n25. *See also* Zapatistas
"El Movimiento intelectual contemporáneo de Mexico," 108–9. *See also* Vasconcelos, José
emblanquecimento. See "whitening"
Enlightenment, 86, 84, 214n18
entre-lugar, o, 162, 163, 164, 168, 188, 235n21. *See also* Santiago, Silviano
"Entre-lugar do Discurso Latinoamericano, O," xix, 129. *See also* Santiago, Silviano
Esquível, Magaña, 99, 100
"ethnographic nationality," 87. *See also* Balibar, Étienne; Molina Enríquez, Andrés
eugenics, 172, 173, 174; aesthetic, 112, 237n36; discourse of, xxi, 127, 129, 148, 157, 178, 181, 186
Eurocentrism, 8, 9, 15, 16, 18, 20, 54, 55, 169, 170, 191n8
Everyday Forms of State Formation, 70, 209n9. *See also* Joseph, Gilbert; Nugent, Daniel
exemplarity, 22–25, 55: "logic of the example," 19, 144, 150; *See also* exceptionalism
exceptionalism: exemplarity and, xvi, 19–20, 22–25; Latin American,

slave: African, 229n19; Muslim,
229n21
slavery: Brazilian, 146–47, 149, 151,
152, 153–54, 158, 183, 184, 185,
186, 187, 228n10
slavery reparations, xv
social class, 30, 90215n1, 230n27
social movements, 38, 39, 68
"sociedade mestiça," 165, 166
Sommer, Doris, 95, 96, 177, 218n17,
236n28, 237n36, 239n47
Sovereign Revolutionary Convention, 221n1
sovereignty, 211n4
space: feminization of, 131, 225n2
space-in-between. *See entre-lugar, o*
Spencer, Herbert, 81, 83, 86, 212n8;
evolutionism of, 79, 80, 112,
223n12
Spivak, Gayatri, xx, 52, 138, 181
Stallybrass, Peter, 49
Stam, Robert, xi, 47–48
Stepan, Nancy Leys, 207n1
subalternism, 195n10
Subalternity and Representation, 33.
See also Beverley, John
syncretism, 4; hybridization and,
28–29; religious, 199n6
S/Z, 162. *See also* Barthes, Roland

teleology, 31, 32, 34–35, 36, 37, 78
Tempo morto e outros tempos, 155,
226n7. *See also* Freyre, Gilberto
temporality, 31, 34–35, 77, 79,
110–11. *See also* multitemporal
heterogeneity
Teresa de Cabora, Santa, 102
texte scriptible, 162. *See also* writable
text
Third Way politics, 27
Tierney, Patrick, 208n8
time lag, xvii. *See also* Bhabha, Homi;
multitemporal heterogeneity

Tomochic, 63, 94–103, 105, 114,
217n11, 217n14, 218n17, 218n19,
235n22; history of, 220n25,
220n26. *See also* Frías, Heriberto
Totem and Taboo, 49. *See also* Freud,
Sigmund
tradition: and modernity, 29, 30,
31, 34, 35, 78, 79. *See also* García
Canclini, Néstor
transculturacíon, xiii, xiv, 4, 5
transculturation. *See*
transculturacíon
Tristes Tropiques, 56, 102. *See also*
Leví-Strauss, Claude
Tupinambá, 179
typification: discourse of, 16, 22, 150

Underdogs, The. See Los de abajo
UNESCO, 153–54
Universopolis, 111–12
Usigli, Rodolfo, 113

Vanderwood, Paul, 100, 221n27
Vasconcelos, José, xviii, 8, 14, 59,
63–64, 105, 106, 107–13, 116–18,
154, 157, 221n1, 222n8, 222n9; law
thesis, 223n10
Vaughn, Mary Kay, 209n9
Veblen, Thorstein, 23
Vespucci, Amerigo, 170–71
Villoro, Luis, 67, 68, 208n6, 216n8

Wacquant, Loïc, 196n21
Wagley, Charles, 153
White, Allon, 49
White, Hayden, 144
"whitening," 132, 151, 152, 173. *See
also* eugenics
woman, indigenous: figure of, 170–74,
177, 178, 179
world-systems theory. *See* center-
periphery model
writable text, 162, 164, 165, 167,

Joshua Lund is assistant professor of Spanish at the University of Pittsburgh. He is coeditor of *Gilberto Freyre e os estudos latinoamericanos*. His most recent essays appear in *MLN*, *A Contracorriente, Race and Class, Journal of Latin American Cultural Studies,* and *Cultural Critique.*